Debates in Physical Education

Debates in Physical Education explores major issues physical education teachers encounter in their daily professional lives. It engages with established and contemporary debates, promotes and supports critical reflection and aims to stimulate both novice and experienced teachers to reach informed judgements and argue their own point of view with deeper theoretical knowledge and understanding. In addition, concerns for the short-, medium- and long-term future of the subject are voiced, with a variety of new approaches proposed.

Key issues debated include:

- What are the aims of physical education?
- What should be covered in a physical education curriculum?
- How should we judge success in physical education?
- Is physical education really for all or is it just for the gifted and talented?
- Can physical education really combat the rise in obesity?
- What is the future for physical education in the twenty-first century?

Debates in Physical Education makes a timely and significant contribution to addressing current contentious issues in physical education. With its combination of expert opinion and fresh insight, this book is the ideal companion for all student and practising teachers engaged in initial teacher education, continuing professional development and Master's level study.

Susan Capel is Professor and Head of the School of Sport and Education at Brunel University, London, England.

Margaret Whitehead is Visiting Professor in the Faculty of Education, Sport and Tourism at the University of Bedfordshire, England.

Debates in Subject Teaching Series

Edited by Susan Capel, Jon Davison, James Arthur, John Moss

The **Debates in Subject Teaching Series** is a sequel to the popular **Issues in Subject Teaching Series**, originally published by Routledge between 1999 and 2003. Each title presents high-quality material, specially commissioned to stimulate teachers engaged in initial teacher education, continuing professional development and Master's level study to think more deeply about their practice, and link research and evidence to what they have observed in schools. By providing up-to-date, comprehensive coverage, the titles in the **Debates in Subject Teaching Series** support teachers in reaching their own informed judgements, enabling them to discuss and argue their point of view with deeper theoretical knowledge and understanding.

Titles in the series:

Debates in History Teaching
Edited by Ian Davies

Debates in English Teaching
Edited by Jon Davison, Caroline Daly and John Moss

Debates in Religious Education
Edited by Philip Barnes

Debates in Citizenship Education
Edited by James Arthur and Hilary Cremin

Debates in Art and Design Education
Edited by Lesley Burgess and Nicholas Addison

Debates in Music Teaching
Edited by Chris Philpott and Gary Spruce

Debates in Physical Education
Edited by Susan Capel and Margaret Whitehead

Debates in Physical Education

Edited by Susan Capel and Margaret Whitehead

Routledge
Taylor & Francis Group

LONDON AND NEW YORK

First published 2013
by Routledge
2 Park Square, Milton Park, Abingdon, Oxon OX14 4RN

Simultaneously published in the USA and Canada
by Routledge
711 Third Avenue, New York, NY 10017

Routledge is an imprint of the Taylor & Francis Group, an informa business

British Library Cataloguing in Publication Data
A catalogue record for this book is available from the British
Library

Library of Congress Cataloging in Publication Data
Debates in physical education teaching / edited by Susan Capel
and Margaret Whitehead.
    p. cm. – (Debates in subjects teaching)
    Includes index.
    1. Physical education and training–Study and teaching.
    2. Physical education and training–Curricula. I. Capel,
    Susan Anne, 1953– II. Whitehead, Margaret, 1940–
    GV361.D38 2012
    613.707–dc23   2012008206

ISBN: 978-0-415-67624-3 (hbk)
ISBN: 978-0-415-67625-0 (pbk)
ISBN: 978-0-203-10018-9 (ebk)

Typeset in Galliard
by Wearset Ltd, Boldon, Tyne and Wear

Contents

Conclusion   233

Contributors

Kathleen Armour is Professor of Education and Sport, Head of the School of Sport and Exercise Sciences, University of Birmingham, England.

Richard Blair is a Lecturer in the School of Sport and Education, Brunel Univeristy, London, England.

Lorraine Cale is a Senior Lecturer and the Director of Learning and Teaching in the School of Sport, Exercise and Health Sciences at Loughborough University, Loughborough, England.

Susan Capel is Professor and Head of the School of Sport and Education, Brunel University, London, England.

Fiona Chambers is Director of Sports Studies and Physical Education, School of Education, University College Cork, Ireland.

Eimear Enright is a Lecturer in Physical Education in the Department of Physical Education and Sport Sciences at the University of Limerick, Ireland.

John Evans is Professor of Sociology of Education and Physical Education in the School of Sport, Exercise and Health Sciences at Loughborough University, Loughborough, England.

Jo Harris is a Senior Lecturer and the Director of Teacher Education in the School of Sport, Exercise and Health Sciences at Loughborough University, Loughborough, England.

Helen Ives is a Partnership Development Manager in West London and is currently undertaking a PhD at the University of Bedfordshire, England.

David Kirk is Alexander Chair in Physical Education and Sport, the University of Bedfordshire, England.

Kyriaki Makopoulou is Lecturer in Physical Education, School of Education, University of Birmingham, England.

Elizabeth Murdoch is Emeritus Professor of Physical Education of the University of Brighton.

Dawn Penney is Professor of Physical Education and Sport Pedagogy in the Department of Sport and Leisure Studies, Faculty of Education, The University of Waikato, Hamilton, Aotearoa New Zealand.

Val Rimmer is an independent education consultant/adviser.

Daniel Tindall is Lecturer in Physical Education, and Course Director for the certificate, diploma and degree programmes in Exercise and Health Fitness and Director of the *i-PLAY* (Inclusive Play and Leisure Activities for Youth) programme for children with special educational needs in the Department of Physical Education and Sport Sciences, University of Limerick, Ireland.

Margaret Whitehead is Visiting Professor in the Faculty of Education, Sport and Tourism at the University of Bedfordshire, England.

Paula Zwozdiak-Myers is Lecturer in Education in the School of Sport and Education, Brunel University, London, England.

Introduction to the series

This book, *Debates in Physical Education*, is one of a series of books entitled Debates in Subject Teaching. The series has been designed to engage with a wide range of debates related to subject teaching. Unquestionably, debates vary among the subjects, but may include, for example, issues that:

- impact on initial teacher education in the subject;
- are addressed in the classroom through the teaching of the subject;
- are related to the content of the subject and its definition;
- are related to subject pedagogy;
- are connected with the relationship between the subject and broader educational aims and objectives in society, and the philosophy and sociology of education;
- are related to the development of the subject and its future in the twenty-first century.

Consequently, each book presents key debates that subject teachers should understand, reflect on and engage in as part of their professional development. Chapters have been designed to highlight major questions, and to consider the evidence from research and practice in order to find possible answers. Some subject books or chapters offer at least one solution or a view of the ways forward, whereas others provide alternative views and leave readers to identify their own solution or view of the ways forward. The editors expect readers will want to pursue the issues raised, and so chapters include questions for further debate and suggestions for further reading. Debates covered in the series will provide the basis for discussion in university subject seminars and meetings between professionals in school departmental meetings and in the context of continuing professional development (CPD) courses. The topics are also appropriate for consideration in assignments or classroom research. The books have been written for all those with a professional interest in the subject and, in particular: student teachers learning to teach the subject in secondary school; newly qualified teachers; teachers undertaking study at Master's level; teachers with a subject coordination or leadership role and those preparing for such responsibility; as well as mentors, university tutors and advisers of the aforementioned groups.

Because of the range of coverage in the series, both in terms of the issues covered and its cross-phase concern, each book is an edited collection. Editors have commissioned new writing from experts on particular issues for debate, which, collectively, represent many different perspectives on subject teaching. Readers should not expect a book in this series to cover the entire range of debates relevant to the subject, or to offer a completely unified view of subject teaching, or that every debate will be dealt with discretely, or that all aspects of a debate will be covered. Part of what each book in this series offers to readers is the opportunity to explore the interrelationships between positions in debates and, indeed, among the debates themselves, by identifying the overlapping concerns and competing arguments that are woven through the text.

The editors are aware that many initiatives in subject teaching continue to originate from the centre, and that teachers have decreasing control of subject content, pedagogy and assessment strategies. The editors strongly believe that for teaching to remain properly a vocation and a profession, teachers must be invited to be part of a creative and critical dialogue about subject teaching, and should be encouraged to reflect, criticise, problem-solve and innovate. This series is intended to provide teachers with a stimulus for democratic involvement in the development of the discourse of subject teaching.

Susan Capel, Jon Davison, James Arthur and John Moss
January 2012

Introduction to the book

This book, *Debates in Physical Education*, is designed to highlight issues which are important in physical education and which physical educators will need to address throughout their professional career. Unlike other books which aim to provide the reader with information, guidance and advice, *Debates in Physical Education* leaves it to each reader to decide where they stand. The challenge for you, as a reader, therefore, is to reach your own informed judgements in relation to the topics discussed, adapting and developing your practice, as appropriate, in relation to these deliberations.

An initial teacher education (ITE) course is only the start in developing as a teacher. Developing as a teacher is a lifelong process which involves developing personal understanding of the teaching and learning process, understanding of wider issues within the profession generally and the subject specifically, as well as understanding of self. It is a process that needs to be addressed explicitly.

Everyone who teaches has a theory of how to teach effectively and of how pupils learn. That this is often implicit, rather than clearly articulated, is of concern, as it is only when teachers can explain their views that real debate, review and change can be effected. You need to be aware both of what your own theory is, as well as of different theories of teaching and learning. You also need to be aware of theories and empirical research on a range of issues in physical education.

Some teachers may feel that they do not have a philosophy of education. What these teachers are really saying is that they have not examined their views, or cannot articulate them. For example, they may not be able to articulate whether they view their job as 'filling empty vessels', transferring the knowledge of their subject to pupils or whether they are there to guide them on a 'voyage of discovery', to lead them through the many and various aspects of the subject. Are you, as a reader, clear about what your philosophy of teaching is?

An articulated, conscious theory of teaching and learning, an ability to address issues within the subject and developing a philosophy of education emerge only if a particular set of habits is developed, in particular, the habit of reviewing your own teaching from time to time. This is what many authors mean when they refer to 'the reflective practitioner'. It is these habits that need to be developed from the start of an ITE course.

Through drawing on the evidence base and reflecting on your own theory of teaching and learning as well as a range of other theories, and theorising about what teachers generally, and you specifically, are doing, you are able to understand your practice better and develop into a reflective practitioner, that is, a teacher who makes conscious decisions about teaching strategies to employ and who modifies their practice in the light of experiences. As a result, you are able to explain more fully your own philosophy of education and what you, as a teacher, are trying to do and why. We hope that this book will provide some support to you in developing your understanding of the value of evidence and theory, integrating theory with your own practice, using evidence to underpin your professional judgement, and using structured reflection to improve practice and develop your philosophy of education.

On an ITE course you can expect not only to undergo *training* but also to be introduced to wider educational issues. We view ITE not as an apprenticeship but as a step on the journey of personal development in which teaching skills develop alongside an emerging understanding of the teaching and learning process, the education system in which it operates and a personal philosophy. This is a journey of discovery that begins on the first day of ITE and may stop only at retirement. Thus, we use the term initial teacher *education* rather than initial teacher training throughout this book.

Teachers are expected to undertake continuing professional development (CPD) throughout their career. We also hope that this book will support your CPD. Teachers in many countries are now expected to have Master's level qualifications. The content and approach taken in this book are intended to support Master's level work whether within an ITE course or in CPD as a practising teacher.

A range of experienced physical educators have contributed chapters reflecting their current views and the research associated with their area of expertise. In the context of there being a variety of views on many issues, you should not be surprised to encounter differing positions presented by different authors. Thus, on some issues authors of different chapters endorse each other's views, while on other issues somewhat different viewpoints are expressed. You are challenged to think through the views and arguments presented and to come to a reasoned decision about where you stand.

The book is set out in five parts each with a particular focus. Part I looks at the nature of physical education; Part II considers issues in learning in physical education; Part III addresses the topic of teaching in physical education; Part IV considers the key players in physical education; and the final Part V is entitled 'Looking ahead' and does just that! A short final conclusion to the book (Chapter 15) draws the different strands of the book together and encourages you to look broadly at the issues and to affirm your own position.

Each part starts with a brief introduction to the part, along with a summary outlining the nature and content of each of the chapters in that part.

Each chapter shares some common features. Each starts with an introduction, outlining how the chapter is to be set out. Each also concludes with a conclusion or summary which emphasises the main points in the chapter. Further, each chapter includes questions for consideration and further reading to guide you in becoming better informed and able to articulate your views about the area under debate. Throughout the text a symbol is included in the margin (Q + a number) to indicate that there is a question for consideration related to that part of the text. The questions themselves are at the end of the chapter.

However, the nature of the presentation of different chapters varies. For example, two chapters (1 and 4) are set out as a dialogue between two physical educators to serve as examples of the nature of debates in which physical educationists might well be involved. As the debate proceeds there are examples of participants being challenged to explain their views in more detail and to defend their positions. These provide an example of the way a debate might proceed.

Other chapters take different formats. For example, some chapters critique a particular view while others set out and justify a specific stance. Some chapters aim to look widely at a situation and share the range of views that exist in relation to the topic. As examples, Chapter 2 provides a model of the way that a position statement or argument can be analysed, subjected to critique and reconsidered from a different perspective. Chapter 3 sets out a particular perspective on the value of physical activity and thus physical education. Here you are challenged to consider the arguments that underpin the position articulated and to review its implications for the physical education profession. Chapter 5 takes the approach of providing an overview of a range of research and evidence to stimulate debate amongst readers about the challenges and opportunities for physical educators in relation to health.

All these ways of working are legitimate approaches in becoming more informed about an important aspect of physical education, in understanding and interrogating the views of others and in coming to a personal position on the issues. However, all of the issues could be the subject of a debate with other teachers, as exemplified by Chapters 1 and 4. Articulating views and defending beliefs are very valuable skills – well worth mastering, not only for physical educationists themselves, but maybe even for the long-term future of the subject.

The authors hope that you will find the chapters stimulating, motivating you to read and discuss widely. We hope that you will question and interrogate the views of others, as appropriate, and formulate your own views on the issues under discussion. In addition we hope that you will reflect on your current views and either reaffirm your positions or rethink where you stand. Having read the book we hope that you will be better able to answer questions such as 'What do you believe?' and 'Why do you believe?' However, these answers should be kept under review. Indeed we hope that the text provides the stimulus for you to want to continue to learn and develop throughout your career as a teacher, and this may well result in different answers to these questions in future.

We have adopted a consistent use of terminology. For example, we call school children *pupils* to avoid confusion with *students*, by which we mean people in further and higher education. We refer to those learning to teach as *student teachers*. Likewise, we call pre-service education *initial teacher education*.

Although the text is designed to be generic and the debates applicable to physical educators in many countries, inevitably, where reference is made to a specific system, that system is England's. However, we would encourage you to view England as an example and apply the issue under discussion to the curriculum in the country (or school) in which you are teaching.

The terms used in the book are understood as having the connotations generally accepted in the United Kingdom. Their use in the UK might not match how the term is used in other countries. Again, we encourage you to consider the terminology as used in your own local context.

Remember, teaching is about the contribution teachers make to their pupils, to their development and their learning and to the well-being of society through the education of our young people. If you see the book and each chapter as potentially an open door leading to whole new worlds of thought about how best physical education can be delivered to enhance pupils' learning in the subject, then one of our goals has been achieved; that is to provide material to support you on your own journey of discovery about, and your ability to debate, physical education. We hope the text will help you in your own development and to play a part in developing the subject in future years.

Susan Capel and Margaret Whitehead
January 2012

Part I

The nature of physical education

Introduction to Part I

The three chapters in Part I – 'What is physical education?,' 'What is the education in physical education?' and 'What is physical literacy and how does it impact on physical education?' – challenge you to reflect in depth on the nature and purpose of physical education. Chapter 1 raises questions about the way the history of physical education has shaped current practice. Chapter 2 involves you in a critical examination of the role of physical education in education as a whole, while Chapter 3 asks you to consider the impact of new thinking in relation to the justification of, and practices in, our subject.

Chapter 1, 'What is physical education?' is designed to set the scene for the debates in this book. It opens by debating the key concepts that are often confused with physical education: recreation and sport. Having made the distinctions between these three clear, the chapter moves on to discuss, briefly, the way physical education has changed throughout recent times in England and the way the subject has had to respond to the culture of the day and the prevailing priorities in education. A significant aspect of our history relates to the introduction of the National Curriculum for Physical Education in 1992, the first statutory curriculum since 1933. Finally the chapter will consider the current nature of physical education in school today. The chapter is presented as a dialogue as an example of the way a debate could be conducted.

Chapter 2, 'What is the education in physical education?' considers a long standing articulation of the value of physical education as part of education. The seminal work of Arnold (1979) is used as an example of this articulation. Arnold's three claims that the subject can educate *about movement*, *through movement* and *in movement* are explained and then subjected to critical evaluation. Building from a monist philosophical position, Arnold's claims are re-examined and re-presented in a form that underlines the unique contribution of physical education to education. The chapter provides an example of the way that a position statement or argument can be analysed, subjected to critique and reconsidered from a different perspective. You are advised both to consider how this process has been conducted and to form an opinion as to whether the counter arguments are valid and acceptable.

Chapter 3, 'What is physical literacy and how does it impact on physical education?' presents the relatively new concept of physical literacy, explaining its philosophical roots and its relationship to physical education. It is argued that physical literacy can play a key role in justifying physical education in the curriculum, serving as a goal to be worked towards and providing a clear rationale for the inclusion of the subject in education. Finally the chapter sets out the responsibilities of the physical education teacher in respect of promoting physical literacy. The chapter proposes a particular perspective on the value of physical activity, particularly purposeful physical pursuits and physical education. You are challenged to consider the arguments that underpin the position articulated and to review its implications for the physical education profession.

What is physical education?

Susan Capel and Margaret Whitehead

Introduction

This chapter is designed to provide a context for the debates raised through-out this book. In conducting a debate it is always valuable to be clear about the definition of key terms related to the area under discussion and this is the first task of the chapter, that is, to define the nature of physical education, recreation and sport. Second, views and opinions are very often closely related to the social and cultural context surrounding the issues under consideration. The chapter will also, therefore, briefly describe the social and cultural context of the development of physical education in schools in England. Significant changes in physical education will be identified and reasons for these pro-posed, including the changing justifications for including the subject in the curriculum. The introduction of the National Curriculum for Physical Educa-tion (NCPE) in England and its effect on practice in schools will be debated. Finally the chapter will review the current nature of physical education in England today.

The issues in this chapter are presented as a dialogue to serve as an example of the nature of a debate in which physical educationists might well be involved. As the debate proceeds you will find examples of the participants being challenged to explain their views in more detail and to defend their positions. It is hoped that this chapter will encourage you to question and interrogate the views of others, as appropriate, and to formulate your own views on the issues under discussion. With the exception of Chapter 4, other chapters in this book are not written in this format; however, many of the issues introduced in other chapters could be the subject of a debate with others. Articulating views and defending beliefs are very valuable skills, well worth mastering.

Key concepts in physical education

MARGARET WHITEHEAD (MW): Debates about the nature of physical education are often made difficult because there is some confusion about the meaning of the terms being used.

SUSAN CAPEL (SC): I agree there is confusion about the nature of the subject – indeed, there does not seem to be clear agreement here, it means different things to different people and for some people their definitions are implicit; in other words they have not considered, explicitly, what they understand by physical education. Many people seem to regard physical education as a range of physical activities which take place on playing fields, in the gym, the dance hall or the swimming pool. Others focus on the contribution the subject makes to the school curriculum, citing it as where attention is given to learning physical skills and/or where young people are encouraged to learn how to work with others and manage both winning and losing. Another problem is that people often confuse physical education with recreation and/or sport. In order to help us to define what physical education is and distinguish it from other modes of physical activity, can we differentiate between the concepts of physical education, recreation and sport?

MW: This is a very contentious area. However I agree that we need to understand very clearly the nature of these concepts so that we all know to what we are referring. Misunderstandings often arise on account of people talking at cross purposes or without being explicit about definitions. It certainly needs to be made clear that the subject of this book is not sport per se, nor is it recreation, although both are closely related to physical education in different ways.

SC: It also needs to be understood that the definitions we propose will relate specifically to language used in the UK. Other countries use different terms, for example in some countries 'sport' and 'physical education' are synonymous.

MW: Yes that is true. Readers from outside the UK should consider carefully how terminology is used in their country and how this relates to the way the concepts are employed in UK.

Looking first at physical education and recreation, I would suggest that physical education is a term that applies to work in the movement field carried out schools. It is a compulsory subject in which all pupils have to take part. I would also suggest that recreation is usually understood to be a self-chosen activity. Physical education as part of education is seen to be important and to have value within the school curriculum, whereas recreation is usually understood as engaged in by the individual for pure enjoyment.

Physical education has a place in education on the grounds that it can foster physical development and movement competence. The subject works towards involving learners in a range of physical activities such as games, gymnastics and dance that use large muscle groups. Furthermore physical education has a role to inform learners about the knowledge and understanding that underpin a healthy lifestyle.

Definitions of physical education that have been formulated in key literature focus on the centrality of the movement experience in physical education and/or on the subject as contributing to education of the whole child. In respect of the first, the NCPE in England (Qualifications and Curriculum Authority (QCA), 2007a: i) defines physical education for 11- to 16-year-old learners as a subject:

> which develops pupils' competence and confidence to take part in a range of physical activities that become a central part of their lives, both in and out of school. A high-quality physical education curriculum enables all pupils to enjoy and succeed in many kinds of physical activity. They develop a wide range of skills and the ability to use tactics, strategies and compositional ideas to perform successfully. When they are performing, they think about what they are doing, analyse the situation and make decisions. They also reflect on their own and others' performances and find ways to improve them.

In respect of the second approach, Bucher (1983: 13) defined physical education as 'an integral part of the total education process,... a field of endeavour that has as its aim the improvement of human performance through the medium of physical activities that have been selected with a view to realising this outcome'. Others have extended this definition to include the development of physically, mentally, emotionally and socially fit citizens. Arnold (1979) defined physical education as: education *through* movement, *about* movement and *in* movement (this is covered in Chapter 2). Similarly the Association for Physical Education in the UK (afPE, 2009) advocates that:

> the learning experiences of physical education should focus on young people 'Learning to Move' and 'Moving to Learn'. Learning to move is about the learning of the movement skills required for participation in different types of physical activities. Moving to learn is not only about the learning needed for participation in physical activities but also the learning integrated with other aspects of school learning within and beyond the curriculum.

While these definitions take slightly different approaches they stress the value of physical education as part of education. I believe that the value of physical education lies in its unique contribution to education in developing our physical capabilities. This development should facilitate lifelong participation in physical activity. In addition the subject area plays a role in education by fostering self-confidence and self-realisation, and by sharing the responsibility with other subject areas to help learners to master personal skills such as co-operation, creativity and independence.

In contrast definitions of recreation tend to refer to it as a way of 'enjoying yourself when you are not working' (*Cambridge Advanced Learner's Dictionary*, http://dictionary.cambridge.org/dictionary/british/recreation_1? q=Recreation) or to an activity through which individuals can be free of pressure, in the interests of enabling them to relax and subsequently re-engage in their 'work activities' with renewed energy and application. Recreation is closely related to leisure activities, to having fun or being involved in a pastime. Other definitions focus on re-creation, being a time when individuals can shed their responsibilities, indulge in self-chosen activities and live for the moment. This can be seen to foster a sense of self with the benefit of becoming reinvigorated and refreshed.

It is a worry that physical education is sometimes viewed as being just a break from the 'serious' work of education and is valued only for the benefits it brings to 'rest' cognitive faculties in the interests of learners being able to work better in lessons that follow. This gives the impression that cognitive functions are not used in physical education, which is certainly not the case, and it can lead to the attitude that physical education is just for fun and has no significant contribution to make to education. This attitude can have unfortunate implications for arguing for the place of the subject in the very overcrowded curriculum and should be challenged.

SC: The argument you put forward lays great stress on the value of physical education, you are surely not arguing that recreation is without value? I would see recreation as an essential part of life – an enriching experience which can, in a sense, 'rebalance' lives. Indeed one of the arguments for having physical education in the curriculum is in the interests of learners being motivated to take part in physical activity in their leisure time, outside school and after schooling is finished.

This is surely part of the role of physical education – to prepare young people for participating in physical activity throughout life?

MW: I agree that recreation is of value and I would hope that young people will be inspired to be active in their leisure time. A key role of physical education is to foster the development of physical competence so that individuals will have the motivation and confidence to continue with activity outside school. Physical education is very important in this respect as it offers the unique opportunity for all to learn from expert practitioners who are trained to establish and improve movement skills. This opportunity should not be lost. It is certainly true that in the later years of schooling physical educationists need to anticipate the changing contexts that young people will encounter with respect to access to physical activity when they leave school. However I do not advocate physical education becoming viewed solely as recreation with these older learners, but rather that learners are given more choice of activity and opportunities to further their movement competence in a wide variety of contexts, within and outside the school setting. Opportunities for working with expert practitioners can be expensive and are less easy to find outside the school and we must use all the time we have in school to encourage learners to gain confidence and real satisfaction from engaging in physical activity and mastering physical skills.

SC: I think we should now look at the definition of sport and how this relates both to recreation and to physical education. Surely sport can itself be recreation?

MW: Yes, sport can be seen as a subsection of recreation alongside activities such as stamp collecting, watching DVDs and window-shopping. Sport is generally understood as physical activity in a competitive setting. Individuals, small and larger groups compete against each other with the goal to win. In team sports co-operation is also needed to outwit the opponents. Other concepts that are related to sport are elite performance, high levels of skill, practice, rewards and acclaim. Younger and older people take part in sport either in their leisure time as recreation or in a professional or semi-professional capacity. Involvement in sport may be a job or a recreational activity. Those who take part in sport in their leisure time do so for a wide variety of reasons. For example some thrive on the competitive element, others enjoy the social side while others see sport as a vehicle to keep fit.

SC: There seems to be a great deal of debate about the place of sport in physical education, even though sport clearly promotes the development of movement skills as well as being valuable as a worthwhile use of leisure time outside of school. Competitive sport in school provides the foundation both for worthwhile adult recreation and professional sport and it undoubtedly appeals to some learners. It is also true that competitive sport can serve a range of valuable educational ends such as developing movement competence, fostering co-operation and learning self-management and self-assessment. However I would assert that it should not be the dominant experience in physical education. Perhaps the problem lies in an over-emphasis on competitive sport in physical education at the expense of a wider range of experience in different activity contexts. Physical education is not sport, it is far wider than sport. The Department of Education and Science (DES, 1991: 7) explains:

> Sport covers a range of physical activities in which adults and young people may participate. Physical education on the other hand is a process of learning, the context being mainly physical. The purpose of this process is to develop specific knowledge, skills and understanding and to promote physical competence. Different sporting activities can and do contribute to the learning process, and the learning enables participation in sport. The focus in physical education, however, is on the child and his or her development of physical competence, rather than on the activity.

Notwithstanding this clear statement many see sport as synonymous with physical education. Again the DES (1991: 7) document is helpful here in stating that

> The place of games and sport in schools has been widely misinterpreted by some commentators in recent times, particularly in the national media. There are those who have argued (although very few in number) that competitive physical activities provided through sport should have no part in the educational process and should be discouraged in schools. Others appear to think that the physical education programme should consist solely of competitive team games. We accept neither of these views, nor is either an accurate description of what currently happens in schools.

In the context of the two quotations above it has perhaps not been helpful that, in the recent past, our subject has frequently been referred to as 'Physical Education and School Sport'. This wording can be read in two ways. It can either be read as indicating that the two concepts are separate, there being two aspects of the subject area covered in curriculum time – physical education and sport. Or it can be read to mean that physical education takes place in curricular time and sport takes place in extra-curricular time. Neither interpretation is accurate or helpful. The first reading is inaccurate as sport is part of physical education not a separate area. The second reading is counter-productive as it implies that extra-curricular work should focus solely on competitive team sports for the most gifted. This seriously narrows the extra-curricular opportunities the school might offer 'out of hours'. Chapters 4 and 11 consider extra-curricular physical activity/sport provision.

MW: You are not denying that sport has a place in the curriculum of physical education?

SC: Certainly not. What I am arguing is that physical education is not sport as defined above. Sport describes a particular form of physical activity that young people should learn as part of their physical education. Sport is part of physical education, but only a part. And when sport in the form of competitive games is taught in physical education it should not be engaged in, in such a way that winning at all costs is seen as acceptable.

While sport is undoubtedly an important element of physical education, I believe that it has been the predominance of sport in the form of competitive games in the physical education curriculum that has resulted in many, both boys and girls, becoming disillusioned in our curriculum area. In fact involvement in sport can erode their confidence and motivation in respect of taking part in physical activity. The predominance of competitive games in the physical education curriculum is well documented (see below). There are at least three reasons for this: first, many physical education teachers join the profession wishing to pass on their enthusiasm for games to learners (the impact of socialisation on physical education teachers is looked at in Chapter 8); second, there are generally ample facilities available for games in most schools; and third, the NCPE in England has encouraged competitive games in the curriculum through the requirements it has identified. For example, in curriculum specifications in 1992, 1995 and 1999 games were compulsory from early schooling to learners of 15 years old (Table 1.1 provides a brief overview of the requirements in each of the NCPE documents at each key stage). The 1999 curriculum made games compulsory throughout schooling. The 2007 curriculum does not specify which activities should be taught, leaving it open for teachers to select what they will teach. With games so firmly established in physical education in schools for very many years, this freedom has tended to result in more time being given to games rather than a wider range of activities being offered (see, for example, Evans and Davies, 1986; Green, 2003).

MW: Would I be correct to sum up the definitions we are proposing by saying that while physical education, physical recreation and sport share a number of features in common, such as involving active physical participation and providing opportunities for a healthy active lifestyle, they are distinct. Physical education is a compulsory school subject that is designed to make an important and unique contribution to education in developing learners' physical abilities and encouraging lifelong participation in physical activity. In addition the subject plays a part in promoting education as a whole, both in respect of fostering self-esteem and confidence and in nurturing personal skills such as co-operation, problem-solving and communication. Physical recreation takes place out of the school context and is freely chosen by participants. Sport, as physical activity in a competitive setting, is a legitimate element of physical education and may be chosen as a recreational activity by individuals or indeed taken up as a career. It should, however, be only one aspect of physical education and not the predominant physical activity in physical education. (Capel *et al.* (2006) consider an alternative presentation of the similarities and difference in these concepts.)

Q1

Looking back to early forms of physical education

MW: It is interesting to note that the subject we now call physical education in England has, over the years, been known by other names, such as drill or physical training. What are these, why were these names used, what was different about these in comparison to physical education?

SC: This is a good question. The answer will show how physical activity in schools has been related closely to the social situation in the country and will begin to reveal some of the roots of the subject that persist today. Some key historical texts are listed in the further readings if readers would like to get a fuller understanding of the history of physical education in England.

Table 1.1 Activity areas specified in NCPE documents

	Key Stage 1	Key Stage 2	Key Stage 3	Key Stage 4
1992	Five areas of activity: athletic activities, dance, games, gymnastic activities, outdoor and adventurous activities + swimming at Key Stage 1 or Key Stage 2	Six areas of activity: athletic activities, dance, games, gymnastic activities, outdoor and adventurous activities and swimming, if not covered in Key Stage 1	Minimum of four areas of activity: games compulsory + three from athletic activities, dance, gymnastic activities and outdoor and adventurous activities (swimming can be part of some of the above)	At least two activities, from same area of activity or two different areas of activity
1995	Dance, games and gymnastic activities + swimming at Key Stage 1 or Key Stage 2	Five areas of activity: dance activities, games, gymnastic activities, plus two from athletic activities and outdoor and adventurous activities and swimming if not covered in Key Stage 1	Four areas of activity: games compulsory + dance or gymnastic activities and athletic activities, outdoor and adventurous activities or swimming	Two activities from different areas of activity
1999	Dance, games and gymnastic activities + swimming at Key Stage 1 or Key Stage 2	Dance activities, games, gymnastic activities, plus some time for athletic activities and outdoor and adventurous activities and swimming if not covered in Key Stage 1	Games – full unit plus one full unit and two additional half units. One half unit must be dance or gymnastic activities. Games in each year of the Key Stage	Two activities, one of which must be a game
2007	Dance, games and gymnastic activities + swimming at Key Stage 1 or Key Stage 2	Dance activities, games, gymnastic activities, plus some time for athletic activities and outdoor and adventurous activities and swimming if not covered in Key Stage 1	Based on key processes, key concepts and curricular opportunities. Activities selected to ensure these three are addressed	Based on key processes, key concepts and curricular opportunities. Activities selected to ensure these three are addressed

To explain briefly, in the late nineteenth century drill or physical training was adopted in state elementary schools to meet both physical needs of poor health and social needs such as improving discipline to prevent unruly behaviour and encourage obedience. This curriculum area was under the auspices of the Department of Health.

Many schools took a militaristic approach which favoured military drill, comprising marching, parading and standing exercises (leg, arm and trunk movements), carried out in unison, under the command of a teacher. It combined physical exercise with strict discipline for children who could get 'awkward and restless'. Drill could be carried out in the classroom or outside by the whole class or as a larger group activity (see, for example, http://history.powys.org.uk/school/newtown/drill.shtml).

Physical training had a slightly different focus, being very much concerned with fitness, such as muscle strength, joint flexibility, cardiovascular fitness and endurance. Physical training was rigidly organised with the teacher or instructor following directions given in a manual. The term physical training is still used today, particularly in military settings or in relation to preparation for a particular activity or challenge. In these contexts it is designed to meet a specific end with testing, measurement and comparison with others used to challenge and motivate participants.

As well as drill and physical training, callisthenics and gymnastics were also included in some elementary schools in the nineteenth and early twentieth centuries. Swedish gymnastics was also found in some elementary schools before and after the First World War. The nature of this gymnastics was very different to that which we find in today's schools. It comprised set exercises carried out in unison and had a focus on posture and joint flexibility.

The emphases on these different approaches to physical activity varied at different times and in different contexts and circumstances. For example, military drill and physical training were particularly prominent in the period immediately after the Boer War (1899–1902), largely as a result of reports of recruits being medically unfit for service (Bailey and Vamplew, 1999: 19–20). Likewise, there were renewed demands for physical drill and physical training as a result of the First World War and hence they were a staple for boys at this time.

MW: You indicate that this focus on Swedish gymnastics was in elementary schools? What was happening in secondary schools?

SC: Secondary education was not available to all at this time. It was largely the preserve of the wealthy and growing middle classes. Physical education in secondary schools in England started in public schools for boys around the mid-1850s. The focus was on sport, particularly team games such as cricket, fives, football, racquets, rowing and rugby. These sports were designed both for physical and social needs, including developing character traits such as loyalty, self-control, perseverance, fairness and courage (both moral and physical) and leadership; these together being described as a magnificent preparation for life (see Mangan, 1983). What has been described as a games ethic or cult of athleticism reached a peak around 1914. According to Bailey and Vamplew (1999: 4) 'the mythology of Thomas Arnold's Rugby School, and the hero of Thomas Hughes novel *Tom Brown's Schooldays*, did wonders for the mid-nineteenth-century spirit of Empire'. As a result, sayings such as 'the battle of Waterloo was won on the playing fields of Eton' (often attributed to the Duke of Wellington, but which is probably apocryphal) and clichés such as 'play the game' and 'it's not cricket' became commonplace.

MW: Am I correct in saying that movement work or physical training in elementary schools was directed to promoting health and discipline of the masses, while it was sport that featured at the secondary level as it was believed that this fostered loyalty, courage and leadership; these qualities being needed by the upper classes to fulfil their roles as leaders both nationally and in the British Empire?

SC: Yes. In both cases activity was a means to a specific end. Games also spread from the public schools into grammar schools in the Victoria and Edwardian eras because, as Mangan (1983) argued, concerns for social status and prestige were uppermost. Hence, grammar schools were modelled on the public schools.

With respect to girls the situation was slightly different. By the 1880s and 1890s girls' public schools took up the games ethic in much the same way as boys' schools had done, albeit largely with different games, for example, netball and lacrosse. In addition, the emphasis of these games was different, with the co-operative and therapeutic aspects of play being emphasised as opposed to the more competitive and physically active emphasis of boys' activities. As well as games, Swedish gymnastics was also firmly established in the emerging girls' high schools in the latter part of the nineteenth century.

MW: It would certainly be true to say that overall the way boys and girls experienced physical activity in secondary schools at this time differed significantly. While the traditions of men and women in physical education follow trajectories which have some similarities there are also clear differences. In fact it was the training of physical education teachers in the women's physical education colleges which were established in the latter part of the nineteenth century and early part of the twentieth century that was responsible for the development of what is often described as the female tradition of physical education. Fletcher (1984: 134) went as far as to say 'here is the origin of that split which has been one of the most striking phenomena of recent educational history'. The first physical education colleges for men were not established until the 1930s. Many of those teaching boys were either from a military background or were expert athletes in their own right. Thus, due to their lack of appropriate training, in the late nineteenth century men were on the periphery of what had been created by women. Women's influence on physical education survived until after the Second World War.

Q2

The name of the subject as physical education was established at the end of the Second World War. This change of name was the result of the responsibility for the subject being moved from the Department of Health to the Department of Education. Physical education was now acknowledged to be firmly part of education. The new perception of the role of physical education as an integral part of overall education created a dilemma for the subject. All previous work in state schools, exemplified in the 1933 syllabus, had been developed mainly with elementary schools in mind, this being directed towards physical fitness and the promotion of discipline. With physical education becoming recognised throughout education, new thinking was needed.

A significant influence on physical education at this time was that, as a result of the introduction of mass secondary schooling in 1945, men joined the profession in large numbers for the first time. They brought with them vastly different experiences of combat and commando training. They introduced developments in the subject such as the physiological approach to gymnastics, strength and stamina training, circuit training and more outdoor activities and, of course, they extended the influence of games/sports. Despite competitive team games and sports being part of British life for a century or so, it was only after the end of the Second World War, and the advent of mass secondary education, that they became established as a substantial part of secondary school physical education programmes. Indeed, they came to dominate and form the core of physical education within a short space of time. While this was resisted by the women, the adoption of the 'private school' model of physical education in the state sector signalled the beginning of sport dominating physical education.

SC: This was surely also the time, at the end of the Second World War, that Rudolf Laban came to England and his system of movement analysis and approach to teaching made an impact on physical education.

MW: Yes indeed Laban's work challenged the approach to physical education, particularly for girls. This was on account of women's training colleges being enthusiastic about Laban's approach, not least as it chimed well with the then current learner-centred philosophy of education. As a result, by the 1960s Swedish gymnastics was challenged in secondary schools by women teachers whose work became strongly influenced by modern educational dance and modern education gymnastics inspired by Rudolph Laban. Work arising from Laban's philosophies was child-centred and based on an understanding of movement comprised of the elements of weight, space, time and flow. According to Fletcher (1984: 98), though the 1933 syllabus

(Great Britain, Board of Education, 1933) had offered more freedom than earlier directives, modern educational dance and gymnastics 'seemed to supply what had long been wanting: a means to develop with older learners the movement training given at the primary stage'. It would be true to say that the decade of the 1960s and the early 1970s saw the most marked difference between physical education for boys and that for girls. Physical education for boys combined sport with aspects of physical training while physical education for girls covered a broader range of activities and was concerned to promote personal attributes such as creativity and independence.

SC: How long did the Laban influence last and what was the cause of its demise?

MW: The Laban influence lasted until the mid-1970s. As the child-centred focus of education lost favour and was replaced by a concern for a more didactic knowledge-focused curriculum, so physical education moved increasingly to an activity-centred focus. Schools began to look to national governing bodies of sports (NGBs) to lead the way in how many of the activities were taught. NGBs were being led mainly by men which, together with the sceptical attitude to Laban's work held by many male teachers, resulted in physical education becoming predominantly games skills based.

SC: So what happened then? How did the curriculum as we know it today develop?

MW: I suggest that from the mid-1970s there has been an ongoing debate as to whether physical education should be activity-centred, with a focus on sport/team games, or whether it should be learner-centred and comprise a wide variety of activities. To some extent men favoured the former approach and women the latter. That there still remains a strong sport ethic in today's physical education for boys and girls can be explained by considering the following changes that occurred, all providing opportunities for men to take the lead.

- State schools amalgamated their boys and girls sections into one institution or became co-educational.
- The male and female physical education departments merged.
- New heads of department were appointed, and these were mostly men.
- The pattern of teaching physical education to mixed sex groups became generally accepted.

There were, of course, some differences between experiences of boys and girls at this stage. For example girls took part in dance and played sports such as netball. Boys had very little opportunity to experience dance, maybe because of lack of training/confidence of male teachers to teach dance and the cultural expectations that dance was not for boys. In addition boys learnt sports such as football and cricket. Notwithstanding some variety, physical education had a clear focus on sport.

SC: While much of physical education remained the same we need to remember that from the 1980s learners in many sixth forms were offered a wider range of activity options in physical education. This development was introduced to enable learners to experience a range of activities from which they would find one they might like to pursue as recreation outside school and/or after they left school. This may have been partly a result of numerous surveys over a period of time which showed the very high drop-out from physical activity after learners left school (starting with the Wolfenden Report, 1960). This introduction may begin to explain why physical education was seen by some as recreation rather than education. Indeed it would seem at this time that physical education for older pupils was a combination of sport and recreation. This was surely the context in which the first NCPE was introduced? How did this new curriculum change the nature of physical education in secondary schools?

The nature of physical education today

MW: I think it is true to say that, perhaps surprisingly, there has been very little change. The pattern of experience in physical education described above seems to have persisted in spite of all the recommendations in the succession of NCPE documents. The reasons for this could include the following:

- The committee appointed to create the initial NCPE Curriculum in 1992 included men and women, traditionalists and innovators, strong sport supporters and those seeing physical education very much as part of education as a whole.
- The outcome of their deliberations were bound to represent a compromise (what might be called a curriculum by committee).
- Subsequent curricula in 1995, 1999 and 2007, while proposed by physical education specialists, had to incorporate directives from non-specialists in government departments.
- The presentation and language of the curricula have been so written that schools had considerable choice in how they reached the aims identified.
- Teachers in schools interpreted the NCPE curriculum in ways that matched school tradition, school facilities and their own beliefs about the nature of PE.
- While overall educational aims were specified, to guide decision making, so were the activities through which these aims could be realised (see Table 1.1).
- Teachers felt secure in that they were delivering activities as required by NCPE and made little change to their school curricula or schemes of work.

SC: This is both surprising and disappointing as in all cases the NCPE curriculum was carefully devised to realise key educational aims: aims that were common with other subjects; aims that underlined the contribution phys-ical education could make to education, aims, the achievement of which, depended on a broad and balanced curricular programme. These can be set out briefly as follows:

- The underlying aims of the National Curriculum in England (NC) in 1992 were concerned with learners developing knowledge, skills and understand-ing. In the context of NCPE, effective planning, performance and evaluation in the learning of physical activities should support achieving these aims.
- The underlying aims of the NC in 1995 had a clear inclusive focus, with NCPE being charged to promote: (a) physical activity and healthy lifestyles, (b) positive attitudes to physical activity, and (c) safe practice in ways that catered for all learners.
- The underlying aims of the NC in 1999 again had a focus on equality of opportunity and articulated a requirement to respect the diversity of society. Specifically NCPE was to be delivered in ways that ensured all learners were: (a) acquiring and developing skills, (b) selecting and applying skills tactics and compositional ideas, (c) evaluating and improving performance, and (d) acquiring knowledge and understanding of fitness and health.
- The underlying aims of the NC in 2007 were the promotion of successful learners, confident individuals and responsible citizens. NCPE should con-tribute to these ends by fostering competence, performance, creativity and healthy active lifestyles. To achieve these aspirations key processes, range and content, and curricular opportunities are spelled out.

We could argue that all versions of the NCPE curricula have been designed to reinforce the fundamental nature of physical education as presented in the definition of physical education in the first part of this chapter, and to set out a programme that could be seen as physical education rather than sport or recreation. In fact NCPE also described what high-quality physical education should look like. In the 2007 NCPE (CCA, 2007a) the follow-ing is proposed:

> A high-quality physical education curriculum enables all students to enjoy and succeed in many kinds of physical activity. They develop a wide range of skills and the ability to use tactics, strategies and compositional ideas to perform successfully. When they are performing, they think about what they are doing, analyse the situation and make decisions. They also reflect on their own and others' performances and find ways to improve them. As a result, they develop the confidence to take part in different physical activities and learn about the value of healthy, active lifestyles. Discover-ing what they like to do and what their aptitudes are at school, and how and where to get involved in physical activity helps them make informed choices about lifelong physical activity.

Physical education helps students develop personally and socially. They work as individuals, in groups and in teams, developing concepts of fairness and of personal and social responsibility. They take on different roles and responsibilities, including leadership, coaching and officiating. Through the range of experiences that PE offers, they learn how to be effective in competitive, creative and challenging situations.

Notwithstanding statements such as the above, it appears that what has been planned and designed in successive NCPE to deliver a rich and varied physical education experience has not resulted in many schools moving away from a predominantly sport-based programme.

MW: Two further questions come to mind. These arise from two of the considerations that must have underpinned the creation of an NC in England: being (1) to ensure parity of experience for all learners and (2) to raise the standard of learning for all. Has NCPE resulted in all learners having similar experiences in physical education and has it resulted in better taught physical education, with learners being more successful?

SC: It is difficult to generalise here, however anecdotal evidence would indicate that learners' experiences in physical education throughout England remain as varied in nature and quality as they were prior to 1992. The conclusion would seem to be that NCPE has not had a major impact on physical education in secondary schools.

MW: This is worrying as we have advocated that physical education in any period of history has been designed to meet the needs of the society in that era. It would appear to be the case that despite enormous changes in our society, significant advances in science and technology and vastly different ways that young people interact with each other, physical education has not moved with the times. In what ways has physical education adapted to the current social context, for example to our multicultural society, a rise in obesity, a rise in stress-related illness, a growing underclass of unemployed, the expansion of the media with the examples of high-level sports performers and the availability of personal information and communications technology gizmos?

SC: I agree with you that these social and cultural changes do not seem to have had a major impact on physical education and even where they have, the changes have been minimal and in no way altered the nature of the subject. It would be true to say that, generally, over the last 30 years modest changes have taken place in:

- the attention given to health-related fitness (see Chapter 5);
- the introduction of some new dance forms to cater for those from different ethnic backgrounds;
- the use of hand-held video cameras and interactive whiteboards and other information and communications technologies;

- the use of a wide variety of activities to try to promote participation outside school;
- particular attention to learners with potential in an activity to enable them to reach representative levels;
- some efforts to foster work-related skills such as in sport education.

All these modifications have occurred under the aegis of NCPE and in response to changes in society. However the experiences learners are having in physical education are not very different to those learners were having in 1980s. Is there evidence to show that this is the case?

Q3

MW: Yes. Evidence that games and sports still dominate the curriculum today includes, for example, an analysis by Roberts (1996: 49) of the 1994 Sport England survey that led him to comment that 'team games and other competitive sports were alive and well in England's schools' in the mid-1990s … nearly all learners were playing team games at school during every year in their school lives'. He concluded 'not that team games had been dropped, but rather they had been joined by other activities in broader sports curricula than the traditional games regime' (p. 50). Likewise, the Department for Culture, Media and Sport (DCMS) and DfES (2006: 2) found that, in the nearly 17,000 primary and secondary schools in their 2005–6 *School Sport Survey*, competitive sports such as football and athletics remained popular 'with almost all schools offering them' (DCMS/DfES (2006: 15). The vast majority of schools, for example, offered football, athletics, cricket, netball, hockey, rugby and tennis.

Likewise, Green (2008: 56–7) reported that 'although the curriculum diet has changed over the years, physical education curricula in many countries reflect a good deal of continuity (as well as undeniable changes in the form of a broadening and diversity of activities) in the shape of a continued emphasis on competitive team sports'. This seems to be prevalent not only in England but also in other countries. According to Penney (2006: 565)

It is … true to say that there is … a great deal of continuity in many countries between curricula of the past 30 years or so and those of the present. Although physical education curricula have broadened, they continue to be dominated by sport and, in particular, team games.

SC: Has the introduction of sports colleges in England made a significant impact on the nature of physical education?

MW: While it is impossible to generalise, sports colleges have, in many cases, focused on the elite performers and run physical education curricula with a focus on sport. They have not, in the majority, led a move from a sport focus to a learner-centred focus, which is signalled both in the definition of physical education and in the requirements of the NC overall.

There is much more that could be said about the nature of physical education today and how far it has and should have changed. What is perhaps most worrying is that there has been so little change despite the NCPE and the radical changes in society. Historical traditions/roots and teachers' reluctance to change together with public expectations seem to have left us with a curriculum area that appears to be sport and recreation orientated and for various reasons unable to move with the times.

Q4

SC: These points are ably set out by Kirk (2010) and in Chapter 14. Kirk's prognosis is alarming in that he is of the view that physical education in its current form may not have a future. Some of the possible reasons for lack of change are covered in Chapter 8.

Summary

This chapter opened by looking at the definitions of physical education, recreation and sport, arguing that, while closely related to each other, they are distinctive.

It then continued to look at a brief history of physical education, highlighting when the subject changed and, more importantly why. The importance of considering historical background is set out by Kirk (2010: x) who writes:

> without a historical analysis, we can know only part of our 'webs of significance' [Dening (1993)] … ignorance of the past means we are trapped in and transfixed by the immediate present. Preoccupation with the here and now might create an impression of being 'up with the pace' in a manner consistent with so much of the frenzied 'innovation' in physical education over the past two decades. A wealth of research literature has revealed, however, that this preoccupation has not brought about real, substantial or desirable change.

This brings us full circle because, as we discussed early in the chapter, although physical education is different from sport and recreation – it is often seen as synonymous with sport (and indeed, in recent years, the term physical education and school sport is often used). On the other hand, a concern to make the physical education curriculum relevant – particularly for older secondary learners, and therefore to widen activities and choices, with taster courses in later years of schooling, has often been seen as recreation. We stress that it is important that readers understand what physical education is and how it differs from sport and recreation (and any other terminology used) to enable deliberate decisions to be made so that the subject is relevant to all learners in all years.

Although the brief history has touched on both primary and secondary education, the focus of much of the chapter has been largely on secondary education. While this is important, it is also necessary to consider what primary physical education should look like to provide a firm foundation for physical education in secondary schools.

Questions for consideration

Q1 Critically discuss the definitions of physical education, recreation and sport as set out in the first part of the chapter. Articulate clearly (a) in what ways physical education is not recreation and (b) the disadvantages of sport being the predominant activity in physical education.

Q2 Fletcher (1984, 134) says 'Divisions in a discipline are common enough, but they are not usually aligned with sex'. She quotes Graham who says 'I find it difficult to conceive of men's/women's geography, mathematics etc.' She continues 'In fact, historically, there is no other subject where the split could have happened as it did in physical education. In this field, where women were leaders, the war brought not only a change of direction but a chance for the men' to take the lead.

What impact does this split have on physical education as we know it today?

Q3 Critically consider in what ways physical education, in your experience, has changed over the last 20 years and suggest modifications that might make it more relevant to today's young people.

Q4 Kirk (2010) describes the current focus of physical education in secondary schools in England as 'physical education as sports-technique'. How far, and why, do you agree with this definition of physical education as it is delivered in secondary schools in England today?

Further reading

Capel, S., Breckon, P. and O'Neill, J. (eds) (2006) *A Practical Guide to Teaching Physical Education in the Secondary School*. London: Routledge.

Chapter 1 includes useful exercises to differentiate between physical education, sport and recreation.

DES (Department of Education and Science) (1991) *Physical Education for Ages 5 to 16*. London: DES.

Chapter 4 includes a valuable discussion on the relationship between physical education and sport.

Fletcher, S. (1984) *Women First: The Female Tradition in English Physical Education 1880–1980*. London: Athlone.

This book looks at the female tradition in physical education through the women's physical education colleges. As Fletcher says 'the history of what has been called the female tradition raises pertinent questions for anyone concerned with the balance of influence between men and women in a mixed society' (p. 156).

Kirk, D. (1992) *Defining Physical Education: The Social Construction of a School Subject in Postwar Britain*. London: Falmer Press.

This text focuses on the social construction of physical education and considers both the defining of physical education and its curriculum history – including games, gymnastics, health, fitness and scientific functionalism.

The following physical education journals should support further reading. There are also many education journals which contain articles related to relevant topics across education more generally, which are useful to extend debate further. They may also contain physical education specific articles.

- *European Physical Education Review*
- *Journal of Teaching in Physical Education*
- *Quest*
- *Physical Education Matters*
- *Physical Education and Sport Pedagogy*
- *Sport, Education and Society.*

Chapter 2

What is the education in physical education?

Margaret Whitehead

Introduction

There has long been debate about the educational value of physical education, for example whether it can be justified on the grounds of its unique contribution to the curriculum or whether the subject is best seen as supporting wider educational goals. This is an important issue for physical education teachers, challenged, as they often are, to justify their subject within the school. This chapter critically considers the place of physical education in education.

From the basis of defining what is to be understood as 'education', the focus moves to the work of Arnold (1979). In his landmark treatise, which is frequently referred to and forms the basis of many arguments regarding the value of physical education (Department for Education and Skills (DfES)/Department for Culture, Media and Sport (DCMS), 2004; Talbot, 2008) he claims that movement experiences in physical education can offer a threefold contribution to the compulsory curriculum. He asserts that physical education has the potential to educate *about* movement, to educate *through* movement and to educate *in* movement. Arnold's arguments will be set out briefly and will then be subject to analysis. This analysis reveals some contestable issues as well as identifying dangers for physical education. Using the foundation of a holistic approach to the nature of the human condition Arnold's three claims are re-examined. This leads to an assertion that movement or physical education is valuable and educative in its own right. In respect of reference to wider educational goals it is argued that the subject has the potential to make a valuable contribution on account of our holistic nature, but that this will only be realised through informed, sensitive and effective teaching of movement work. The conclusion outlines the benefits of this approach. Readers are encouraged to form their own opinion as to how far the profession can benefit or otherwise from Arnold's treatise. The full text referred to in this chapter (Arnold, 1979) and his other work are worthy of study.

Nature of education

The place of physical education in education and the significance of having 'education' in our subject name have been the focus of wide debate. Perhaps the first question to ask is 'What is understood by *education?*' Until that question is answered it will be impossible to identify whether or not physical education can make a contribution to its realisation. There are a number of issues around the nature of 'education'. Pertinent to this chapter are two particular considerations: first, the context of education and second, the nature and purpose of education.

In the respect of the first consideration education can be conceived either as a lifelong journey or as the responsibility of schools and schooling. From the former perspective education is viewed as the responsibility of parents, schools, the government, the community at large, and indeed in adult life, the responsibility of each individual. From the latter perspective education is seen as synonymous with schooling, being focused on learners of compulsory school age and solely the responsibility of teachers, schools and the appropriate government department. Thinkers such as Claxton (1984) hold the former view while Hirst (1974) would hold the latter.

With respect to the second consideration, there is a range of perspectives. However, in relation to the debate about the value of physical education, it is useful to differentiate between two particular views. One sees education as having an extrinsic purpose, while the other asserts that its rationale is the intrinsic value it offers to individual learners. The former view sees education as initiation into that which a country or culture sees as worthwhile (e.g. Hirst, 1974). Here it is the passing on of what is seen as valuable knowledge, skills and understanding that is central to education. This concept has an undercurrent of an instrumental role for education in preserving and perpetuating that which the country sees as important. Education must ensure that the country thrives, compares well with other countries and is economically strong. The other view of education is focused more on the learners and what it is in their interests to nurture. Put simply it is learner-centred. Education is the vehicle by which individuals are supported in reaching their unique potential through developing a wide range of capabilities with which each is endowed (e.g. Dewey, 1922; Claxton, 1984).

In this chapter education is understood as that which takes place in schools, as physical education is a term that is, in most cases, used specifically in the context of schooling. The following discussion will look at the value of physical education during the years of compulsory schooling. In addition the chapter will look at schooling as an enterprise with learners at its heart. This is in line with the overall tenor of Arnold's position and challenges readers to look in depth at the intrinsic value of movement experiences for the participants. This approach underpins much that is written about the subject but is seldom accorded extended consideration and debate. The deliberations in this chapter aim to make a contribution to redressing this situation.

Education *about*, *through* and *in* movement

To debate the question 'What is the education in physical education?' it is valuable to consider the seminal work of Arnold (1979, Chapter 6). Arnold took for the central plank of his argument a notion that had been articulated by a number of writers with respect to physical education but had not been subject to serious interrogation (for example see Williams, 1970). He bases his discussion of the educative nature of physical education by considering three ways in which movement can be seen as making a significant contribution to education as a whole, these being 'education *about* movement', 'education *through* movement' and 'education *in* movement'.

In his terms education *about* movement 'can be looked upon as a rational form of enquiry' (Arnold, 1979: 168) covering knowledge in the fields of 'anatomy, physiology, physics, psychology, sociology, anthropology, aesthetics and philosophy' (p. 169). He sees these areas of knowledge being referred to, and exemplified, in physical education at different stages of schooling: for example at primary level scientific principles can be highlighted in the movement context and also applied in appropriate classroom lessons. At the secondary level aesthetic principles, for example, can be introduced and discussed in physical education and again applied to other subjects such as the arts. In examination work in physical education or sports studies, for those learners who opt for these courses, there is the opportunity to learn and appreciate a wide range of theoretical principles such as those related to anatomy, biomechanics, health and theories concerning the acquisition of movement skill. He accepts that what he calls rational movement knowledge is mainly of a propositional kind, that is knowledge that includes theories, beliefs and data. He sees merit in the fact that this knowledge is objective, shareable and communicable and that it provides 'a theoretical background of understanding which helps make coherent and meaningful that which is performed' (p. 170).

With respect to education *through* movement, Arnold refers to Andrews (1970) who claims that it is legitimate to argue that physical education can contribute to the broad enterprise of education in respect of, for example, cognitive development, aesthetic and moral education, fostering sound social relationships, education for leisure and fitness for 'positive living'. Arnold is mindful of the ambitious claims he is making and the problem of verifying this broader contribution to education. For example, can it ever be proved, without a shadow of doubt, that experiences in physical education are significantly responsible for improved cognitive function or the development of enhanced social skills? He also acknowledges that 'what is actually accomplished is always dependent upon a set of transactions between the teacher and the learner', and that effectiveness 'will entail the intelligent utilization of those situations that arise' (p. 173). Here Arnold is alerting teachers to the potential of taking up opportunities in teaching as they occur, such as highlighting moral issues in respect of games playing and giving time to look at personal and social skills that facilitate productive co-operation in groups. Arnold elaborates his argument by suggesting that education *through* movement can also relate to education *in* two specific ways – that is having either an illustrative or referrent function. His examples of illustrative functions include situations in which the working space becomes a laboratory in which scientific principles can be experienced and understood first hand. His examples of referent functions include the suggestions that games can be a valuable context within which to debate the need and value of rules and that dance can provide opportunities to raise issues concerned with aesthetics. In these situations physical education is being used as a vehicle for learning, learning that can be acquired in other settings. Physical education is serving ends that are not necessarily intrinsic to its core responsibilities.

Arnold justifies the value of education *in* movement in arguing that movement activities are worthwhile in themselves, are intrinsically rewarding and should be engaged in 'for their own sake' (p. 178). He writes that physical activity permits a person to actualise his physical dimension and to become more aware of himself and the world he inhabits. The knowledge acquired is substantially 'know how' or tacit knowledge (Polanyi, 1966). Tacit knowledge is the knowledge we have of how to carry out habitual movement tasks such as riding a bicycle, climbing a ladder or brushing our hair. This type of knowledge is seldom articulated but is undoubtedly a source of information on which our ability to move effectively relies. Furthermore Arnold argues that education *in* movement enables the individual to become part of 'exemplifications of a culture's sporting and dance heritage' (1979: 178). That is, it introduces the individual to aspects of the culture of which the learner is part. He concludes by saying that

> The world of movement for the agent or the moving being, is a world of promise towards self-actualization.... It is a world in which the mover can come to understand an aspect of his socio-cultural world and in doing so discover more perfectly his self and his existential circumstances.
>
> (p. 179)

In this context involvement in activities has a twofold value, one being an introduction into physical activities in which an individual can take part outside schooling and the second that, in participation, the individuals can realise and develop their physical potential with the satisfaction this brings.

Arnold closes with the assertion that while education *about* movement, education *through* movement and education *in* movement arise from taking different perspectives on the work in physical education that can be considered separately, in actuality they are closely interrelated in the learning that takes place in school.

A review of Arnold's position

For many years this approach has generally been seen as useful and uncontentious. For example it has been used as a basis of numerous government publications (e.g. Department for Culture, Media and Sport (DCMS), 2004) and has featured in views expressed by the professional association for physical education in England (Talbot, 2008). It has been referred to and valued as providing grounds for justifying our place in the curriculum by identifying ways that, broadly, would seem to describe different aspects of our work. While this approach has enabled the subject to remain in the curriculum, it has not been able to establish the uniqueness of physical education, nor improve the respect shown to the subject as a significant aspect of schooling. There are indeed some serious questions to ask about this approach.

Education *about* movement

Looking first at education *about* movement, is it the case that curriculum physical education in the secondary school contributes to education in a substantial way by covering aspects of propositional knowledge in the fields of, for example, anatomy, sociology and aesthetics? From where does this claim arise? In one sense there is no difficulty in answering this question. As learners prepare for a lesson with some form of warm-up activity the teacher may highlight the way that particular muscles and joints need to be activated and loosened. In addition attention may be drawn to the cardio-vascular system and how a lesson preparation needs to take account of this bodily function. Similarly in teaching folk dance, aspects of anthropology might be mentioned and in teaching creative dance issues of an aesthetic nature might be considered briefly. Whether or not these fleeting references to knowledge in specific disciplines can be classed as significant educational experiences is dubious. This is not to dismiss the value of drawing attention to these issues in a practical situation where learners can reflect on their own experience.

However beyond the reference to related areas of theory as an adjunct to teaching various aspects of physical education, there is a more substantial issue of whether it is the responsibility of physical education teachers to address propositional knowledge in the areas identified. This is a more complex question. The teachers' own knowledge of these areas is important as schemes, units of work and lesson plans are devised and indeed as she observes the learners in lessons. For example knowledge of anatomy is essential in observing movement and appreciation of the physiology of our embodied dimension is critical in devising appropriate challenges for learners. Psychological knowledge will inform the nature of the teacher's interaction with the learners and an understanding of sociology can guide decisions about aspects of teaching such as class management and group organisation. However, that the teacher has the responsibility to pass on this knowledge to learners seems beyond what would be expected. It can be argued that the role of the physical education teacher must be first and foremost to provide appropriate learning experiences in the form of physical activity to enhance learners' movement competence. In most cases any real depth of understanding would need an extended amount of time in lessons for explanation, exemplification and discussion, and, it is argued, this would seem out of place in physical education.

In conclusion it seems very grandiose to claim that propositional knowledge is effectively presented, understood and learnt in physical education, outside studying for an examination at the age of 16 or 18 years. That physical education teachers have the opportunity to highlight aspects of these fields seems acceptable, but to claim that an important contribution is made to education in this way by physical education is both overstating the case and trivialising these important areas of study. Chapter 7 in this book looks in detail at the knowledge content for teaching physical education.

Education *through* movement

Education *through* movement seems problematic from a different perspective. The tenor of this claim is that movement work in physical education is instrumental in learners attaining broader educational goals. Physical education on this justification becomes a means to other ends and not an end in itself. There are at least two dangers related to any claim of this nature. First, it is almost impossible to prove that experiences in physical education have a positive impact on, for example, cognitive development or moral education.

Claims such as these are seldom taken seriously except in the sense that all teachers, whatever their subject area, have a responsibility to contribute to the all-round education of the learners. The second danger is that, in different ways, most other curriculum subjects are making a contribution to these broader educational goals. If physical education lays particular stress on this contribution to education, there could be rational grounds to leave it out of the curriculum – other subjects being well able to achieve these goals. The profession is to be reminded that physical education has, in its history, too readily taken the opportunity to jump onto educational bandwagons, which, when these become out-of-date, can leave the subject somewhat beleaguered. For example when learning through discovery was in vogue, physical education argued that this was its main vehicle for learning and when life skills were championed as crucial to learning in school, physical education teachers claimed that these skills underpinned all physical education learning and teaching.

The claim that physical education contributes to education *through* movement experiences has another problem in that the impression is given that simply by taking part in, for example, gymnastics, swimming or competitive team games, broader educational benefits will be accrued. This has been contested and rightly so (e.g. Whitehead with Blair, 2010). In what ways will learning gymnastics in and of itself promote independent thinking? How will competitive games automatically foster appropriate moral development and is it the case that group work in dance will enhance social development? Similar questions can be asked in respect of the current UK government key principles within the *Every Child Matters* Agenda (DfES, 2003a) and the cluster of personal learning and thinking skills that have featured in a variety of ways in recent UK national curricula programmes (e.g. see Qualifications and Curriculum Authority (QCA) 2007b). Is it the case for example, that athletics will of itself, foster self-management and that outdoor and adventurous activity will by its nature, nurture communication skills?

The answer to all these questions must be in the negative. Examples are not hard to find.

For example a didactically taught gymnastics lesson will not foster independent thinking skills. A competitive games lesson in which learners are allowed to win at all costs will not foster moral development and a dance lesson in which group leadership is insensitive and domineering will not enhance social development. There is no guaranteed relationship between forms of physical activity and the acquisition of broader educational goals.

It is true that Arnold includes a word of caution in respect of this claim in writing that the achievement of contributing to education *through* movement will depend on 'transactions between the teacher and the learner', and 'will entail the intelligent utilization of those situations that arise' (Arnold 1979: 173). These observations are wise and need to be clearly understood. While it seems without doubt that physical education can make a contribution to wider goals, this is not because physical activities per se are being taught, but because of the way they are taught. It is suggested that it is not the *what* of physical education but the *how* that can be effective in promoting wider goals. The onus is firmly on the teacher, first, to plan schemes, units of work and lessons in which learning is designed in such a way that wider educational goals can be addressed, and second, to make sure that, in the pupil–teacher interaction in the lesson, attention is paid to the achievement of these goals. For example if group work is being employed in a lesson to promote social skills, the teacher will not only give feedback about how the movement work is developing but will also reinforce co-operative pupil behaviour. In a dance lesson that is also aiming to promote creativity, feedback should consider both movement outcomes and also imaginative ideas. Achieving these goals does not spring solely from *what* physical educationists are teaching but depends on the way teachers work with learners, the nature of interaction with learners and the methods of teaching used.

A cautionary word is needed here in that the focus of physical education is generally understood to be movement development. There could be a danger of so much attention being given to achieving broad educational goals such as developing communication skills, that less actual physical activity takes place. A balance needs to be struck.

It is indeed the case, as indicated above, that work in the movement field has the potential to make a significant contribution to the educational enterprise as a whole. However, this is not on the grounds that movement learning is somehow a separate aspect of our human nature which can be related to other areas of learning, rather it is based on the appreciation of each individual as a whole, or in other words on an acceptance of a monist philosophical position. This is a belief that we, as humans, are, each one of us, an indivisible entity. We are comprised of a variety of capabilities – cognitive, affective, interpersonal, embodied – that function in concert, mutually enriching each other. Any action we take, any experience we have, whatever capability or capabilities we are drawing on, will affect all other capabilities and resonate throughout all aspects of the individual. From this position it goes without saying that education, in the broadest sense of developing each individual's potential, will be affected by all experiences in school. Learning in music or art can permeate ways in which we see and appreciate the world at large, success in understanding mathematical procedures can add to our self-confidence and taking part in a debate in a history lesson can make us more sensitive to listening to the opinions of others. Experiences and learning are not compartmentalised, they change us as a whole person. Experiences in physical education are no different.

In conclusion, with respect to the claim that physical education provides education *through* movement, it is suggested that a stress on this justification for the subject paints a picture of a need to justify ourselves as a means to ends outside our unique contribution to the curriculum. Furthermore it is not the case that wider goals will automatically be achieved simply by participating in physical activity. However, it needs to be remembered that as teachers it is our responsibility to address wider goals; we are teachers first and physical education teachers second. All that having been said there is a sense, from a monist standpoint, that the claim is stating the obvious. Our nature as human beings is such that all experiences change us, for better or for worse, whatever capability or aspect of our human potential we may be engaged in exercising.

Q1

Education *in* movement

In respect of Arnold's discussion of 'education *in* movement', he addresses three themes. In relation to the individual these are concerned with:

- initiation into sporting and dance activities in which learners can take part beyond school;

- involvement in activities that are engaged in for their own sake, the experience being intrinsically rewarding, interesting and satisfying;
- realisation of self and self-actualisation.

On first reading, all three themes could be accepted without contention. However it is suggested that there have been some worrying implications of the first theme, being a focus on the initiation into forms of physical activity. A stress on the centrality of activities as the prime role of the subject has led to an activity-centred curriculum. Physical education becomes no more and no less than learning activities and the techniques and skills of those activities. Teachers see themselves as teachers of activities rather than teachers of learners. The experiences of the pupils are not judged as central to the work. Pupil needs, interests and motivation are seldom a concern. It is of course true that this introduction is in 'the interests' of learners, facilitating their ready participation in sport and dance activities in the 'adult world', beyond the years of schooling. However where physical education becomes synonymous with learning named activities there can be further limiting outcomes. If named activities and initiation into those activities that have the highest profile in a culture, together, become the focus of physical education, the result could be, as in, for example, the UK, a curriculum directed to participation in competitive team games, such as football and rugby. Furthermore this approach can all too readily 'dance to the tune' of those who see physical education as instrumental in bringing prestige to the country through international sporting success in key activities such as Olympic events. An insidious corollary of this is a focus on the identification and promotion of talent in physical education, at the expense of the majority of the learners.

Care also needs to be taken with respect to the second theme. The claim that physical activity can be justified on the grounds of the pleasure it brings, via intrinsically rewarding experiences, can in fact work against the subject. This is because this assertion is often interpreted as arguing that the purpose of physical activity is simply to have fun. Is this a sound basis for a subject to be included in the curriculum? Enjoyment or fun experienced by participation in an activity does not necessarily add weight to its inclusion in education. Do we employ teachers to provide enjoyment above all else? There is no doubt that taking part in physical activity can be enjoyable and exhilarating, but this of itself does not justify its inclusion in the curriculum.

The third of Arnold's themes – that of self-realisation and embodied experiences enabling learners to become 'more fully human' has been subject to little attention and development.

This is most unfortunate as it is argued that it is with this insight that Arnold puts his finger on the real value of physical education and the intrinsically rewarding experiences it offers. Indeed it can be argued that herein lies the unique value of embodied activity, the realisation of a distinctive human capability. The nurturing of this aspect of human endowment has far-reaching effects on the development of learners, development that can be supported as significantly educative in the sense of being learner-centred and nurturing learner potential. There is little doubt that Arnold would unequivocally see this contention as at the heart of our work.

It is most unfortunate that in attempting to clarify the 'educative opportunities' related to physical education, many in the profession have selected some or all of education *about* movement, education *through* movement and education *as initiation into* culturally relevant activities as their guiding principles. As can be seen above, each of these justifications leaves the profession open to a series of dangers, for example, claiming too much for the subject, rendering it without a unique contribution and resulting in a focus on specific named activity based work.

Arnold himself is careful to articulate the complex interdependence between all the ways that physical education can be seen as being 'educative'. He is also careful to stress where the significance of movement experience can be located. However these points seem to have been disregarded by the profession in favour of the more easily articulated aspects of his treatise. It is argued that the physical education community needs to move on from these more readily understood claims, appreciating their inherent problems and dangers, and work to understand and articulate the unique and invaluable contribution that physical education can make to the education of every learner.

Q2

The individual as a holistic being: taking a different perspective

Notwithstanding the above concerns about Arnold's seminal work, he provides the springboard for identifying the unique contribution of physical education to education and thus its justification. Indeed building from an element of his third theme of 'education *in* movement' – that of nurturing individual potential – a very different picture comes into being, that, far from rendering his treatise problematic, in fact, underwrites his ideas without their being open to misuse.

This argument rests on the premise, as stipulated at the start of this chapter, that education is essentially learner-centred. Education, it is argued, is the vehicle that enables every individual to reach their potential, by developing a wide range of capabilities with which they are endowed. Furthermore the claim is founded on an holistic understanding of the nature of persons and the way that all human capabilities function in concert. In line with the thinking of existentialists and phenomenologists, as well as numerous modern-day philosophers, psychologists and cognitive scientists, the individual human being is, by nature, a whole (Whitehead, 2010a). Scholars such as Gallagher (2005) and Lakoff and Johnson (1999) support a monist concept of being and refute dualism, this latter being the view that humans are comprised to two separable 'parts' the mental and the physical. It is argued that each person has to be appreciated as a whole before any consideration of his various abilities can be considered. And indeed, when these capabilities are examined, it is found that they are intricately interrelated. For example cognitive capabilities, embodied capabilities, musical capabilities and interpersonal capabilities are not 'free standing'; they feed from and into each other. Exercise of any of these capabilities provides experiences that resonate throughout the whole person. Experiences are not compartmentalised. In this situation the crude dualist view that a person is comprised of mental capabilities and embodied capabilities, with the former vastly superior to the latter, is exposed as seriously flawed. Indeed some of the recent research proposes the contrary view, that the development of cognitive concepts relies on embodied experience before they can be understood and established (see Gallagher, 2005; Edelman, 2006; see also Lakoff and Johnson, 1999).

It is argued that each human capability is of value in its own right, being a human endowment. Each is worthy of respect, appreciation and development. Human embodiment is not an inferior aspect of our personhood but a vital component in our human make-up.

The spectre of the usually unquestioned superiority of the mental faculties in comparison with the inferior status of our embodied capabilities would seem to be the underlying cause of the profession's lack of confidence in its own work, and as a consequence its ready use of arguments that justify physical education as a means to achieving what might be seen as 'more worthwhile' educational ends. Nurturing an individual's embodied potential is valuable in its own right, its justification does not rest on its contribution to the development of other capabilities. Interestingly Leder (1990: 153–4) writes about our being trapped inside a dualist picture that has limited our self-development and self-realisation. There is a great deal written, not least in relation to the concept of physical literacy (see Chapter 3), that spells out the value, per se, of nurturing embodied potential. This soundly grounded case for the significance of the embodied nature of the human condition, should be the profession's starting point in setting out the contribution of physical education in education.

Revisiting education *about*, *through* and *in* movement

Education about *movement*

In respect of this notion of the role of physical education in education it is recommended that the focus should be on the development of an understanding of the nature of movement. Concepts of intrinsic importance in movement learning such as control, balance and co-ordination should be highlighted, discussed and grasped. Sensitive self-awareness of movement as experienced and an ability to analyse and articulate aspects of movement are both of significant value to the central project of learning in physical education. This knowledge and understanding have the potential to develop thinking, independent learners who have the confidence to evaluate their progress in the movement context, take responsibility for their own learning and plan strategies for improvement.

This task relates closely to an appreciation of oneself as an embodied, moving being. There is a fine line between education *about* movement, in Arnold's terms propositional knowledge, and education *in* movement in the sense of understanding the principles underlying effective movement. In fact the knowledge and understanding of movement are better seen as an element of education *in* movement.

As indicated above, claims to contribute to education though the enhanced understanding of certain academic disciplines and their attendant propositional knowledge are highly questionable and are perhaps better forgotten. There is, however one exception, being the knowledge and understanding of the effect of exercise on the functioning of body systems and on health as a whole. Physical education is an ideal situation in which to inform learners of this important area of theory. Developing this knowledge in the context of taking part in physical activity certainly makes an invaluable contribution to education. This aspect of education *about* movement would seem to be wholly legitimate to our work and can indeed help to show the importance of physical education and legitimise its place in the curriculum.

Education **through** movement

From the standpoint described above of the holistic nature of the person, together with the significance of all human capabilities and the way in which all capabilities function in concert, the broader contribution of physical education to education can be seen in a different light. *On account of* our holistic nature, experiences in physical education can, without doubt, influence other capabilities such as cognition, aesthetic appreciation, musicality and interpersonal skills. The use of the notion of '*on account of*' moves away from the impression that physical education is principally of value in education by serving ends beyond its principal focus. Learning in physical education is an end in itself, not a means to other ends.

It would seem to be in the profession's interest to drop the notion of education *through* movement or *through* the physical, with its dualist connotations and the impression it gives of needing to rely on aims beyond its central remit to justify its place in the curriculum.

The profession needs to argue with conviction that *on account of* the holistic and embodied nature of the learner, physical education not only fosters our unique embodied capability, but alongside all other aspects of schooling, can have a profound influence on the total educational experience of every learner.

Q3

Education **in** movement

Looking at the areas of unease about elements of Arnold's notion of 'education *in* movement' the explanation needs to take a different approach. The rationale for the coverage of a range of activities, it is argued, should be less focused on introducing learners to culturally established movement forms and more concerned with providing an appropriate range of experiences for learners to deepen and extend their embodied potential.

In order to foster each individual's embodied potential, experiences of physical activity need to be broad, in respect of both the range of movement skills or patterns that are nurtured and the variety of environments in which these patterns can be challenged and extended. Issues of depth and choice in the coverage of different activities are debated in depth in Chapter 4.

Arnold's inclusion of the educational contribution of 'education *in* movement' as providing opportunities that are rewarding and satisfying is not straightforward to unpack. However it needs to be understood not as justifying physical activity simply because it is fun, but because successful involvement in embodied activity enables learners to come to know themselves as embodied beings and to appreciate the fulfilling experience of celebrating an aspect of their human nature. This experience is profoundly rewarding and can contribute significantly to the enhancement of self-confidence and self-esteem. Herein lies the seat of pleasure, satisfaction and enjoyment. In this context it needs to be remembered that individuals will be working within the potential of their particular embodied endowment. Any notion of success must be understood as related to the individual learner, not as the achievement of reaching pre-ordained benchmarks, and teachers should reinforce this.

Conclusion

It has been proposed in this chapter that reference to the trilogy of 'education *about* movement', 'education *through* movement' and 'education *in* movement' as the guiding principle in answer to the question 'What is the 'education' in physical education?' is less than helpful and can have dangerous consequences.

Considering the role of physical education in education from a holist or monist perspective and taking account of the concerns expressed in this chapter it is recommended that:

- the notion of education *about* movement should be confined to knowledge and understanding of aspects of health that relate directly to physical activity;
- the concept of education *through* movement should be dropped and a rationale based on our holist human nature should be articulated to explain our potential for making a significant contribution to education as a whole;
- education *in* movement should stress the development of personal embodied potential and the enrichment of self-confidence and self-esteem that this can bring. Notions of initiation into activities and the fun of participating, as justifying physical education should be played down. Also part of education *in* movement is the knowledge and understanding of the nature and principles underlying human movement.

Fundamentally physical education is educative in that it develops the embodied potential of the learner. The subject area needs no further justification. We are, by nature, embodied. Our embodied dimension is irrefutably involved in almost all aspects of education and life, and as such it is worthy of respect and nurturing in the same way as any of our other capabilities. The uniqueness of physical education lies in its ability to enable each individual to realise, nurture and develop his embodied capabilities and thus become more fully human.

The benefits of the approach suggested in this chapter in relation to the 'education' that can be addressed in physical education are that, as a profession, we:

- can state and justify, with confidence, the value of physical education in its own right;
- can claim with confidence that we make a unique and distinctive contribution to the education of all learners;
- are not reliant on dubious claims that the subject's principal contribution in the curriculum is to achieve wider educational goals;
- have a clear rationale for devising curricula that are learner-focused, not activity-focused and respect each learner as an individual.

This chapter has looked at Arnold's (1979) seminal presentation of the values of physical education and raised serious doubts as to the validity of some of the claims he makes. It has been argued that the educational value of physical education is founded on its principal concern with education *in* movement. The nurturing of our embodied potential has value of itself, which *on account of* our holistic nature has resonance with and contributes to the enrichment of many other aspects of our nature as humans. The position set out in the latter part of this chapter lays the ground for the discussion of the concept of physical literacy, which is the subject of the next chapter.

Q4

Questions for consideration

Q1 Critically consider the suggestion that it is counter-productive to claim that physical education has the capacity to deliver a wide range of educational ends.

Q2 Critically analyse the concerns expressed in the chapter in respect of Arnold's views, identifying criticisms with which you agree and those with which you disagree.

Q3 Critically consider the benefit of using the expression *on account of* rather than *through* to address the way that physical education has the potential to contribute to broad educational goals.

Q4 Discuss the notion that the place of physical education in schooling can be most strongly justified on the grounds that it makes a unique contribution to the curriculum.

Further reading

Arnold, P.J. (1979) *Meaning in Movement, Sport and Physical Education*. London: Heinemann.

Chapter 6 in this text sets out Arnold's reasoning behind his support for education about, through and in movement. It is valuable to refer to this treatise in debating the validity of the challenges raised in this chapter.

Whitehead, M.E. (2000) Aims as an issue in physical education, in S. Capel and S. Piotrowski (eds), *Issues in Physical Education*. London: RoutledgeFalmer, pp. 1–21.

Chapter 1 addresses a range of issues in respect of the aims of physical education. Particularly of interest in respect of the discussion above is the consideration of aims as ends in themselves rather than means to other aims.

Whitehead, M.E. (ed.) (2010) *Physical Literacy: Throughout the Lifecourse*. London: Routledge.

This text sets out the philosophical position that underpins the arguments put forward in this chapter. Part I provides a valuable insight into the rationale behind advocating a monist approach to the human condition. This supports the claim that it is *on account of* our nature that physical activity can have a profound impact on many aspects of human achievement and life.

The following Physical Education journals should support further reading. There are also many Education journals which contain articles related to relevant topics across education more generally, which are useful to extend debate further. They may also contain physical education specific articles.

- *European Physical Education Review*
- *Journal of Teaching in Physical Education*
- *Quest*
- *Physical Education Matters*
- *Physical Education and Sport Pedagogy*
- *Sport, Education and Society*.

Chapter 3

What is physical literacy and how does it impact on physical education?

Margaret Whitehead

Introduction

Physical literacy is a relatively new concept in the world of physical education. The concept is founded on philosophical principles and provides a clear rationale for the importance of the subject. The concept identifies a unique value for physical activity as well as clarifying how physical education can make a significant contribution to the education of young people.

This chapter is concerned with considering whether and how the concept of physical literacy can play a part in articulating, with conviction and clarity, the significance and value of nurturing our embodied capability, and at the same time, in line with suggestions made in Chapter 2, provide the means by which the profession no longer needs to rely on extrinsic factors to justify the subject area in the curriculum. Work in the movement field is of value in its own right and has both a unique contribution to make to education as well as potential, in and of itself, to make a broader contribution to the development of young people.

The chapter opens with a short background to the concept of physical literacy. The concept is based on a monist approach to human nature and two philosophical schools of thought – existentialism and phenomenology. Each of these is explained briefly. The overarching value of fostering our embodied capability is drawn out from these views and this provides the springboard for the definition of the concept of physical literacy to be presented.

Building from this explanation, the value of physical literacy as a human capability that can enhance and enrich the quality of life is briefly outlined. The relationship between physical literacy and physical education is then explained and the way that the concept can support the value of physical education is presented. The responsibilities of the physical education teacher in promoting physical literacy are then outlined. Finally the implications for the teaching of physical education, where the goal of nurturing physical literacy has been adopted as the fundamental goal of the subject, are presented.

Readers should examine the arguments in detail, ideally carrying out further reading as suggested, and then consider both the claimed value of physical literacy and the assertion that it can contribute to supporting physical education within the school. Finally readers should interrogate the pedagogical recommendations concerning the implications for teaching physical education.

Philosophical foundations

Physical literacy is a concept developed from a commitment to a monist approach to the nature of human being and a philosophical study of existentialism and phenomenology.[1]

A monist or holist approach to our nature is in opposition to the dualist position that sees us as comprised of two distinct and separable parts – the 'body' and the 'mind', with the 'body' being relegated to secondary status in relation to the 'mind' or the intellect. From a holistic perspective we are one indivisible whole, with every experience we have and every action we take being influenced by, and influencing, all aspects of our personhood. We are each comprised of a variety of capabilities,[2] all of which function in concert with each other – reciprocally interacting, influencing and enriching each other.

The philosophy of dualism dates back to the work of Descartes (1972 in Leder, 1990) who claimed that the intellect is indisputably our dominant feature on account of the fact that the only thing about which he could be certain was that he was thinking. He argued that he could doubt the reality of all other functions that he could perform. Hence, he concluded, we are at root cognitive beings. This attitude to our nature has become so embedded in western thought that it is taken for granted, notwithstanding challenges from philosophers, psychologists and cognitive scientists such as Leder (1990), Strawson (in Gill 2000), Lakoff and Johnson (1999) and Gibbs (2006). For example Leder (1990: 153–4) describes this situation well in writing that we are trapped inside a picture, a dualist picture of ourselves. He goes on to say that this has limited our self-development and self-realisation. Similarly Strawson (1964, in Gill 2000: 18) asserts that the person is logically prior to any description of the dimensions, such as cognitive, affective and physical, from which the individual is comprised. In other words he asserts that as humans we are manifest in the world as composite beings, fostering the capabilities that arise from developing our different areas of potential or dimensions to live our lives to the full. Any consideration of these constituent 'dimensions' of our nature must start from the notion of a whole person. No aspect of human nature exists as a discrete function prior to the existence of a person. It is similar to saying that, for example, a vase is comprised of clay, colour, texture, shape and weight and then trying to conceive how each of these constituents is merged to make the vase. You have to start with the vase and then identify its characteristics.

Q1

The philosophies of existentialists and phenomenologists are grounded in this monist concept of our human nature and build their theories from this perspective. The other key aspect of these philosophies, from the standpoint of physical education, is that they both see great significance in the fact that we are embodied and judge that our embodied nature plays an all-pervading and fundamental role in the development of life as we know it. The concept of physical literacy grew from the respect shown by monists, existentialists and phenomenologists for our 'body'. Significantly these thinkers arrived at these views from their wider philosophical deliberations, in no way concerned to support work in physical education.

The belief on which existentialism is founded is that existence precedes essence. Put simply this means that humans create their individual being through interaction with the world they inhabit. Every interaction provides new perceptions, new experiences, new knowledge about the world. As we interact with the world we are ourselves enriched and changed. We not only come to know more about the world, but at the same time realise more of our potential and our capabilities. We can interact with the world in a variety of ways. Each mode of interacting with the world carries the potential to contribute to the full realisation of human being and so it follows that all modes that offer this interaction should be nurtured. The human embodied dimension is one such mode and is therefore worthy of serious study, attention and development. Far from being a minor player in existence, our embodied nature is implicated in all we do.

For example many writers are now convinced that the development of cognitive concepts depends on embodied interaction with the world. Burkitt (1999: 12) writes that meaning is created through our embodied interaction with the world and also says:

> What we call mind only exists because we are embodied and this gives us the potential to be active and animate within the world ... we can only become persons and selves because we are located bodily at a particular place and time in relation to other people and things around us.

Leder (1990: 114 and 126) writes that 'the lived body is mentalised through and through, all of its organs participating in a uniquely human intelligence' and refers to the 'lived body as the seat of vitality, action and thought'.

Phenomenology adds further support for the significance of the embodied dimension, championing 'the embodiment-as-lived' perspective of this dimension. These philosophers assert that we perceive the world from the perspective of how we have interacted with it on previous occasions. The meaning it has for us is based on experience. We make sense of the world by assimilating what is perceived so that it builds from our prior knowledge, in a way 'seeing' the world in a particular way. We accommodate this new information about the world by adapting aspects of existing knowledge and understanding. Each of us has a slightly different world and each of us is changed by what we experience. The richer the understanding and appreciation of the world, accrued through interaction with the environment, the more sensitively perceptive the individual becomes, the more the individual learns about the world and at the same time learns about him/herself.

Given the key role that the embodied dimension plays in interacting with the world and the monist views of the human as a whole being, further support is provided in respect of the importance of our embodiment. It is the case that an element of the meaning of most of our surroundings springs from our embodied relationship with features in our environment. Unfortunately this meaning is seldom realised or articulated. Polanyi (1966) describes this as tacit meaning or knowledge: meaning that is inherent in our dealings with things. Tacit knowledge is seldom articulated, partly because it is founded on experiences in childhood prior to the development of language, partly because it is acquired throughout life in our embodied interaction with the world – an interaction much of which takes place at pre-conscious levels – and partly because the experience is, by nature, subjective. Tacit knowledge is taken for granted. For example, we know how to ride a bicycle but would have great difficulty to put this into words. Similarly we may know how to use a paper clip, climb stairs, perform a forward roll or throw a javelin, but it is almost impossible to explain how we do these things. Nevertheless knowledge of this nature is constantly called on as we live our lives and, as suggested above, is the foundation of cognitive development and the acquisition of propositional knowledge.[3] Merleau-Ponty, referred to in Leder (1990: 7), suggests that abstract cognition itself may sublimate but never escapes its inherence in a perceiving, acting body.

Monism, existentialism and phenomenology give unequivocal support for the significance of the embodied dimension in human life as we know it. As such it is not appropriate to 'write off' our embodied dimension as a subordinate servant to our intellect. *We are as we are* on account of our embodied nature and we interact with the world essentially from an embodied perspective. The world is for us a world viewed by an embodied being.

Q2

Philosophical considerations, physical literacy and physical education

How do the above views relate to the work of physical educationalists? Unequivocally these views demonstrate the importance of the subject area. There are no grounds for the profession to see itself as nurturing a subsidiary or inferior aspect of our learners. The learners' embodied dimension is as worthy of development as any other human dimension. Education, as a vehicle by which potential is developed in order to live a full and rewarding life, should address all aspects of our human nature. Individuals should be aware of the potential of their various dimensions and be motivated and confident to foster the capability each dimension affords, deploying it as appropriate throughout life. This includes our embodied dimension and its resultant capability and is pertinent to all learners, whatever their physical endowment. From this standpoint physical educationists have a clear, underpinning justification for their work as making a significant contribution to education.

Our role is to nurture learners' motivation and confidence in capitalising on their embodied dimension in realising their embodied capability. It is suggested that promoting positive attitudes to physical activity in the interests of establishing exercise as a lifelong habit should be our ultimate goal. This positive disposition to activity has been described as being physically literate. Physical literacy is a disposition all can achieve, it has far-reaching benefits for the young and the old, for those with particular needs as well as the able-bodied.

The definition of physical literacy can be set out briefly as follows:

> As appropriate to each individual's endowment, physical literacy can be described as a disposition acquired by individuals encompassing the motivation, confidence, physical competence, knowledge and understanding that establishes purposeful physical pursuits as an integral element of their lifestyle.
>
> (Whitehead, 2010a: 11)

In more detail the attributes evident in a physically literate individual can be described as follows:

A   Physical literacy can be described as a disposition characterised by the motivation and confidence to capitalise on innate movement/physical potential to make a significant contribution to the quality of life and a commitment to maintaining purposeful physical pursuits[4] throughout the lifecourse.

   All humans exhibit this potential, however its specific expression will depend on individuals' endowment in relation to all capabilities, significantly their movement potential, and will be particular to the culture in which they live.

B   Individuals who are physically literate will move with poise, economy and confidence in a wide variety of physically challenging situations.

C   Physically literate individuals will be perceptive in 'reading' all aspects of the physical environment, anticipating movement needs or possibilities and responding appropriately to these, with intelligence and imagination.

D   Individuals will have a well-established sense of self as embodied in the world. This, together with an articulate interaction with the environment, will engender positive self-esteem and self-confidence.

E   Sensitivity to and awareness of embodied capability will lead to fluent self-expression through non-verbal communication and to perceptive and empathetic interaction with others.

F   In addition physically literate individuals will have the ability to identify and articulate the essential qualities that influence the effectiveness of their own movement performance, and have an understanding of the principles of embodied health, with respect to basic aspects such as exercise, sleep and nutrition

(Whitehead 2010a: 12)

These attributes need to be understood from the background of the monist nature of the individual and the way in which developing physical literacy has an impact on the wider development of other capabilities such as cognition and social interaction.[5]

It is important at this stage to make it clear that the concept of physical literacy offers no threat to physical education. Physical education is an element of the school curriculum, while physical literacy is a goal to be reached. Physical literacy provides a clear focus for our work in physical education. In addition its sound philosophical roots open up the opportunity of providing a clear articulation of the value of movement work in school and a justification for the inclusion of physical education in the curriculum.

Questions are often asked about the relationship between being physically educated and being physically literate. It is suggested that there has never been real consensus about what is meant by being physically educated and this is not surprising given that other subjects do not use this type of terminology. For example, the notions of being of geographically educated and historically educated are not used. Efforts to define being physically educated have usually resulted in a list of physical skill achievements realised by an individual by the end of schooling.

There are a number of problems with any effort to describe an individual as being physically educated. Of particular note is that, with such a wide variety of physical endowments, it is all but impossible to have a single benchmark against which to judge attainment in respect of every pupil. The second problem is that the notion of being physically educated gives the impression that there is an end state which cannot be built on in the future.

There is considerable advantage in referring to individuals being physically literate as this implies that they are making progress, as appropriate to their individual endowment, across all or most of the attributes of physical literacy. The notion acknowledges that they are on a lifelong journey and that progress is always possible. Critically, being physically literate encompasses the expectation that this progress is very likely to occur. It is interesting to note that other areas of the curriculum have adopted a 'literacy' approach, for example music – music literacy – and politics – political literacy.

While there have been various references to physical literacy in the context of discussing the nature and aims of physical education, such as in the Declaration from the National Summit on Physical Education (Talbot, 2007), Hardman (2011) uses the concept of physical literacy to define being physically educated in writing:

> Physically educated persons might be described as being physically literate, having acquired culturally normative skills enabling engagement in a variety of physical activities, which can help to maintain healthy well-being throughout the full life-span; they participate regularly in physical activity because it is enjoyable; they understand the value physical activity and its contribution to a healthy lifestyle.

While this is a useful way to relate the two concepts it is not wholly satisfactory in that it does not make clear that all can be physically literate, in a form appropriate to each individual's physical endowment, nor does it highlight the key aspects of physical literacy of being motivated and confident in respect of taking part in purposeful physical pursuits.

Q3

The value of physical literacy

There is not space here to go into great detail of the value of physical literacy (see Whitehead 2010b). However two approaches can be suggested, either of which can be a starting point from which values can be identified.

First, taking a broad view from the perspective of the philosophical positions that have been covered, the value of making progress in becoming ever more physically literate enables each individual to:

- foster the development of the embodied dimension and thus benefit from realising a human capability;
- capitalise on an aspect of human potential – thus becoming more fully human;
- engage in a wide range of interactions with the world, including interacting with others, thus having experiences through which to gain personal knowledge and understanding as well as a richer appreciation of the world.

Second, the value of physical literacy can be expressed from a more practical standpoint, that is, its potential in making a significant contribution to human flourishing in its widest interpretation.

On account of our holistic nature, making progress in respect of all the attributes of physical literacy will promote:

- the development of physical competence;
- confident participation in a wide variety of purposeful physical pursuits;
- effective interaction in a wide variety of situations and environments;
- the development of self-confidence and self-esteem;

- sensitive interaction with others;
- knowledge and understanding of the importance of physical activity in maintaining health;
- the commitment to participate in a range of purposeful physical pursuits;
- the ability to reflect realistically on personal strengths and to select appropriate purposeful physical pursuits in which to take part;
- an appreciation of the value of purposeful physical pursuits in their potential to enhance the quality of life.

Physical literacy has the potential to enhance life in many respects. Some of the outcomes of being physically literate relate closely to our specific embodied potential, however others relate to broader human functioning and thus can be significant to human flourishing and to individuals enjoying a rich quality of life.

Physical literacy and physical education teaching

While the nurturing of physical literacy needs to be addressed throughout the lifecourse, with a variety of significant others being involved from the early years through to later life, it is suggested that physical education teachers have both a unique opportunity and a clear responsibility to nurture this capability (see Whitehead with Murdoch, 2006). It is certainly the case that physical education in school is the only place where every young person is assured of having experiences in purposeful physical pursuits and therefore it represents perhaps the one and only opportunity for every young person to develop their motivation, confidence and competence in respect of their participation in these activities. This unique opportunity puts the onus on physical education teachers to use this time to effect to promote physical literacy. The expertise that the teacher brings to this area of the school curriculum is substantial and significant. School physical education may be the only time when all young people work with those who are best prepared to enable every pupil to thrive in the physical activity context. It is argued that, as highly qualified professionals, physical education teachers have a responsibility to support all learners in their physical literacy journeys and to launch them on the road of a lifelong habit of participation in purposeful physical pursuits.

Implications of promoting physical literacy for physical education teachers

Where teachers set themselves the goal to promote physical literacy what are the implications for teaching?

The implication for teaching can be seen to cover four areas: knowledge of the nature of physical literacy, the development of a productive relationship with learners, the employment of appropriate teaching approaches and the selection of apposite lesson material.

Knowledge of the nature of physical literacy

It is suggested that a prerequisite for taking up the challenge is a sound understanding of the nature of physical literacy and its philosophical foundations (see Whitehead, 2010a) Teachers need both to understand and support the concept of physical literacy and to appreciate the range of attributes of which it is comprised. They need to take a monist approach in their appreciation of the human condition and to acknowledge, as argued in Chapter 2, that, on account of our monist nature, promoting physical literacy can have far-reaching effects on the whole person.

Relationship with learners

The promotion of physical literacy is founded on the acceptance of each individual as an holistic being with unique potential. Each individual should be viewed as a whole, a unique person with particular characteristics and potential. Each individual should be respected and acknowledged as of value. Each is worthy of support, attention and guidance. Each is on a personal physical literacy journey and progress should be judged from this perspective. Comparison with others is less valid than an evaluation of individual learning, hence the use of ipsative assessment, where judgements are made in relation to the individual's previous attainment, is recommended. There is no reference to benchmarks or comparison with others. This respect for each young person should be reflected in all interaction between pupil and teacher and this compassionate understanding and acceptance should extend to the ways learners relate to each other. The teacher's example is paramount. Learners should be encouraged to show empathy and appreciation of the efforts of their peers as displayed by the teacher.

Physical education requires learners to display, very publicly, an aspect of their personhood and to expose more of their physicality than is normally the case, outside the physical education setting. The embodied dimension is an integral and highly significant aspect of the nature of young people and they can feel exposed, embarrassed or ashamed of this aspect of themselves. Any criticism of the embodied dimension can be read as a criticism of themselves – for both boys and girls. Great care needs to be taken to show that each is accepted as they are and to build appropriately from this starting point. Presentation of self is highly significant to young people at the secondary stage and this needs to be borne in mind when deciding on the dress for physical activity. Sensitivity should be shown to all and of course to those from certain cultures/faiths that have strict dress codes. In the context of respect for persons, listening to the learners' voices demonstrates the teacher's real interest in the experiences of young people. Acting, as appropriate, on their views is a clear indication that the learners are seen as having a contribution to make to decisions relating to the learning/teaching in lessons. As far as possible teachers should know their learners, and, being sensitive to their family circumstances, encourage ways the learners can participate in purposeful physical activity beyond the school.

How teaching is conducted

The overall nature and atmosphere of lessons have been described above and the way teaching needs to be conducted follows closely on these recommendations.

It is argued that all learners should be confident that physical education is a context in which they can make progress and succeed, in respect of their own physical literacy journey. All learners should leave the lesson with a 'can do' attitude to physical activity, a feeling of satisfaction in their work in the lesson and a positive attitude to the next lesson. This can be engendered by the teacher being encouraging and supportive. Effort and progress need to be acknowledged as much as achievement. This enthusiastic appreciation of learners' work does not mean that the teacher has low expectations and is easily satisfied. On the contrary the teacher should set realistic goals and demand application from all. Praise should be earned. Learners themselves are very much aware of how hard they are working and rewarding casual efforts can be seen as something of a joke (see Whitehead, 2011).

Q4

Assessment for learning should be adopted at all times including recognition of effort, as appropriate, as well as an identification of the next goal and advice on how this goal can be achieved. Feedback should display appreciation, understanding and empathy. Criticism should be avoided where possible, with reprimands focusing on the deed not the person, stressing behaviour that should be adopted rather than the inappropriate behaviour. With the embodied dimension being such a key aspects of personhood, negative comment on learners' abilities or progress can lower self-perception, self-confidence and self-esteem. Nurturing of this triumvirate is absolutely critical to the promotion of physical literacy, having at its heart confidence and motivation.

As indicated above, the experience of success is essential in nurturing individuals' physical literacy. This points towards effecting differentiation through task, outcome or teaching approach, in some or most episodes of the lesson. The concept of mastery learning where the goal for each pupil is to reach a particular goal, rather than to reach a pre-specified class-wide standard, would seem to be the most likely to offer success.

A particularly challenging aspect of differentiation is management of ability grouping with its inherent overt recognition of differences in pupil potential. The success of an ability grouping approach, where some learners can feel identified as less able, will depend on lesson experiences in which a 'respect for persons' climate pervades between the learner and the teacher and between the learners. Learners should accept that it is in their interests to work on particular tasks. In fact learners themselves know how they compare with others. However this should not prevent all participants feeling that they can improve and that sometimes this means working on different tasks. All mixed ability grouping and teaching is challenging and needs to be carefully presented and managed.

With the goal of involvement in purposeful physical pursuits becoming a lifetime habit, learners should be given increasing opportunities to take responsibility for their own learning. They should be supported in being realistic in their self-assessment and in the acknowledgement of strengths and areas that need to be developed. They need to be able to self-assess and be intrinsically motivated to work to make progress. When learners complete compulsory education they should to be able to make informed decisions about the physical activity regimes they adopt. This points to the need to use strategies that involve independent learning in physical education, with the reliance on the teacher being decreased.

The recording of progress throughout schooling with respect to physical literacy is a challenging area and one that is currently the subject of study and research. While charting personal progress with respect to movement competence will be of central importance, all attributes of physical literacy should be monitored. Any record should document a personal journey rather than the success or otherwise of reaching pre-specified targets. It is suggested that learners should be involved in this exercise, both because affective elements of physical literacy such as motivation and self-esteem will involve gathering the views of learners, and because realistic self-assessment and setting own goals is an important element of being physically literate.

While a highly controversial suggestion, it is worth considering if, given the marked variation in physical development at certain stages of schooling, age-related physical education is the best way to teach the subject. For example in adolescent boys chronological age is not always a good indicator of limb development or muscular strength. Timetabling two year groups together and sub-grouping according to height, size and strength might be an approach to explore.

Content of teaching

Once again this topic needs to be considered from the perspective of each learner being on a personal journey, through which the promotion of motivation and self-confidence are paramount. However this should be balanced against providing a broad and balanced experience of Movement Forms (see also Chapter 4) and the need to prepare learners to make choices from the wealth of opportunities available in the context of purposeful physical pursuits within and beyond school.

In the early years and through the first stages of schooling up to the age of 11 years a broad and balanced experience of movement competence needs to be effected. As detailed in Chapters 9 and 15 of Whitehead (2010a), movement competence should build from the young child's movement vocabulary described as generic movement patterns. Movement patterns are seen as the building blocks of physical competence and the root of all purposeful physical pursuits. An essential aspect of teaching should be the development of generic movement patterns so that they become refined and then specific to different activity contexts. This sophistication of movement patterns depends on the application of movement capacities such as balance and control. This honing of movement patterns into activity specific forms is a long-term and challenging enterprise. (Movement patterns and movement capacities are explained more fully in Chapter 4.)

It is proposed that the focus of pre-secondary school experience should be on the confident use of generic and refined movement patterns rather than being concerned with specific patterns. Specificity is needed when the adult form of an activity is engaged in and this is seldom appropriate for the majority of younger learners. It is argued that a curriculum that looks widely at movement competences in relation to, for example, functional body management, expressive body management, manipulative learning and learning in the outdoors, is more appropriate than a curriculum comprised of named activities. Working in these broader categories of movement experience, younger participants can learn through discovery and problem-solving and acquire the necessary co-ordination and control to facilitate later more specific and demanding movement patterns.

In the secondary years of schooling difficult decisions have to be taken on how best to enable all to make progress and at the same time open doors to future involvement in purposeful physical pursuits. This calls for a carefully designed curriculum in school that builds on earlier work in developing movement patterns. In the main the focus will be on fostering the development of movement capacities enabling patterns to develop from refined to specific. Learner involvement in examples of adult physical activities and sports should be introduced as the context for specific patterns to be practised and established. As indicated above, the intention in all this work is to ensure that every learner is being appropriately challenged and making progress. Situations to be avoided are:

- those in which previous work is repeated, for example, the learning outcomes of a lesson on throwing in athletics being the same as those covered in an earlier module or year;
- lessons in which the demands of work are unrealistic, for example the expectation of younger secondary phase learners to play a full game of hockey;
- lessons in which insufficient time is given for specific movement patterns to be established, for example a very brief introduction to the tennis serve with no time for practice and individual guidance, or the challenge in dance to use different levels in movement without enough time to improve control and precision in the execution of the movements identified.

All the above should be avoided as they can engender frustration and disillusionment and hinder the development of motivation and/or confidence.

Teachers have a dilemma here. There is a strong desire in curriculum time to introduce learners to as many adult forms of physical activity as possible, thus enabling learners to have a wide experience from which to select in their participation after schooling. While these sentiments are valid, the outcome for most learners is seldom effective. As discussed by Kirk (2010) there is no evidence that this approach is either fostering motivation in physical education or encouraging lifelong participation in purposeful physical pursuits. Short blocks of time are given to a series of activities with learners rarely getting to grips with the movement demands. When this organisation is repeated year after year, learners have to revisit old work before they can begin to move on to new work. Overall little progress is made, with the danger of learners becoming bored, losing motivation and achieving no gain in confidence.

A new approach will be needed if all are to make progress in their individual physical literacy journey. This is not an easy problem to solve. However one approach would be to see curricular and extra-curricular work as a whole. Curriculum time would be spent on fewer activities that involve learners in participating in different Movement Forms such as the athletic form, the competitive form and the aesthetic and expressive form (these are detailed in Chapter 4). An equal amount of time would be given to each Form, with learners experiencing exemplar activities from each Form. Extra-curricular time would be planned as an extension of curricular work to provide opportunities for all to take part. Some learners may wish to widen their experiences of activities, some may favour doing further work in an area of the curriculum they are finding challenging, while others may want to challenge themselves in competitive and/or team situations. Learners themselves would be free to plan this aspect of the physical education curriculum. (This proposal is discussed fully in Chapter 4.)

In deciding on the content of teaching, teachers should also be mindful of the attributes of physical literacy that

> individuals will have the ability to identify and articulate the essential qualities that influence the effectiveness of their own movement performance, and have an understanding of the principles of embodied health, with respect to basic aspects such as exercise, sleep and nutrition.
>
> (Whitehead 2010a: 14)

This knowledge and understanding need to permeate the curricular work with records kept by the teachers of the ways in which this has been covered in each year of schooling with each class. As far as possible these records should be readily available to other teachers so that subsequent teaching can both reinforce and build on earlier consideration of these issues.

This section of the chapter has presented a variety of recommendations, some very challenging, for aspects of teaching physical education in school. All arise from a commitment to the philosophy underpinning the concept of physical literacy. It is for the reader to consider both if these are feasible and if, together, they represent a route to enable all to make progress, laying the ground for participation in purposeful physical pursuits throughout the lifecourse.

Q5

Conclusion

This chapter has set out the philosophical background to the concept of physical literacy by briefly outlining monist, existential and phenomenological positions. These reveal the centrality of our embodied nature in life as we know it and lead to a clear justification for serious attention to be paid to this human dimension throughout life. The concept of physical literacy was then explained, with a concise definition and a list of the attributes likely to be demonstrated by a physically literate individual. Using these definitions as a background, the value of physical literacy was briefly touched on both from a philosophical standpoint and from the perspective of human flourishing.

The relationship between physical literacy and physical education was then explained as were the ways the concept of physical literacy, with its roots in established philosophical thought, can support the value of physical education in the curriculum. This was followed by a consideration of the pedagogical implications of promoting physical literacy.

Underpinning the views expressed in this chapter is the notion that physical literacy is a disposition relevant to all, throughout life. It is argued that lifelong participation should be at the heart of all work by practitioners with participants in school and beyond. Physically literate individuals, drawing on the motivation, confidence, movement competence and knowledge and understanding they have developed, will be more likely to:

- be energised to be active;
- establish involvement in purposeful physical pursuits as a lifespan habit;
- understand the value of physical activity in maintaining health;
- value purposeful physical pursuits as a part of a full and satisfying life;
- reflect on this value and make informed choices relating to the nature of physical pursuits in which to be involved.

Individuals who have developed these propensities will be highly likely to self-manage their involvement in purposeful physical pursuits and take steps to foster their own physical literacy. This can, without doubt, provide opportunities for a richer, fuller life.

Readers are encouraged to consider where they stand in relation to the potential of physical literacy to add legitimacy to physical education and to debate if the pedagogical approaches suggested to achieve this goal for all learners are apposite and feasible.

Q6

Questions for consideration

Q1 It has been suggested that dualist beliefs work against the appreciation of the importance of work in physical education. Reflect on ways in which you have experienced problems on account of a devaluing of the embodied dimension in comparison with other aspects of education. Construct an argument to advocate the importance of physical education using a monist approach to support your position.

Q2 Critically consider the concept of physical literacy, debating how far it is legitimate to claim that the concept is grounded in the philosophical views presented in this chapter.

Q3 Differentiate clearly between physical education and physical literacy, critically considering if physical literacy should be the goal of physical education. What grounds would you identify in your support, or otherwise, of the suggestion that there are advantages in using the term physically literate over the concept of being physically educated?

Q4 This chapter has stressed that key to physical education is the development of the motivation and confidence to promote continued involvement in purposeful physical pursuits throughout life. Discuss how feasible it is for physical education to achieve this aspiration.

Q5 Discuss whether the pedagogical approaches suggested above are feasible and have the potential to foster physical literacy in all learners.

Q6 Critically consider what might be the chief barriers to the acceptance of the concept of physical literacy as the fundamental goal of physical education.

Notes

1 For further detail see Whitehead (2010a).

2 A capability is the outcome of fostering the potential of a human dimension. Examples of dimensions are cognitive, affective and physical. Nussbaum (2000: 5) defines capabilities as 'what people are actually able to do and to be'. As Whitehead (2010a: 18) explains, Nussbaum 'argues that each capability is valuable in itself and should not be seen as a means to other ends. ... While she does not describe them as human rights she asserts that all humans should be at liberty to exercise each capability and express themselves in ways that they choose. She talks of each capability as being an opportunity for functioning in a fully human way and argues that in nurturing the capability each person should be treated as an end in themselves and not a means to the ends of others'. For further detail see Nussbaum (2000).

3 Propositional knowledge is that concerned with theories and cognitive concepts, typically involving statements that express notions that can be true or false.

4 Purposeful physical pursuits are understood to include the wide range of developed and organised physical activities within a culture such as dance, swimming and competitive team games. Also included here are activities such as walking, gardening and DIY activities in the home.

5 Descriptions of physical literacy are often interpreted as if the capability is a state of being; that is an individual is or is not physically literate. This is not the case. Physical literacy is not a capability that is achieved at a particular time and then persists throughout life. All can achieve physical literacy. There are no benchmarks that have to be reached. Each individual will be on their own physical literacy journey which will be unique, with twists, turns and maybe setbacks along the way. The key issue is that teachers and significant others are supporting individuals in *making progress on their individual journey*. This relates both to the short definition and to the attributes described later in the chapter. The relationship between physical literacy and literacy per se is discussed in Whitehead (2010a).

Further reading

Burkitt, I. (1999) *Bodies of Thought: Embodiment, Identity and Modernity*. London: Sage.
  Chapter 1 in this text has a useful discussion of dualism and monism.
Gill, J.H. (2000) *The Tacit Mode*. Albany: State University of New York Press.
  Chapter 3 includes a useful discussion of Polanyi's philosophy relating to tacit knowledge.
Nussbaum, M.C. (2000) *Women and Human Development. The Capabilities Approach*. Cambridge: Cambridge University Press.
  Chapter1, 'In Defense of Universal Values' discusses the background to the concept of capabilities and includes a list of capabilities on pp.78–80.
Whitehead, M.E. (ed.) (2010) *Physical Literacy. Throughout the Lifecourse*. London: Routledge.
  This text sets out, in detail, the concept of physical literacy. Part I looks at the philosophical background to the concept. Part II is entitled 'Contextual Connections' and includes chapters from professionals working in the fields of, for example, early years, special needs and the older adult population. Part III discusses the practical implications of applying the concept in practice.

The following physical education journals should support further reading. There are also many education journals which contain articles related to relevant topics across education more generally, which are useful to extend debate further. They may also contain physical education specific articles.

- *European Physical Education Review*
- *Journal of Teaching in Physical Education*
- *Quest*
- *Physical Education Matters*
- *Physical Education and Sport Pedagogy*
- *Sport, Education and Society.*

Part II

Learning in physical education

Introduction to Part II

The three chapters in Part II relate closely to the issue of aims that was central to the debate in Part I and consider aspects of pupil learning. Chapter 4, 'What should pupils learn in physical education?' presents a particular model of the content that learners should experience, while Chapter 5, 'Physical education and health: considerations and issues' puts the spotlight on the ways in which a focus on health can be incorporated into physical education.

Chapter 6, 'What is success in physical education and how can this best be achieved?' argues that the current aims and practices of the subject should be reviewed in order to ensure that all pupils can experience success.

Chapter 4, 'What should pupils learn in physical education?' looks at issues concerned with the subject matter of physical education. It suggests that new thinking could be valuable to encourage all learners to develop the motivation and confidence that will lead to participation in physical activity throughout life. Having considered what might be the aims of physical education, the chapter addresses three aspects of content. These are the movement content, the activities experienced and the inclusion of elements of theory. Also discussed are the notion of choice of activities in curriculum time and the best use of extra-curricular time. The chapter is presented as a dialogue to provide an example of how a real-life conversation could be conducted. You are encouraged to formulate your own views on the issues under debate, considering arguments to support the positions you hold.

Chapter 5, 'Physical education and health: considerations and issues' focuses on the role of physical education in promoting health and highlights some of the key considerations and commonly debated issues within the literature concerning the area of health within the physical education curriculum. The chapter takes the approach of providing an overview of a range of research and evidence to stimulate debate amongst readers about the challenges and opportunities for physical educators in relation to health. The chapter starts by considering physical education's role and responsibilities in relation to health and then obesity. Issues including the place, expression, organisation, content and delivery of health within the physical education curriculum are then explored.

Chapter 6, 'What is success in physical education and how can this best be achieved?' is designed to raise questions about what counts as success in physical education. You are asked to consider the relationship between assessment and the aims of the subject and to reflect on the long unquestioned focus on high-quality performance skills as being the way that pupils should be assessed in physical education. The chapter then asks you to conceptualise assessment that is as concerned with process as with product and which moves away from norm-referenced assessment procedures to assessment that can chart individual progress. The notion is proposed that our fundamental aim should be that all learners are motivated to continue with physical activity throughout the lifespan and implications for achieving success in this respect are outlined. Recommendations for enabling all learners to be successful in achieving this aim are briefly proposed and the chapter ends with a challenge for you to devise and implement appropriate strategies to judge success that recognise individual progress.

Chapter 4

What should pupils learn in physical education?

Elizabeth Murdoch and Margaret Whitehead

Introduction

This chapter is designed to raise issues concerned with what might be called the 'subject matter' of physical education. Other chapters such as Chapter 8, address aspects of *how* physical education might be taught. This chapter considers *what* might be taught.

There are three principal aspects of content that will be considered as significant in respect of the material covered in lessons. These are, first, movement skills such as throwing, rolling, jumping, diving and running; second, physical activities such as dance and athletics; and third, theory related to human movement within disciplines such as anatomy and physiology.

In conjunction with this debate there are issues concerned with whether the pupils should have any choice in the activities they follow and whether extra-curricular work should be seen as an opportunity to extend physical education experiences for all pupils (see also Chapter 11).

The debates that are raised in this chapter are closely related to issues considered in other chapters. Different views will be expressed and persuasive arguments presented. The challenge for the reader is to reflect on the relative validity of the positions presented and to come to a reasoned personal view on each of the issues. Without belittling the good work being carried out in physical education in many schools, the chapter is written as a critique of a current practice. The rationale here is that some learners could make more progress in physical education than is currently the case. The chapter is presented as a dialogue.

Background – the aims of the subject

ELIZABETH MURDOCH (EM): Chapter 1 looked at the nature of physical education and some of the aims the subject has worked towards throughout its history. Our debate moves on from this to look at what might be the appropriate content of the subject. What is taught should spring from the aims of the subject. In this context would it be useful to start our debate by proposing the overall aims of physical education? How would you describe these?

MARGARET WHITEHEAD (MW): This is a challenging and potentially contentious area, since there are widely varied and strongly held opinions concerning the role of physical education in the curriculum. However I might suggest that the following represent a cluster of aims with which the majority of the profession would concur.

All pupils should leave compulsory physical education having made progress in respect of developing:

1   a positive attitude to physical activity through having experienced a sense of achievement and enjoyment in the subject;
2   the motivation and confidence to continue active participation in physical activity;
3   movement competence, commensurate with their physical potential;
4   experience of a range of movement activities;
5   realistic self-knowledge and self-awareness enabling them set appropriate personal goals in respect of physical activity;
6   an understanding of the nature of movement and of the importance and value of physical activity as contributing to a healthy lifestyle;
7   an understanding of how to access physical activity beyond the school.

While a broad 'ladder' of development can be devised there can be no pre-scribed benchmarks with regard to the specific level of attainment that should be reached when learners leave compulsory schooling. This depends very much on the physical endowment of each learner. The critical factor is that each learner has made, and is making, sustained progress in respect of the aims set out above.

EM: The above aims provide a very useful framework from within which to discuss content in the secondary phase of schooling. It would seem that while lesson material will contribute to the realisation of all aims, the most significant ones for us are numbers 3, 4, 6 and 7. Aim 3 would seem to demand coverage of movement skills, Aims 4 and 7 have implications to the activities to be covered and Aim 6 indicates that some attention to theory might be needed. The other aims would seem to be principally reliant on the teaching methods used.

MW: Yes, true. While elements of our discussion will touch on Aims 1, 2 and 5 a full consideration of these, in respect of content, would involve debate from perspectives different to that adopted in this chapter (for example see Chapters 6, 12 and 14).

QI

Movement competence

EM: If we look first at Aim 3 and movement competence, I presume you are referring to the fundamental movement vocabulary upon which all physical activity relies? Are we talking about movement skills?

MW: I find the concept of 'skills' problematic as they are sometimes understood as the application of technique in an activity setting. I prefer to refer to fundamental movement vocabulary in terms of movement patterns. Movement patterns are the basic building blocks of all movement and the constituents of all physical activity and all physical activities in the form of purposeful physical pursuits. These foundation or generic patterns emerge as part of the maturation process and are developed in the early years of growth and learning through a variety of play situations, both free and semi-structured. Patterns evident in the early years can be located in categories such as loco-motion/running, flight/jumping, projection/sending (see Whitehead, 2010a: 108). As the learner develops, these patterns have the potential to be established, refined and made more specific. For example patterns in the projection category become established as the generic movements involved in 'sending away'. Sending away patterns become refined into throwing, bowling and shooting. These refined patterns become specific when they are further developed in an activity context such as bowling in rounders or cricket or, in athletics, in the disciplines of javelin and discus. This development is show in Table 4.1.

The progression of movement patterns from generic through refined to specific, depends on the appropriate application of movement capacities such as co-ordination, dexterity, use of power and precision (see Whitehead, 2010a, Chapter 15). As a general rule I would recommend that refined movement patterns should form the core of primary school work while specific movement patterns are developed in the secondary school and beyond.

EM: I agree that, in the primary phase, we would hope that learners had experienced, become familiar with, and hopefully mastered, a wide range of

Table 4.1 The development of movement patterns from generic through refined to specific

Generic movement patterns, e.g.	Refined movement patterns, e.g.	Specific movement patterns, e.g.
Sending	Throwing, bowling, shooting	Bowling in baseball
Striking	Batting, dribbling, driving	Forehand in tennis
Receiving	Trapping, catching	Catching in netball
Running	Sprinting, dodging	Running 100 metres
Jumping	Leaping, hopping	Hurdling
Rotating	Turning, spinning	Turns in swimming

refined movement patterns. The development of the more complex specific movement patterns is seen as a key role of work in the secondary phase when full adult forms of activities should be introduced. Experience of a range of different activity contexts is recommended at the primary stage, however, these should be appropriate to the age of the pupil. Adult forms of activities with their imposition of complex rules and the involvement of large groups of people are not appropriate. Small sided games and simplified activities provide opportunities for maximum activity for younger learners who should be exploring movement possibilities rather than being limited by strict rules and protocols.

Developing effective specific movement patterns is closely related to participation in recognised physical activities. There is an interesting interplay here. On the one hand effective participation in a recognised activity depends on the mover's facility to adapt and hone refined movement patterns so that these patterns conform with the requirements, including the rules, of an activity. On the other hand it is within the context of physical activities that specificity is challenged and established. There is a lively debate, for example in respect of the 'Games for Understanding' approach, about whether specific movement patterns are best taught in a 'practice' situation, or whether their introduction is most effective in the context of taking part in the activity. In whatever way these specific patterns are developed it is important to realise that this learning relies on the mastery of a wide range of movement capacities, as you mentioned above. As exemplified by Whitehead and Murdoch in Whitehead (2010a: 185) specific movement patterns in dance will depend on the development of poise, control and fluency; in hockey key movement capacities will be use of power, moving at different speeds and co-ordination; in Pilates the movement capacities of flexibility, balance and precision will be paramount.

However it needs to be stressed that learners will seldom master movement capacities or specific patterns just by taking part in the activity. In most cases these capacities and patterns will need to be taught through demonstration, observation and practice. This learning must be a significant focus of physical education content in the secondary phase for Aim 2 to be realised.

Activities covered in physical education

MW: I agree with your views here. What follows from this is that an appropriate mix of activities should be introduced so that learners are challenged to master a wide range of movement capacities as they acquire a bank of specific movement patterns. This seems to bring us to the point of addressing the achievement of Aim 4, that of providing learners with a rich variety of contexts in which to take part in physical activity. The question to be asked is 'Which activities should be learnt in physical education in the secondary phase?' The answer could be that the activities covered should be a range of established physical activities relevant to the 'parent culture'. Is there any room for debate?

EM: Yes, there is room for debate! Not least because, while this is the general approach being taken at the moment, it does not seem to be enabling the majority of learners to achieve the aims suggested above by the time they leave compulsory schooling. Many learners, other than those who are talented, have a negative experience of physical education and as a result are not motivated to continue to take part in physical activity out of school or after they leave school. They may lack confidence in their physical ability and have experienced little success or satisfaction in the subject. Many learners leave school without a positive attitude to physical activity and an appreciation of the value of physical activity as contributing to quality of life.

MW: What could be the cause of this situation and, more importantly, what might be the solution?

EM: The cause of the problem might be either the selection of activities that are included, or maybe the problem lies in the way the activities are presented.

MW: We need to address both issues. If we start with the activities that are included, are you suggesting that in some way they do not appeal to, or are not appropriate for, the learners?

EM: I would suggest it is the case that, currently, many of the activities included are not particularly enjoyed by all learners. Many of these have become unquestioned elements in the curriculum. In fact there has been little change in the activities covered in the last 30 years. For example as a result of tradition, team games form the backbone of the curriculum. These predominate in curriculum time – with, generally, lesser attention being given to activities such as athletics, swimming, dance and gymnastics. Ironically most additions to the physical education curriculum have been the introduction of a wider variety of team games. This stress on team games flies in the face of a good deal of anecdotal evidence that many learners, particularly, but not exclusively, girls, do not rate team games highly in their preferences (see, for example, Penney and Evans, 1999; Department of Culture, Media and Sport and Department for Education and Skills (DCMS/DfES), 2006; Flintoff and Scraton, 2006).

The social and cultural context also influences learners' interest and I suggest that many young people nowadays are looking for thrill and excitement. This is evidenced by the popularity of games on computers and Play Stations. And there are a number of new activities that have emerged in the last decade that are very popular with young people. In order to cater for the interests of today's young people and to equip them with experiences relevant to opportunities beyond school, I wonder if the physical education curriculum should include activities such as skate boarding and mountain biking. And perhaps the frequently televised sports such as snooker, crown bowling or golf should have a place in the curriculum. In addition there is a great and developing interest in what are coming to be known as 'extreme sports', all of which incorporate an element of risk. It can be this danger that is attractive to young people.

It is fair to say that, in comparison, participation in the activities that feature on the school curriculum do not reflect what is shown on television and mostly fall far short of this experience of excitement and controlled risk. The difficulty of providing teaching and supervision of extreme activities within the school curriculum makes it obvious that they cannot feature as a regular part of a school programme. It is nevertheless important that we take note of what it is in these activities that make them pleasurable and challenging to young people. The combined elements of joy and fear keep the participants on the edge and provide satisfaction in achievement.

Q2

MW: While I accept your observation about the attraction of extreme sports and high-risk activities, I do not think that the school curriculum is the right place for these to be introduced. I would hope that well-grounded movement competence and confidence that learners develop in physical education would stand them in good stead should they wish to take up these sports outside school. We must certainly open doors for learners so that they are as well equipped as possible to take part in whatever activities they choose when they leave school. Can activities be categorised in such a way that a selection can be made that introduces learners to a range of different experiences?

EM: Yes. Over the years a number of categorisations have been proposed. For example the UK National Curriculum in 1999 identified athletic activities, dance activities, games activities, gymnastic activities, outdoor and adventurous activities and swimming activities and water safety as their categorisation of activities. Bedford College of Higher Education in the late 1990s used an 'Areas of Experience' categorisation, being Body Management; Artistic and Aesthetic; Interaction; Adventure and Challenge; and Health and Wellbeing. Six Movement Forms are proposed by Murdoch and Whitehead in Whitehead (2010a, Chapter 15). These are: Adventure; Aesthetic and Expressive; Athletic; Competitive; Fitness and Health; and Interactional/Relational. Each Form has a unique 'essence' and takes place in a different situation in respect of both the physical environment and the relationships with others. Each Form makes particular demands on the embodied dimension in drawing from particular clusters of movement patterns and each Form affords the realisation of a number of motives or outcomes, such as social contact, health and fitness or personal challenge. For example most competitive activities demand movement patterns such as sending and receiving and rely on capacities such as hand–eye co-ordination. In addition they have the potential to satisfy participation motives of social contact and testing oneself against others. Each activity found within a Form has the potential to offer participants a particular type of experience that is characteristic of the Form. The characteristic nature or 'essence' of activities within each of the six Movement Forms can be described as follows:

- Activities in the '**Adventure Form**' have a main focus on *meeting risk and managing challenge* within the natural and often unpredictable environments, for example in orienteering and climbing.
- Activities in the '**Aesthetic and Expressive Form**' have a main focus on the *embodied dimension being used as an expressive instrument* within a creative, aesthetic or artistic context, for example dance and rhythmic gymnastics.
- Activities in the '**Athletic Form**' demand a main focus on the performer reaching *personal maximum/optimal power, distance, speed and accuracy* within a competitive and controlled environment, for example gymnastics and long jump.
- Activities in the '**Competitive Form**' have a main focus on the achievement of predetermined goals through *outwitting of opponents while managing a variety of implements and objects* in a challenging and changing context, for example, hockey, cricket and tennis.
- Activities in the '**Fitness and Health Form**' have a main focus on *gradually improving the function of the body both qualitatively and quantitatively* through regular, repetitive participation, for example aerobics and Pilates.
- Activities in the '**Interactional/Relational Form**' are characterised by a main focus on *recognition and appreciation of empathy between people and groups* as they move together in a social context, for example country dance, line dance.

MW: This is a useful clustering. However, am I correct in thinking that according to the way activities are presented they could, on occasion, 'belong' to different Forms?

EM: Yes, indeed. Take swimming, for example. Swimming could be an example of an Athletic Form where the presentation and teaching focus on specific movement patterns and relevant movement capacities. Alternatively swimming could fall within the Competitive Form where optimal performance is demanded to out-perform another swimmer. Swimming could also be seen as an Aesthetic and Expressive activity in synchronised swimming work or within the Health and Fitness Form if stamina and endurance are the focus.

What is important is that learners have experience of activities that together exemplify *all* Movement Forms. This will ensure a comprehensive coverage of a range of movement patterns and challenges in a wide variety of situations and environments. I would argue that this is the best way to enable all learners to realise their potential. Each individual will find satisfaction and success within some Movement Forms rather than in others, as the essence of one Form may hold greater appeal in relation to the personal characteristics and aspirations of that individual. Some involvement in all Movement Forms will extend the participant's experience and provide all learners with a rich repertoire from which they can select activities out of school. In addition to activities serving to ensure that the demands of each Form have been introduced and established, they also provide opportunities for individual needs to be met throughout the lifecourse. Should individuals want to test themselves out against others, should they wish to be part of a group or should they wish to be involved in artistic and creative activity they will have had experiences that will inform their choice of activity.

MW: You make a strong case for learners to have as broad and balanced experience across all Movement Forms as possible. Is this feasible in the school curriculum context?

EM: Yes it should be. I would propose that to realise Aim 4, work in curriculum time must cover activities representing all six Movement Forms. This should ensure that learners experience a programme that provides all pupils with the distinctive experience offered by each Form. The presentation within the curriculum of each activity (from each Movement Form) should be such that the participants are very clear why this activity has been chosen and why it is being delivered in a particular way. For example dance should be introduced as predominantly an Aesthetic and Expressive activity with teaching including opportunities for creativity and problem solving. Athletic activities, such as gymnastics and long jump, should be viewed as challenging movement skill with the teaching encouraging learners to improve on their previous performances.

I accept that this will present a significant challenge to many schools. However, unless changes are made in the nature of the activities experienced in the physical education curriculum there seems little chance of the aims listed at the start of the chapter being reached. It is regrettable that, despite encouragement from curriculum recommendations to deliver a broad and balanced curriculum, many schools in the UK continue to include a great many Competitive activities at the expense of a wider range of activities from other Forms (see Chapter 1 for the background to this situation).

MW: How might a curriculum be constructed incorporating this recommendation? Would such a curriculum be feasible?

EM: I accept this may not be straightforward for teachers. As far possible, time should be divided equally between Movement Forms with perhaps three Movement Forms being covered in each year and no more than two activity examples from each Movement Form being covered during each year. Time allocation will always be an issue, as will staffing and facilities. However I suggest that if the time was used on fewer activities, learners would experience more progress, enjoyment and satisfaction. Activities from within each Form would have to be selected carefully. I envisage two periods of physical education a week and this would give the equivalent of a term's work in each of the three Movement Forms. An example of the time allocation to the Forms is set out below in Table 4.2.

Table 4.2 An example of this coverage of all Movement Forms in years 7–11

Movement form	Adventure	Aesthetic and expressive	Athletic	Competitive	Fitness and health	Interactional and relational
Year 7		✓	✓	✓		
Year 8	✓			✓	✓	
Year 9		✓	✓		✓	
Year 10	✓			✓		✓
Year 11		✓			✓	✓

In Year 7 learners might have a period a week for two terms of gymnastics, a period a week for one term on each of creative dance, synchronised swimming, hockey and tennis.

MW: While I strongly support this type of programme could there be a danger that learners might still be demotivated if the participation in fewer activities across the range of Forms is not rewarding and enjoyable? Does this relate to the earlier issue that we have not yet considered about the way that learners are introduced to and taught activities?

EM: Yes, I believe that one of the problems in many current curricular programmes is that teachers introduce learners to a very wide range of activities, and pupils never have the time to develop the necessary appreciation of the activity, the specific movement patterns required in each and an understanding of how these patterns are employed in context. The pleasure of being active, and thus the motivation to take part, is very significantly rooted in success in performance of that activity: 'I can do it! I am good at this!' Brief coverage of a large number of activities, whatever these activities might be, has, I believe, resulted in lack of motivation and confidence, as well as little development of movement competence. Teachers should realise the value of consistent and sustained experience in the learning process and not be afraid to pursue this course of action, on the understanding that the learners will benefit from more time devoted to fewer activities.

MW: I agree with you in that the intention of keeping pupils engaged and motivated through introducing them to a great many different activities has backfired and indeed the practice is demotivating learners. A wide range of different activities covered each year in short blocks never allows the learners to have any real satisfaction from being able to participate effectively. An annual six-week block of, for example tennis, has little time to do more than try to recap the material covered in the previous year. Kirk (2011) adds other reasons for this outcome, for example the predominant focus on isolated movement patterns at the expense of developing these in activity contexts.

Clearly a balance needs to be struck between too many activities being covered for a few weeks at a time and too few activities being addressed for longer periods.

EM: While there are potential problems with this approach, with imaginative teaching it should be possible to sustain interest, through the satisfaction learners experience as a result of their progress. There could perhaps be individuals who find a particular activity unattractive and thus learners might be seriously demotivated even to a point of being disruptive. In this situation a reflective teacher should be able to shift the focus of that learner's participation from the essence of one Movement Form to another Form. For example if a pupil is clearly not motivated in an Aesthetic context or a Competitive context the teacher could, for that learner, change the focus to, respectively, health and fitness or leadership within the activity.

Q3

MW: Yes, I agree this would be a possibility but, I hope, the exception.

EM: While I advocate the division of time equally between the Movement Forms, I wonder if this prescription should be sustained right through the secondary phase of schooling? Should choice be introduced at some stage?

MW: This is clearly an issue. I feel strongly that there should be sufficient time for learners to become familiar with, and develop movement competence in, activities from all Movement Forms. Without a reasonable length of time I doubt if they will have sufficient experience either to take part effectively or to have sufficient grounds on which to base decisions about which activity, or type of activity, they might want to pursue in their own time while they are at school or in later life. I think that a broad coverage should last for four or five years.

EM: I think this might be too long and would favour perhaps just three years. Choice thereafter would be guided in that learners would select three Movement Forms within which to work in each year. This would retain breadth but allow learners to design their own programme. The opportunity to select activities would surely promote motivation, interest and commitment, all essential if physical activity is to be continued after the years of schooling. Learners would engage in the type of decision-making, with respect to activity choice, they will be involved in once they leave school. While I accept there may be timetabling constraints, I would like to see learners taking more responsibility for planning their physical activity experiences as soon as possible.

MW: You make some persuasive points. I would still favour compulsory coverage for five years, as I feel that time is needed to develop and establish movement patterns in different Movement Forms and environments. The last two years of schooling could certainly offer elements of choice, but again blocks of work in an activity should stretch across a whole term, no less. There would be additional opportunities in extra-curricular time for learners to take part in activities of their choice from all Forms, throughout the secondary phase (see below).

EM: There is surely a range of solutions to this issue. Admittedly they would depend on timetable flexibility. For example using Table 4.2 above, two of the Forms identified in each of Year 10 and Year 11 could remain compulsory, with opportunity for choice in respect of a third. If whole year groups were timetabled together once a week this could facilitate opportunity for choice.

Q4

MW: This is a useful way forward and it could be up to each school to decide how best to design the curriculum. My point remains, however, that curriculum physical education should cover fewer activities which represent experiences across all Forms, allowing sufficient time for effective and rewarding participation.

EM: Whatever the decision about when choice is given, the outcome of our proposal would be to limit significantly the number of different activities to which learners are introduced.

Use of extra-curricular time

MW: Yes, I accept this outcome, but would argue that unless significant changes are made we are unlikely to turn the tide of demotivation all too common in many learners. My solution would be to use extra-curricular time in a different way. I feel that we should move the focus away from extra-curricular provision as being principally 'team practices and matches' for the gifted, and develop a programme relevant to all. There has, in fact, been a gradual collapsing of the boundaries between the curriculum and its 'extra' dimension. There is increasingly, particularly with policy-makers, a strong tendency to couple the two together and consider them as one provision, each supplementing/complementing the other.

EM: I have long felt uneasy with this inclusion of extra-curricular work in the provision of statutory requirements. Even the title of this aspect of physical education would seem to differentiate it from core curriculum work. In my view, by definition, learning in the physical education curriculum should be adequate to meet the demands of the subject and whatever is undertaken in extra-curricular time is not a necessity but a desirable extra. Extra-curricular work, by definition is an added, additional opportunity. 'Extra' is normally used to mean 'more than usual'; 'over and above the usual or necessary'; 'greater in degree, extent or quality'.

MW: Of course your analysis is correct, but this is not currently how extra-curricular work is viewed. In fact the use of extra-curricular time is now acceptable in achieving the present target of four hours high-quality physical education per week that learners should experience, as laid down by the UK government (see also Chapter 10). That said, I do not feel current extra-curricular provision is effectively complementing the curriculum experience of the vast majority of learners. I would suggest that fewer than half of the pupils in most secondary schools take part in any extra-curricular provision. I would like to see five changes in extra-curricular provision, in respect of:

1   the expectation of learners to take part;
2   the motivation of learners to take part;
3   the relationship between what is offered in curricular and extra-curricular time;
4   the title/name of this experience;
5   the nature of the experience.

EM: Why are these changes needed and can you give more detail about the changes you advocate?

MW: The changes are needed to encourage every learner to take part in physical activity beyond the curriculum. I would like to see every learner involved in additional, appropriate and rewarding experiences that would encourage all to see physical activity as a positive option for them to pursue out of school. The changes would involve:

1   the expectation that all learners would take part in physical activity after school hours at least twice a week. This would depend on 2 and 3 below;
2   there being at least three clear purposes for, or motivations to take part in, this participation. Provision would be made for learners to:

   •   widen their experience of activities beyond those in the timetabled curriculum;
   •   establish movement patterns introduced in curriculum time which they are finding demanding;
   •   challenge themselves to apply movement patterns in more demanding situations, often involving competition;

3   there being a clear rationale for the way work in out-of-school hours comple-ments work in curriculum time. That is, as alluded to above, physical activity after school could add activities to those introduced in the curriculum, for example a new competitive team game or another form of dance; alternatively this time could be spent on improving an aspect of work from the curricu-lum, such as swimming, in which the learner would benefit from more prac-tice, or finally, this time could be devoted to developing high-level skill in a competitive context. Teachers would be actively involved in encouraging all learners to be involved in activity out of curriculum time, discussing which type of opportunity might be in each individual's interests;
4   the acceptance of a new name/title for this work being the 'extended cur-riculum' rather than referring to it as 'extra-curricular' provision;
5   the nature of the experience being one that is learner-centred and respects the motivation of the participants. I would see the nature of the learner–practi-tioner relationship being, predominantly, one of teaching not coaching. That is that the learner is at the centre of the interaction. All learners are catered for, whatever their level of expertise, and there is no sense that the practitioner is teaching the activity rather than the learners. Planning and teaching are

designed in relation to the needs of the learners rather than strictly adhering to the technical requirements of the activity.

I believe a programme of this nature could be attractive to all. It would no longer be seen as designed specifically for competitive team sport for the most talented. The activities would be open to all. Learners from different year groups would work together. I accept that this proposal creates challenges concerning staffing, facilities and transport. However I also believe that the effects of such a programme would be significantly beneficial and far reaching.

EM: You seem to imply that this type of extra-curricular programme would be a completely new way to organise this time – a big step for many schools.

MW: Yes, it would be a radical change for some schools. However this type of programme does exist is some schools. One example is The Coopers' Company and Coborn School in Upminster, Essex, who have a successful positive approach to involving all learners in the extra-curricular pro-gramme, through encouraging everyone to take part in these activities, with participation being recorded in a Passport of Entitlement. In fact pro-grammes of this nature are commended for the way they complement cur-ricular work, and are viewed more as an 'extended' curriculum as opposed to an extra to the curriculum.

EM: I think that you make a strong case here and I accept that there is promis-ing potential for this type of programme, alongside a remodelled experience in the curriculum, to engage, enthuse and motivate all learners.

Q5

Theoretical study in the physical education curriculum

EM: This moves us on to the last content issue relating to the achievement of Aim 6 – an understanding of the importance and value of physical activity as contributing to a healthy lifestyle. This would seem to suggest that some theoretical study should have a place in physical education.

MW: I feel this needs careful discussion. As I have written in Chapter 2, I am not comfortable in justifying the place of physical education in the curricu-lum, to any significant degree, on the grounds of the acquisition of propo-sitional knowledge, other than that related to issues concerned with health and fitness.

EM: My approach to this area is concerned with the value of theoretical know-ledge and understanding from a different perspective. I am referring to the value to learners of an understanding of the nature of movement in the context of their developing movement competence. I see this as a necessary aspect of their learning.

An appreciation of aspects of the 'theoretical' underpinning to 'practice' is critical if learning is to be effective. Within the curriculum this relationship can be seen to be of benefit along a continuum which is grounded in a learn-er's own actual movement experience and is subsequently refined into reflec-tion *on* movement from a more objective perspective. The continuum might be expressed as a number of steps. Learners in all phases should be expected to engage thoughtfully in their practical work with input from the teacher in respect of steps one, two and three gradually becoming more detailed and demanding. Step 4 has a somewhat different focus (see Figure 4.1).

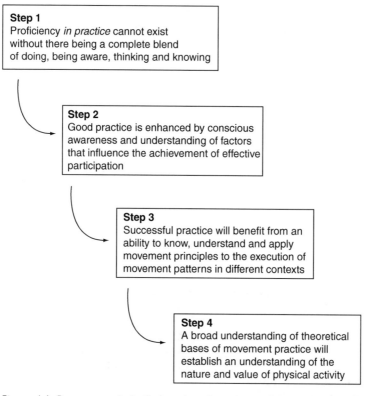

Figure 4.1 Recommended Steps in the awareness and understanding of movement.

Step I is based on the principle that proficiency in practice cannot exist without there being a close relationship between the practical and the theoretical – *being active means to do, think and know simulta-neously.* This first step surely permeates physical education learning and teaching from the early years. Learners are encouraged to become aware of the way their embodied dimension is involved in developing movement patterns and how capacities such as balance and co-ordination are essential for effective movement performance. They become aware of aspects of movement such as the use of space, direction, speed and force, can appreciate the differences between these elements of movement and realise how they contribute to effective participation in physical activity. Alongside this appreciation is an awareness of the effect of exercise on the body.

Step 2 builds from Step 1 and relies on the principle that movement practice will be greatly enhanced by the ability of participants to allow themselves to become consciously aware, in a theoretical sense, of what is going on during practice. This refines knowledge and understanding from Step 1 and is likely to be introduced in the later primary years and through the secondary phase. For example, it will enhance the quality of learning if the pupil is able to appreciate, *in a practical way*, that the ability to balance successfully will be helped by shortening the length of the limbs in relation to the centre of the body. Or again that the 'line' of the body during a balance will have a positive impact on the aesthetic pleasure enjoyed by the spectator. Learners will also become increasingly knowledgeable about the effect of exercise on embodied functioning. They will understand the value of exercise and be able to articulate and debate issues concerned with health and wellbeing.

Step 3 moves out from the learner and concerns knowledge and understanding, per se, of the context and structure of movement. It is based on the principle that practice is enhanced by an understanding of the demands of the situation in relation to the role of others, the nature of the physical environment and the routines and expectations of the activity. For example, an understanding of the principles of buoyancy should help the participant to realise why the body is not floating easily. Similarly a sound understanding of the nature of gravity will explain why landing on hard surfaces demands the ability to absorb impact. The ability to apply this *during practice* will enhance the potential for a successful performance. While elements of Step 3 may be touched on in the primary years, this type of knowledge and understanding will feature particularly in the secondary phase.

Step 4 sees the learner reflecting on movement rather than being actively engaged in the movement. This is based on the principle that there is a wealth of well-established knowledge from many recognised theoretical disciplines that relates to movement and offers a fascinating study in its own right. For example, there is extensive literature on physiology, kinesiology and biomechanics that informs the functioning of body systems; readings in aesthetics provide insights into the nature of dance; and literature in psychology can promote the understanding of group dynamics and can inform the development of the leadership skills needed to become an effective team leader or captain.

MW: This is a very useful continuum relating to the practice–theory relationship in movement learning. The first and second steps in your presentation of theory would seem to support not only Aim 6 but also Aim 3 – movement competence.

I presume that the knowledge and understanding referred to in the first three steps would permeate all learning/teaching and be explained as movement patterns and activities are developed and refined. Thus we are not looking at situations in which practical activity is suspended to focus on theoretical issues?

EM: No, that is the case in essence, although establishment of knowledge and understanding will always involve the teacher's time in explanation and the learners' time in questioning and/or discussion. These short periods of time, however, would be minimal and would feature alongside the movement learning. All learners would be expected to be engaged in this theoretical appreciation which is covered in the interests of improving intelligent participation and promoting learner decision-making and independence. It could well be the case that some aspects of the theory touched on in physical education might be picked up in other areas of the curriculum.

I would suggest that in many cases physical education teachers are integrating 'theoretical' aspects into their teaching although, in my experience, it is perhaps, surprisingly, Step 1 that is addressed less well. There is a danger that teachers do not encourage their learners to reflect on their movement experiences, ever being concerned to move on to further challenges. This could be on account of some lack of confidence on the part of the teacher regarding appropriate descriptive movement language. Self-awareness and self-reflection through highlighting aspects of movement are essential to learning and pupils need to be helped to focus on proprioceptive feedback.

MW: Should Step 4 be an experience for all learners or are you really referring to examination work in physical education? Is there any justification for all to be involved in this depth and extent of theoretical study?

EM: Step 4 does describe the acquisition of knowledge generally associated with examination work. There is difficulty in justifying the time spent in pure theoretical study, as an alternative to practical experience, when the curriculum is so limited in terms of hours per pupil per week. However, examination opportunities in physical education and sport are important and should be available, as pupils may be motivated to study aspects of movement and physical activity. This can be particularly the case for learners who thrive in the practical areas, and who are interested to look more deeply into the theory behind, for example, skill development or health promotion. In addition such study may provide a route into higher education and subsequently offer career opportunities.

Looking broadly, the issue of the balance between practical and theory in physical education needs to be carefully considered throughout the years of schooling, in relation to each group of pupils and adapted to meet their needs, as far as possible, within the constraints of the curriculum. Debate about the place of theory in physical education must be addressed far more widely than a discussion about the nature and content of examinations. Theoretical considerations are relevant to all learning in a physical activity context.

MW: I have sympathy with your sentiments and agree that theory enhances experience, learning and understanding in physical education. However I would caution against too much time being spent on theoretical input in curriculum time. Focus must always be on participation, with any theory enhancing this practical experience. Nevertheless you have made a strong and convincing case for aspects of theory related to the experience and understanding of movement being an integral part of physical education in all phases of schooling.

Q6

Summary

This chapter has taken a critical look at an aspect of physical education that has generally been taken for granted, that is, the content of the subject. Following a proposal of the aims for physical education against which learners might be expected to make progress throughout their time in school, the necessary content in respect of achieving three of the aims was the subject of debate, namely:

- the acquisition of specific movement patterns was recommended to achieve Aim 3 – movement competence;
- the experience of activities from all Movement Forms was supported to achieve Aim 4 – experience of a range of movement activities;
- attention given to awareness and understanding of theory, or propositional knowledge was advocated to achieve Aim 6 – an understanding of the nature of movement and the importance of physical activity.

In addition the issues of learner choice of activities and the use of extra-curricular time as a planned extension to the timetabled curriculum were debated.

There was not room in this chapter to look in detail at how content can influence all the proposed aims of the subject. This would involve an in-depth examination of the relationship between content and method (see Chapters 6, 12 and 14) and Haydn-Davies (2010). However, as indicated in our discussion, enabling learners to develop secure specific movement patterns and thus effectively participate in purposeful physical pursuits will of itself promote a positive attitude to physical education and increase the motivation and confidence to continue to be physically active throughout life (Aims 1 and 2). Participation in physical activities off the school site will provide some awareness of how activities can be accessed beyond school (Aim 7). Steps 1 and 2 in the presentation of the theoretical content will support self-knowledge (Aim 5).

Throughout the chapter a wide range of challenging questions were raised that warrant serious debate among the profession.

Questions for consideration

Q1 Critically consider the proposed aims of physical education against which learners might be expected to make progress during their time in secondary school, debating how far they are feasible and if this progress is, in general, evident. Where aspirations are not met, identify reasons for their not being achieved. Are there other aspirations you would like to add?

Q2 'Physical education cannot provide a curriculum which includes extreme sports – which might seem attractive and appropriate to adolescents in the twenty-first century.' Discuss this statement and consider if is possible to prepare learners in physical education to take part in these activities outside school.

Q3 Consider how far it would be possible to deliver a curriculum in physical education in which the time is divided equally between experience of all Movement Forms. Identify the challenges and barriers presented by this approach, possibly completing a SWOT (Strengths, Weaknesses, Opportunities, Threats) analysis.

Q4 Formulate a reasoned argument for the length of time all pupils should follow a compulsory curriculum before being able to select activities.

Q5 Carry out a SWOT (Strengths, Weaknesses, Opportunities, Threats) analysis on the suggestions relating to the use of the extended curriculum. Be prepared to explain the reasons for the detail of this analysis and compare your views with those of a colleague.

Q6 In relation to theoretical study as part of physical education, critically debate whether Step 4 (as described above) should be an element in the core curriculum for all and if so how this might be achieved.

Further reading

DfEE/QCA (Department for Education and Employment and Qualifications and Curriculum Authority) (1999) *Physical Education: The National Curriculum for England*. London: DfEE/QCA.
This National Curriculum document details the activities that should be covered in the physical education curriculum.

Kirk, D. (2011) *Physical Education Futures*. London: Routledge.
There is useful debate in this book discussing reasons why learners may lose motivation in physical education on account of the nature of their experiences in school.

Maude, P.M. (2003) *Observing Children Moving* (CD). Worcester: afPE.

Maude, P.M. and Whitehead, M.E. (2006) *Observing and Analysing Learners' Movement* (CD). Worcester: afPE.
These CD-ROMs are designed to promote effective movement observation and to provide teachers with the movement vocabulary to facilitate learning in physical education.

Whitehead, M.E. (ed.) (2010) *Physical Literacy: Throughout the Lifecourse*. London: Routledge
Chapters 9 and 15 in this text discuss in detail the concepts of movement patterns, movement capacities and Movement Forms.

The following physical education journals should support further reading. There are also many education journals which contain articles related to relevant topics across education more generally, which are useful to extend debate further. They may also contain physical education specific articles.

- *European Physical Education Review*
- *Journal of Teaching in Physical Education*
- *Quest*
- *Physical Education Matters*
- *Physical Education and Sport Pedagogy*
- *Sport, Education and Society.*

Chapter 5

Physical education and health

Considerations and issues

Lorraine Cale and Jo Harris

Introduction

The role of physical education in promoting health and producing a 'healthy nation' has been increasingly recognised in recent years (Shephard and Trudeau, 2000; Cale and Harris, 2005; Stratton *et al.*, 2008). Indeed, physical education has been viewed as the most suitable vehicle for the promotion of healthy, active lifestyles among young people (Shephard and Trudeau; 2000) and contributing to public health via promoting health-enhancing lifestyles. Increasing physical activity has been seen to be one of, if not the, most important objectives of the subject (e.g. Shephard and Trudeau, 2000; Cardon and de Bourdeaudhuij, 2002; Green, 2002; Fox *et al.*, 2004; Fairclough and Stratton, 2005). Further-more, a number of government policies and initiatives in England over the past decade have identified physical education to be instrumental in providing oppor-tunities for young people to improve their health. A few notable examples include *Game Plan* (Department for Culture, Media and Sport (DCMS), 2002), *Every Child Matters* (Department for Education and Skills (DfES), 2003a), *Healthy Weight, Healthy Lives* (Department of Health and Department for Chil-dren, Schools and Families (DoH/DCSF), 2008) and *Healthy Lives, Healthy People* (DoH, 2010).

This chapter focuses on physical education and health and highlights some of the key considerations and commonly debated issues associated with the area of health within the physical education curriculum. Firstly, physical education's contribution to health and addressing obesity are considered and then issues including the place, expression, organisation, content and delivery of health within the curriculum are explored.

Physical education's role and responsibility in health

According to Harris (2010), physical education's role in public health is based on the premise that it provides opportunities to be active and educates about and through physical activity (via its dual focus on 'learning to move' and 'moving to learn'). In this way it sets the foundation for lifelong participation in physical activity and sport (Association for Physical Education (afPE), 2008). Put simply, physical education provides opportunities for pupils to be, and to acquire and develop the knowledge, skills and understanding to be, physically active. This educational function is important given mounting evidence of the health benefits to be gained from engagement in physical activity and the knowledge that a sizeable proportion of young people are inactive and lead relatively sedentary lifestyles (Cale and Harris, 2005; McElroy, 2008). Recent comprehensive reviews of the health benefits of physical activity for children and young people have revealed that physical activity can lead to better cardiovascular and metabolic health, improved cardiorespiratory endurance and muscular fitness, improved skeletal health and more favourable body fat composition, as well as provide psychological benefits such as enhanced self-esteem and cognitive function and reduced symptoms of anxiety and depression (National Institute of Clinical Excellence (NICE), 2007a; Stensel et al., 2008; United States Department of Health and Human Services (USDHHS), 2008). In addition, physical activity has been found to have a role in the prevention and management of overweight and obesity in young people (Stensel et al., 2008).

Physical education (and schools generally) provide a very suitable setting in which to promote physical activity and health for a number of reasons. They have a captive audience and provide access to all young people, provide a context for learning at a time of high receptiveness, and have a workforce with the appropriate knowledge and expertise (Fox and Harris, 2003; Cale and Harris, 2005; 2009a). Furthermore, in England under the 2002 Education Act and the requirements of the National Curriculum, physical education (and schools) have a statutory responsibility to promote the 'physical' development of pupils and learning about health. Details of the place of health within the National Curriculum in England are outlined in the following section. There is also evidence to suggest that physical education can be successful in the promotion of healthy lifestyles. For example, reviews of school-based physical education and physical activity programmes have reported positive outcomes including improvements in activity during physical education classes, in fitness levels, and in knowledge, understanding and attitudes towards physical activity (e.g. Kahn et al., 2002; Cale and Harris, 2006; Salmon et al., 2007).

Despite the above, it is also important to be realistic about what physical education can achieve given that it has a range of objectives, only one of which is concerned with health, and that it accounts for only a small proportion of young people's time. Physical education represents less than 2 per cent of a young person's waking day (Fox and Harris, 2003), at least half of which can justifiably involve only light or physically passive activity (Stratton et al., 2008). Furthermore, many countries around the world have witnessed a progressive decrease in physical education time (Hardman and Marshall,

2005). Exceptionally, physical education time in England has increased in recent years (Ofsted, 2005; Quick et al., 2010), though of course more time does not necessarily equate to increased attention to and emphasis on health. Physical education clearly needs to do what it can in the time available to contribute to the promotion of healthy, active lifestyles. In this respect, its role and responsibility should be to stimulate interest, enjoyment, knowledge, competence and expertise in physical activity and sport for health and well-being (Fox et al., 2004), by providing pupils with high-quality teaching, and positive, meaningful and relevant physical education and physical activity experiences.

In addition, it is important to be aware of the numerous factors within and beyond physical education (and schools) which influence young people's physical activity and health, and to appreciate the complexities involved in changing health behaviours (NICE, 2007b). It is known, for instance, that knowledge and understanding of the importance of an active lifestyle is not sufficient to inspire young people to be physically active (Smith and Biddle, 2008). Tinning (2010) notes that it is unrealistic to expect individuals to change their lifestyles and behaviours simply because they acquire some new knowledge, and that to expect that knowing will translate into doing is naïve. Thus, whilst it is generally accepted that physical education has a responsibility and important role to play in health, it clearly cannot meet all physical activity and health needs, nor be held responsible for improving the health status of all children and young people (Cale and Harris, 2011a) or of the nation as a whole. In short, improving health is a far more complex aspiration.

Physical education's role and responsibility in addressing obesity

Whilst physical education's role and responsibility in health has been and continues to be debated, an even hotter topic of debate at the moment is its role and responsibility in addressing obesity. We are bombarded on a daily basis with government, media and scientific reports and messages concerning the growing 'problem' of childhood obesity and the possible health consequences of this for young people's current and future health (Cale, 2011). The World Health Organization (WHO) (2011) claims that childhood obesity is one of the most serious public health challenges of the twenty-first century, reporting the problem to be global and increasing at an alarming rate. The most recent childhood obesity figures in the UK reveal a rise in obesity levels since 1995 in both boys and girls (from 11 per cent to 17 per cent for boys and from 12 per cent to 16 per cent for girls) (Craig and Shelton, 2008).

Perhaps not surprisingly therefore, the role of physical education in tackling obesity has also been increasingly recognised (Fox et al., 2004; Kirk, 2006; Barlow and the Expert Committee, 2007; Davidson, 2007; Zieff and

Veri, 2009). In England this is evidenced by various policies, strategies and responses from government which have highlighted schools, including physical education, to be instrumental in addressing the issue. For example, a Public Service Agreement target was established in 2004 to halt the increase in obesity among children under 11 by 2010. In association with this, the National Child Measurement Programme was introduced which involves measuring children's weight in reception (ages 4–5 years) and year 6 (10–11 years). Following on, *Healthy Weight, Healthy Lives* (DoH/DCSF, 2008) set out the government's ambition for addressing obesity and overweight, the initial focus of which was on children and schools, including physical education, and more recently the current government's strategy for public health in England, *Healthy Lives, Healthy People* (DoH, 2010), continues to highlight the role of schools and physical education in the promotion of health, pledging continued commitment to the National Child Measurement Programme.

Clearly then, physical education teachers are under pressure to address the issue and consequently seem to be responding in varied and different ways (Cale and Harris, 2009a). There is concern however, that some of the reports, messages, measures and practices being advocated and implemented in response to government policy on this matter are exaggerated, misleading and misguided and could do more harm than good (Evans *et al.*, 2008; Cale and Harris, 2009a). Indeed, a number of researchers question whether there is an obesity 'problem' at all and express grave concerns over the discourse surrounding the condition and the impact of this on both practice and pupils in schools (e.g. Gard and Wright, 2001; Evans *et al.*, 2004; Gard; 2004a; 2004b; Evans *et al.*, 2008).

One practice which could do more harm than good, and yet which often features within health-related fitness or fitness testing programmes, is the routine measuring and weighing of pupils in physical education to calculate their body mass index. This would seem to be a pointless exercise in that it is not necessary to weigh or measure any child to tell them something that they already know, and no child needs to be measured to be helped to enjoy being physically active (Cale and Harris, 2009a). Examples of other questionable practices cited in the literature include inspecting pupils' lunch boxes, issuing health report cards, fitness testing regimes and fat laps and fat clubs for overweight or obese pupils (Wright and Dean, 2007; Evans *et al.*, 2008; Cale and Harris, 2009a; Rich, 2010). The worry with these is the potential damage they can do to a pupil's self-esteem, body image and potentially mental health. Research has highlighted, for example, girls and young women with anorexia and bulimia who have been deeply affected by the way such policy and practice transmit what are referred to as 'body perfection codes' (Evans *et al.*, 2004; Evans *et al.*, 2008). Such responses also represent an overly simplistic and narrow view of obesity and of the role and responsibility of physical education (and schools) in addressing the issue and have the potential to further stigmatise overweight and obese children, which is a problem that is reportedly growing (Latner and Stunkard, 2003).

Taking the above into account, the question remains as to what role physical education can realistically, appropriately, sensibly and safely play in addressing obesity. Given the health benefits of physical activity highlighted earlier, some of which are particularly relevant to obese children (e.g. better metabolic health, more favourable body fat composition, enhanced psychological health), it is clearly important to try to effectively engage obese children in physical activity, including physical education. It is contended that every child can benefit from regular engagement in physical activity and physical education and therefore as a profession we have a responsibility to provide this and to ensure that the experiences we offer are just as positive, meaningful and relevant for obese pupils. Whilst there are some specific practical considerations and sensitivities to take into account which are likely to affect obese children's enjoyment, attitude towards and ability to perform physical activity, and thus the approach to promoting physical activity with these youngsters, the same general messages, advice and principles should equally apply (Cale and Harris, 2009a). Considerations and sensitivities which have implications for practice, for example, relate to the orthopaedic problems obese children may encounter, their generally lower tolerance to exercise, poorer movement efficiency and body management, lower self-esteem and self-confidence and feelings of self-consciousness, embarrassment and isolation (Cale and Harris, 2009a, 2011b). In light of the above, Cale and Harris (2009a) have identified a number of practical recommendations to support physical education teachers in effectively engaging all pupils, including those who are obese, in physical activity. The recommendations take into account the considerations and sensitivities outlined and also draw on formal guidance and recommendations from previous literature (e.g. Evans et al., 2004; O'Dea, 2005; Evans, 2007; Evans et al., 2008) as well as those emanating from a specialist seminar, 'Physical Education and Childhood Obesity', organised by afPE in 2007.

Finally, just as it is important to be aware of the numerous factors and complexities involved in influencing children's health generally, it is equally important to recognise the complexity of obesity and the many factors beyond the control of physical education (and schools) which contribute to this particular issue. The term 'obesogenic' has been used to describe the current 'obesity-promoting' environmental circumstances in which we find ourselves these days which promote high energy intake and low energy expenditure (Yeung and Hills, 2007). Indeed, it has been suggested it is hard to envision an environment more effective in producing obesity (Battle and Brownell, 1996). For example, the ready availability of fast food or high sugar foods, king-size portion sizes and the widespread sale of pre-packaged and ready-prepared snack foods all promote high energy intake, whilst the widespread popularity of computer and video games and social networking, the increased reliance on motorised transport, and the greater restrictions placed on children and young people due to concerns over their safety all serve to promote low energy expenditure.

Q I

The place and expression of health within the physical education curriculum

The association between physical education and health is not new. Concerns about children's health and physical condition were instrumental in the introduction of the subject into the education system in England, albeit in the form of prescribed exercises (Harris, 2010). However, by the end of the the Second World War, a range of additional objectives for physical education came to the fore. It was not until the 1980s that there was a return to health as a key objective of physical education, as 'a solution to the problem of improving the healthy lifestyles of children' (Tinning, 2010: 177). In the UK, this renewed interest was expressed as 'health-related fitness' or 'health-related exercise', although other terms such as 'health-related physical education' or 'health-based physical education' have also been adopted for this area. According to Harris (2000), the different terms that have been used to refer to the area of health within the physical education curriculum reflect the varying influences on health issues within the subject over time. Regardless of the term chosen though, the area can broadly be defined as 'the teaching of knowledge, understanding, physical competence and behavioural skills, and the creation of positive attitudes and confidence associated with current and lifelong participation in physical activity' (Harris, 2000: 2). Furthermore, Cale and Harris (2005) advocate that it is concerned with health enhancement and should involve learning through active participation in purposeful activity embracing a range of sport, dance and exercise experiences including individualised lifetime activities. Thus, the emergence of the area attempted to broaden the traditional, competitive team-sport orientated physical education programmes in place at the time to include education about lifetime physical activity (i.e. activity that can readily be carried over into adulthood) and to introduce lifetime physical activities including fitness-related activities such as aerobics and circuit-training (Harris, 2010). (Chapter 4 considers what pupils should learn in physical education.)

The emphasis and interest in health within physical education has continued to flourish. The first National Curriculum for Physical Education (NCPE) in England (1992) incorporated 'health' as a statutory component and as a theme to be embedded implicitly across a range of activity areas (e.g. athletics, games). Whilst its positioning within the NCPE was significant at this time, the themed approach was criticised as it was felt that it marginalised health. However, within subsequent revisions of the NCPE, the health-related focus of the subject has arguably been strengthened (Fox and Harris, 2003; Cale and Harris, 2005; Qualifications and Curriculum Authority (QCA), 2007c). In terms of the coverage of health-related issues within the current (2007) secondary NCPE, for instance, 'healthy, active lifestyles' is a key concept and 'making informed choices about healthy, active lifestyles' and 'developing physical and mental capacity' are key processes. Furthermore, 'exercising safely and effectively to improve health and wellbeing, as in fitness and health activities' represents one of the six areas within the 'range and content' which teachers should draw from when teaching the key concepts and processes.

Whilst the above seems promising, there have and continue to be concerns over the time and status physical education teachers afford to health and their knowledge and understanding of it. For example, Ofsted (2004) has criticised the physical education profession for paying insufficient attention to health and fitness, suggesting that it still remains a marginal area within the curriculum. In addition, a number of researchers have found physical education teachers' knowledge and understanding of health and/or health promotion to be narrow, limited and even flawed and for health to be generally absent from their professional development profiles (Cale, 2000; Armour and Yelling, 2004a; Castelli and Williams, 2007; Armour and Harris, 2008; Kulinna *et al.*, 2008; Ward *et al.*, 2008; Ward, 2009; Harris, 2010; Alfrey *et al.* 2012). Arguably related to this is that many pupils have also been reported to lack knowledge and understanding in the area (Ofsted, 2005: 1) and to have misconceptions about health, activity and fitness (Harris, 1993; 1994; Kulinna and Zhu, 2001; Placek *et al.*, 2001; Stewart and Mitchell, 2003).

Q2

A further concern is that, despite the intention being for the area to broaden the physical education curriculum, its development has been and still appears to be overshadowed by the powerful influence of competitive sport within the subject (Green, 2000a; Kirk, 2010). As a profession we are noted for being resistant to change (Kirk, 2010) and competitive sport, sport techniques and particularly team games which focus on performance and fitness continue to dominate our subject and physical education teachers' philosophies and practices (Green, 2000a; Kirk, 2010). The area of health is no exception in this respect and a number of researchers have highlighted how many teachers adopt a 'sport', 'performance' and 'fitness' focus to the delivery of health within physical education (Green and Thurston, 2002; Leggett, 2008; Ward *et al.*, 2008; Ward, 2009; Harris, 2010; Alfrey *et al.* 2012). For example, a study of health-related policy and practice in secondary schools in England and Wales by Leggett (2008) found minimal change in the expression of health in physical education over an eight-year period and revealed that, whilst many physical education teachers articulated a 'fitness for life' philosophy, their delivery was usually expressed in terms of a 'fitness for performance' discourse, dominated by testing and training. Similarly, Ward (2009) and Ward, Alfrey and colleagues (Ward *et al.* 2008; Alfrey *et al.* 2012) reported concerns about the expression of health within physical education given that most physical education teachers claimed to value health-related learning, yet some had no written scheme of work outlining the nature and progression of this learning and most relied on sport- and fitness-related contexts to deliver it. Thus, it is argued that although physical education represents an ideal opportunity to educate young people about physical activity and health, contradictory philosophies concerning its role in this endeavour have hindered the development of effective health policy and practice (Cale, 2011). This notion and the implications of the focus on sport, performance and fitness are explored later.

Approaches to the organisation of health within the physical education curriculum

Given the concerns just highlighted, it is perhaps no surprise that the organisation of this area within the physical education curriculum has also been reported to be varied, inconsistent and limited (Harris, 2000; Fox and Harris, 2003). Various approaches can be taken to the organisation of health within the curriculum including, for example, permeation or integrated, focused, topic, or combined. A permeation or integrated approach is where health is taught through other practical areas of physical education (e.g. athletics, games, gymnastics); a focused approach involves teaching health through specific focused units of work; a topic approach involves a series of lessons following a specific topic or theme that is taught through physical education and classroom lessons; whilst a combined approach can involve any combination of permeation, focused and/or topic-based delivery. Each approach has specific strengths and limitations and professional judgement is clearly required to decide how best to deliver the content within the context of different schools. According to Cale and Harris (2005), curriculum leaders and heads of department who understand their own school and physical education curriculum and context are in the best position to make appropriate decisions over which approach or approaches to adopt, based on the strengths and limitations of each. Of course, the critical issue in this decision-making should be the effective delivery of the statutory requirements and the effectiveness of the learning, rather than the particular approach adopted (see also Chapter 8 in which teaching strategies are considered).

There has, however, been considerable debate over the years concerning the most appropriate approach to adopt (e.g. Fox, 1992; Harris and Elbourn, 1992; Almond and Harris, 1997; Stratton, 1998; Cale and Harris, 2005). Because, as noted earlier, the NCPE has traditionally included health not as a practical area in its own right, but as a theme to be embedded across a range of specified activities, this has been interpreted by some to indicate that the area should be delivered solely through permeation, rather than in discrete blocks or units of work (Oxley, 1994 cited in Cale and Harris, 2005; Harris, 1995; 1997). Cale and Harris (2005) note how the strengths of a permeation approach are that health knowledge, skills and understanding can be seen as integral to all physical education experiences and thus pupils learn that all physical activities can contribute towards health. However, they also warn that permeation can be rather 'ad hoc', 'piecemeal' and 'hit and miss' (pp. 168, 170) and identify a number of limitations with the approach. For example, knowledge, skills and understanding may become lost or marginalised amongst other information, pupils may be overloaded with information, and much liaison activity is required to ensure consistent delivery and messages. Furthermore, it has been suggested that the approach may deny pupils the opportunity to engage in a variety of popular health-promoting lifetime exercise activities (Fox and Harris, 2003).

As a consequence, and in recognition that all approaches have strengths and weaknesses, Cale and Harris (2009a) advocate a combined approach as it is felt that this builds on the strengths of each and provides a realistic opportunity to more adequately address the associated knowledge base. A combined approach also suggests that value is being placed on the area and allows learning and messages to be reinforced and links to be made to all physical education experiences as well as to other health behaviours and subjects (Cale and Harris, 2005; 2009a). Equally though, the time involved in planning, structuring, implementing and co-ordinating a combined approach is acknowledged. Yet, on a positive note, earlier research by Harris (1995) and Cale (2000) revealed the most popular approach to be through a combination of approaches. If representative of practice today, this suggests that value is being placed on health in many schools and that teachers are taking the time to plan, structure, implement and co-ordinate the area.

Other approaches to the delivery of health in schools that have attracted growing support and interest in recent years are whole school approaches such as the 'Healthy School' and the 'Active School' (see, for example, Fox and Harris, 2003; Cale and Harris, 2005). Whole school approaches consider the role of the broader school environment in promoting and learning about health, thereby making it a collective responsibility for teachers, pupils, parents and others (Stratton et al., 2008). These approaches acknowledge the need to move beyond the 'restrictive, one-dimensional focus on traditional curricular physical education to a model in which the culture and policy of the school is child-centred and health- and activity-driven' (Fox et al., 2004: 344), to recognise the multiple influences within and beyond the school environment which impact on young people's physical activity, such as, the influence of peers, family and the 'hidden curriculum' in the form of policies and other practices (Cale and Harris, 2005). With regard to the latter, Cale and Harris (2005) note how many aspects of the school can either promote or inhibit the adoption of an active lifestyle and understanding gained through the 'formal' curriculum can either be reinforced and supported or completely undermined by other influences. For example, a school with poorly maintained playgrounds or playing fields and 'no ball game' policies at breaktimes and lunchtimes would suggest that it does not value physical activity for its pupils.

Despite the merits and growing support for whole school approaches, environmental and policy interventions are the least studied component of school health promotion (French et al., 2001). It should also be recognised that adopting approaches such as the 'Active School' is challenging given the multiple demands on teachers, competing educational objectives and the need for new skills among teachers (Fox *et al.*, 2004). It is furthermore suggested that these approaches are likely to be more effective if they are informed by improved understanding of the place and significance of physical activity in young people's lives (Wright *et al.*, 2009) and of the views of young people about the barriers to and facilitators of participation in physical activity (NICE, 2007b).

Lastly, and alongside the debate concerning approaches, is the question as to whether health should be delivered via classroom-based or practical sessions in physical education. On this issue, it has been argued that sedentary classroom-based delivery of health-related concepts is limited in that it tends to focus on information transmission rather than the essential combination of understanding, experiencing, decision-making and evaluating. On the other hand, a practical approach is consistent with the physical context of the subject and with messages relating health benefits to frequent physical activity (Harris, 1995). In addition, school-based physical activity intervention programmes which have centred on classroom delivery involving theoretical instruction and information provision have been found to be relatively ineffective (Cale and Harris, 2005; 2006). Consequently, practically-based delivery is recommended over classroom-based delivery. At the same time, though, it is important that physical education teachers avoid some of the poor or undesirable practices that have been associated with practically-based delivery in the past, such as failing to recognise the knowledge base associated with health and merely delivering activity-based units (e.g. blocks of aerobics, cross-country) without imparting learning (Cale and Harris, 2005).

Content and delivery of health within the physical education curriculum

Regardless of the approach adopted, both the content and the way in which health is delivered within the physical education curriculum are clearly critical. If the subject is to be effective in promoting healthy active lifestyles and positively influencing young people's participation, then the teaching needs to be high quality and to involve enjoyable, positive and meaningful physical activity experiences, a practical knowledge base and caring teaching strategies (Fox and Harris, 2003). However, research has also revealed weaknesses and variations in the planning and delivery of health within the physical education curriculum (Harris, 1995; 1997; 2000; Cale, 2000; Ward *et al.*, 2008; Ward, 2009) suggesting that many schools may be falling short of achieving this. In the study by Ward (2009) and Ward, Alfrey and colleagues (Ward *et al.*, 2008; Alfrey *et al.*, 2012), for example, physical education teachers in a number of schools reported that they did not have access to schemes of work, units of work or lesson plans or resources to support their practice which, it was proposed, suggested a generally ad hoc attitude and a possible lack of structure, progression and coherence within the area.

The dominance of physical education teachers' sporting philosophies and how these are applied to, influence, and may even hinder the delivery and practice of health within the physical education curriculum was highlighted earlier (see also Chapter 8 which considers teachers' philosophies). There are a number of reasons why this is a concern. First, it is argued that a focus on sport, performance and fitness in the delivery of health results in a rather narrow curriculum with limited provision of a range of more recreational and individual lifetime activities. In turn, this may limit learning in this context and/or have limited appeal for many young people (Green, 2002; Fox and Harris, 2003; Ward *et al.*, 2008; Alfrey *et al.*, 2012), thus potentially alienating them from the subject and from physical activity participation outside school and later in life (Stratton *et al.*, 2008). The relevance and appeal of competitive sports and team games to many young people have been questioned for some time (Green, 2002; Fox and Harris, 2003) in that continued emphasis on these fails to acknowledge participatory trends in young people towards lifestyle activities and non-competitive, more recreational sport, and away from competitive performance-oriented ones (Cale, 2011).

Secondly, it is suggested that the often narrow focus on sport, performance and fitness results in the delivery of some undesirable or questionable practices which may also be counter-productive to the promotion of healthy, active lifestyles in young people. For example, research has highlighted examples of the area being equated solely with vigorous activity, fitness testing or warming up and cooling down (Harris, 2000) and of physiological issues, such as the physical effects of exercise or fitness testing dominating the teaching of health (Harris, 1995; 2000; Ward *et al.*, 2008; Ward, 2009; Alfrey *et al.*, 2012). According to Harris (2000), such narrow interpretations have the potential to lead to practices such as forced fitness regimes, directed activity with minimal learning, or dull, uninspiring drills.

It cannot be denied that increasing physical activity levels during lessons is inherently a good thing and indeed, as noted previously, reviews have revealed school-based physical education programmes to be effective in increasing activity during lessons. Guidelines suggest that pupils should participate in moderate to vigorous physical activity for at least 50 per cent of physical education lesson time (afPE, 2008; USDHHS, 2010), yet evidence suggests that this target is often not met and concerns have been expressed over the low level of moderate to vigorous physical activity pupils experience during physical education (Fairclough and Stratton, 2005; Stratton *et al.*, 2008). However, Cale (2011) cautions that this target needs to be approached sensibly to avoid prompting some of the inappropriate responses mentioned above, as well as to avoid other teaching objectives being compromised (Fairclough, 2003). Suggestions for achieving this include careful attention to planning and organisation and modifying instructional and organisational strategies to maximise 'active' learning, embracing more inclusive, pupil-centred curricula that place greater emphasis on lifetime physical activity, and the adoption of whole-school approaches (Stratton *et al.*, 2008; Cale, 2011). According to Fairclough and Stratton (2005), establishing a solid foundation for further and future engagement in physical activity requires educational and psychological approaches which focus on young people acquiring the appropriate understanding and behavioural skills to ensure physical activity becomes a routine part of their daily life. Harris (2010) concurs and suggests that these approaches are more likely to have a greater long-term impact than those focusing solely on the volume of physical activity accumulated in physical education classes, or on specific fitness outcomes.

Related to this last point is the issue of fitness testing which is common practice within the physical education curricula within most schools (see American College of Sports Medicine, 2000; Cale and Harris, 2009b; Chen, 2010). Advocates of fitness testing in schools have traditionally claimed that it promotes healthy lifestyles and physical activity, motivates young people to maintain or enhance their physical fitness or physical activity levels, facilitates goal-setting, self-monitoring and self-testing skills, promotes positive attitudes and enhances cognitive and affective learning. Other purposes of testing have been reported to include programme evaluation, tracking of fitness over time, identification of children at risk, in need of improvement or with potential, and screening and diagnosis of fitness needs for individual exercise prescription and improvement (Whitehead et al., 1990; Pate, 1994; Freedson et al., 2000). Despite its popularity and proposed purposes though, controversy has surrounded the fitness testing of young people for a number of years and various issues have been debated and concerns expressed over the use of fitness tests with this group (see more recently, for example, Keating, 2003; Cale and Harris, 2005; 2009b; Cale et al., 2007; Garrett and Wrench, 2008). According to Cale and Harris (2009b), issues debated most frequently relate to concerns with respect to the type, validity and reliability of fitness tests and to the ethics and value or purpose of testing. As a result, questions have been raised as to whether fitness tests do actually serve the purposes for which they are intended.

Q3

Keating (2003) claims that unless youth fitness testing actually improves fitness and increases involvement in physical activity, the need for it is questionable. He cites three facts that cast doubt on its role in this regard: (a) children have failed to show improvements in fitness and have become less physically active; (b) the percentage of overweight youth has increased substantially in recent years; and (c) the proportion of inactive adults has also increased dramatically. Similarly, based on a review of the literature and a study of the views, experiences and observations of stakeholders and experts in the field, Cale and Harris (2009b) considered whether fitness testing in physical education represents a worthwhile or a misdirected effort in the promotion of healthy lifestyles and physical activity. In response, they noted how there is little evidence to support the notion that fitness tests promote healthy lifestyles and physical activity, motivate young people, or develop the knowledge and skills that are important to sustained engagement in an active lifestyle. To the contrary, they highlighted how fitness testing can be counter-productive in that it can be unpleasant, uncomfortable, embarrassing and meaningless for many young people and scores can be inaccurate, misleading, unfair and demotivating (Cale and Harris, 2005). On this basis, they concluded that fitness testing may well represent a misdirected effort and that physical education time could therefore be better spent. By the same token, though, they noted how, if appropriately employed, and provided all relevant factors and limitations are taken into account, there is no reason why fitness testing cannot play a role in supporting healthy lifestyles and physical activity and in educating young people about physical activity and fitness. However, testing should not be allowed to dominate physical activity promotion efforts (Cale *et al.*, 2007; Corbin, 2007). Furthermore, and to achieve this, it is suggested that clear guidance for teachers on the appropriate use of fitness testing in young people is needed (Cale and Harris, 2009b).

Q4

Summary

This chapter has highlighted some of the key considerations and commonly debated issues associated with physical education and health. First, it considered physical education's contribution to health and its role and responsibility in promoting the health of the nation. Physical education's association with health is based on the premise that it provides opportunities to be active, educates about and through physical activity, and sets the foundation for lifelong participation in physical activity and sport. Consequently, it is contended that its role and responsibility should be to stimulate interest, enjoyment, knowledge, competence and expertise in physical activity and sport for health and well-being, and that this be achieved by providing pupils with high quality teaching and positive, meaningful and relevant physical education and physical activity experiences.

Given the current concerns over and attention to childhood obesity, the chapter also explored what role and responsibility physical education can realistically, appropriately, sensibly and safely play in addressing obesity. The importance and benefits of engaging obese children in physical activity, including physical education, were highlighted and it was suggested that as a profession we have a responsibility to provide this and to ensure that the experiences offered are just as positive, meaningful and relevant for obese children as they are for all other children.

The chapter then went on to explore a number of the commonly debated issues associated with health within the physical education curriculum relating to, for example, its place, expression, organisation, content, delivery and effectiveness. This led to concerns being raised in particular with respect to the time and status afforded to health and physical education teachers' knowledge, understanding and traditional sporting philosophies and the influence of these on the content and delivery of the area. It concluded that if health within physical education is to be effective in promoting healthy, active lifestyles and the health of the nation, then these concerns need to be addressed to ensure that all young people experience high quality teaching and enjoyable, positive, meaningful and relevant physical activity experiences.

Q5

Questions for consideration

Q1 In your view, in what way(s) and to what extent should and can physical education be held responsible for the health of the nation? Give reasons for your answer.

Q2 What factors do you feel contribute to physical education teachers' lack of knowledge and understanding of health and what impact do you feel this may have on teaching and on pupil learning about health?

Q3 In your view, what role does fitness testing have in the promotion of healthy lifestyles and physical activity?

Q4 How might fitness testing be appropriately employed within physical education and what guidance would you consider to be useful for physical education teachers?

Q5 From what you have just read, what do you feel are the main challenges with respect to health within the physical education curriculum and what actions are needed to address these?

Further reading

Cale, L. and Harris, J. (2009) *Getting the Buggers Fit: The Complete Guide to Physical Education*. London: Continuum.

This is a very practical text which is intended to be particularly relevant to physical education practice. The book aims to provide answers to a number of important questions concerning physical activity, fitness and health and the promotion of healthy, active lifestyles amongst young people and presents a range of practical ideas, strategies and tips as to how to motivate young people to be physically active.

Cale, L. and Harris, J. (2011a) Learning about health through physical education and youth sport, in K. Armour (ed.), *Sport Pedagogy: An Introduction for Teaching and Coaching*. Harlow: Prentice Hall, pp. 53–64.

This chapter provides a useful overview of learning about health within physical education and youth sport and of a number of the issues that are relevant to learning about health within both of these contexts. For example, issues such as time and status, focus and content, perspectives in learning about health and physical education teachers' health-related knowledge and professional development are highlighted.

Dinan Thompson, M. (ed.) (2009) *Physical Education and Health. Issues for Curriculum in Australia and New Zealand*. Melbourne, Australia: Oxford University Press.

This text draws on contemporary research and a socio-cultural approach to provide an overview of the concepts and issues central to the physical education and health curriculum in Australia and New Zealand. As such it provides a perspective and understanding of physical education and health beyond the UK. It also highlights important social issues including, for example, inclusion, social justice and equity to increase awareness of the relationship between physical education, health and society.

The following physical education journals should support further reading. These often include articles on health and will be useful to extend debate further.

- *European Physical Education Review*
- *Journal of Teaching in Physical Education*
- *Quest*
- *Physical Education Matters*
- *Physical Education and Sport Pedagogy*
- *Sport, Education and Society.*

Chapter 6

What is success in physical education and how can this best be achieved?

Val Rimmer

Introduction

Issues around defining success in physical education have been hotly debated for many years. However it would seem that we are no closer to achieving consensus, *across* groups at least, that is between policy-makers, advisers and teachers of physical education, about the nature of success in physical education. The key issues seem to lie with understanding what the subject is really about. In other words what are its aims? For example is it about nurturing sports skills or promoting health and fitness? Alternatively is it about fostering motivation in participation in physical activity or is it about development for all in and through the physical? How would working to each of these different aims affect the way in which success is described? (See also Chapters 1 and 2.) Certainly, our subject began in secondary schools as sport in the form of boys' games in the mid-1800s. Much has changed in education since then. Those seeking recognition of the potential of our subject to make a difference to the lives of *all* young people have successfully influenced politicians in England, initiating a debate about the value of the subject. Over the years since the 1990s the National Curriculum for Physical Education (NCPE) in England has evolved and programmes have been implemented through a national strategy for physical education and school sport which ran from 2003 to 2011, and yet it would seem that any enlightened understanding about learning and assessment of success is being clouded by historical thinking and practice. It seems that the way we see success in physical education is so deeply rooted in sport culture that high performance is accepted uncritically as our fundamental aim and our criterion for success. This view is seldom challenged and has, indeed, become highly resistant to change.

The intention here, therefore, is to reflect on the impact that developments in our subject area have had on our professional culture and their influence in terms of how judgements regarding success are made. Are the success criteria that were regarded as appropriate in the early to mid part of the twentieth century just as appropriate now? A possible measure for this perhaps lies in the answers to the following questions: what do we really want to achieve and are we being successful? And here is the issue. If, as many advocate, what we want to achieve is for *all* young people to be 'successful learners and confident individuals' (QCA, 2007a) in order that they will lead active, healthy lifestyles, to what extent is this currently the outcome of our work? Furthermore, to what extent is this even considered to be a feasible aim? Indeed, it is often questioned as to whether we can ever know whether or not learners will remain active for life? Some might suppose that there will always be those learners who, in spite of all efforts, will not want to learn or to continue participation in sport or physical activity. Undoubtedly, in England more learners do engage in physical activity than they did a decade ago, largely due to the national strategy, entitled Physical Education, School Sport and Young People (PESSYP) which was operational from 2008 to 2011, but the issue of quality and lifelong participation remains questionable. The chapter therefore closes with a recommendation that we review our aspirations and work to aims that all learners can achieve in physical education. These aims, it is argued, are more likely to promote lifelong participation in physical activity. It is suggested that it is against these aims that we should identify and judge success.

Historical review – prior to NCPE

When 'games' were first introduced into public schools in the mid-1800s, it apparently brought order to rowdy public school boys! The introduction of sport at Rugby School resulted in improved behaviour in school and thus the perception of a more effective education (see Mangan (1981) for further discussion of the nature of physical education in this era). Such was the belief in this link between sport and educational effectiveness that other schools introduced sport into their curricula. Matches between schools became highly competitive with winning seen as reflecting the standing of the school, not just the performance of the boys. 'Physical education' as it has subsequently become known, was all about sport, and success was judged on the number of trophies won for the school and by the discipline it promoted.

For many teachers this perception of success, that is, a focus on high-level skilled performance, was maintained at least through to the late 1980s. Before that, judgements regarding success in physical education were not openly considered or questioned. Physical education lessons in the secondary school continued, in the main, to be games-dominant and provided an opportunity to develop the skills of the major sports, in order to identify those who had talent and to encourage them to play for the school teams. Each lesson would include practices to improve sports skills and would culminate in the playing of a game. The 'picking of teams' by learners was common and, supported by the mantra 'learners can't be good at everything', there was an acceptance by both teachers and learners that some were good at sport and some were not. Physical education was regarded as a break from academic lessons, a chance to let off steam and an opportunity for the less 'academically able' to shine. Regarded as separate from the real business of education, it was perceived predominantly as a subject that provided fun and enjoyment for young people. If success in terms of 'enjoyment' can be judged on the number of learners who choose to participate in extra-curricular activity, then the national average of 25 per cent suggested that the profession was 'failing'. However, the profession did not perceive itself in these terms, nor were the results questioned. Attendance outside curriculum time was considered to be a matter of choice. Teachers could only encourage learners, they could not *make* them attend or participate.

There was no question about teacher commitment during this time. The *raison d'être* of many was to raise levels of skill performance and thereby ensure the school teams were successful. Considerable time was devoted to out-of-school-hours, including weekends, to provide sporting opportunities for young people. However, the teachers' strikes about pay and conditions in the 1980s were to have a significant impact on the amount of time teachers were prepared to give outside curriculum time. This opened up a potential dilemma for physical education teachers since a reduced out-of-school-hours programme was likely to lead to impaired team success. Furthermore, in 1986 the sport fraternity began to challenge physical educationists in their failure to provide a base for men and women to achieve at a national level. In the eyes of the sport fraternity physical education was not being successful. Murdoch (1993) recounts the initiation of the 'great media debate' and how this controversial and somewhat negative press stirred two government departments, the Department for Education (DfE) and the Department of the Environment to take action. They created a task force made up of representatives from sport and physical education, and commissioned a desk study to look into the relationship between these two areas of activity. The resulting document, *The Desk Study: Sport in Schools* (Murdoch, 1987) concluded that each area needed the other and the strengthening of the partnership between physical education and sport was heralded. It was argued that their aims were compatible, albeit arising from different perspectives. However, one of the key issues seemed to lie in the profession's inability to articulate what physical education was essentially about. Elizabeth Murdoch noted that 'Among significant policy-makers, a considerable confusion still exists in clarifying not only the difference between physical education and sport but also the relationship of one to another' (Murdoch, 1993: 66).

Whilst attempts to 'collapse boundaries' were being made at the highest level, the extent to which this debate influenced success criteria and practices in physical education is questionable. Many in the profession may not have even been aware of the debates between physical education and sport since teachers were just 'getting on with the job' of teaching and had little time for philosophical debate. Such academic discussion was rarely undertaken and the difference between the purposes and practices of physical education and sport not only remained unarticulated but may not even have been considered to be an issue for many physical education teachers. However, if the relationship between physical education and sport did not engage teachers the issue was certainly of interest to headteachers! If there was no difference between physical education and sport, headteachers reasoned that it would be cheaper to employ a coach than a teacher. This led to heightened insecurity and physical education teachers began to express real concerns about their perceived diminishing status in schools. The profession was being challenged to consider, perhaps for the first time, what the purpose of physical education really was, and to articulate the success criteria by which the subject should be judged. There was a call to become more accountable.

While success in physical education had not previously been considered from the perspective of examination results, this possibility attracted the profession as a way of legitimising the subject and adding to its status. The profession seemed willing to redefine the aim of the subject and as a consequence its criteria for success, these being a mix of skilled performance and understanding of relevant theory. The outcome was to introduce General Certificate of Secondary Education (GCSE) in 1986 and Advanced (A) Level physical education examinations in 1988. It was believed that the subject's inclusion in the examination system would demonstrate that physical education was clear in its aims, that it could assess its outcomes and stand alongside other subjects as a valued area of study. Learner assessment here included a significant proportion of theory as well as some elements of practical. Some regarded this as the saviour for the profession, others were dubious about the high percentage of theoretical study and its assessment, and how far this matched the aim of being 'physically educated'. Others expressed concern that this would undermine the subject's 'fun and enjoyment' element. However controversial, GCSE uptake grew by nearly 100,000 over the following 12 years and many departments saw the merits of delivering GCSE as 'core' to all Key Stage (KS) 4 learners. Providing results that supported school league tables, physical education teachers began to gain credibility and enjoy increased status in schools. Driven by performance tables, success in physical education was now being judged by some in terms of examination results and since GCSE learners were, and still are, being assessed, in part, on their skills and performance in sport, the historical thread has remained in evidence.

Q1

Alternative foci for success in physical education

In the 1980s, however, there were some in the profession who were uneasy about the single-minded focus on the performance of skills as criteria for success in physical education. Initiatives were introduced by educators and advisers to encourage the profession to rethink their aims, each in their different ways trying to move the focus away from performance per se, for example, games for understanding (GfU) (Bunker and Thorpe, 1982; Oslin and Mitchell, 2006), health related fitness (HRF) (Harris, 2000) and sport education (SE) (Siedentop, 1994).

GfU sought to move the profession away from taking the skills of a particular sport, which were often difficult to master, as a starting point for teaching, towards an approach that applied skills progressively, supported understanding and thus engaged and motivated all learners. Regardless of the fact that the longstanding skills approach tends to reduce motivation, the skill-focused approach remained, and continues to remain, the favourite mode of delivering games. Many who attempted to implement the GfU approach in their teaching would often feel deskilled and revert to a skill-based approach because, in the short term, GfU seemed to have an adverse effect on nurturing the more able and subsequently on school team performance; the dominant performance success criterion was being compromised.

HRF was introduced in the 1980s, proposing that physical education should be concerned with lifelong health and participation in physical activity, and that the focus of assessment should be on health and fitness. Again this was not implemented by all schools, despite its importance being signalled in many of the NCPE recommendations. Some tried to integrate HRF into their lessons but skill development still tended to dominate. Others reorganised the curriculum to have separate HRF lessons but often reverted to the skill-focused lessons because of the perceived loss of time for skills teaching. The drive to maintain skilled performance as the criterion for success and the development of successful school teams were too powerful to override the benefits of fitness and health and lifelong active participation, however rational the case for them may have been.

An SE approach advocated that physical education should address general educational aims and recommended that the development of collaborative skills, learner independence and leadership skills should feature strongly as criteria for judging success in physical education. This approach particularly focused on teamwork in games but could be applied in other activity settings. Learners worked in groups and shared responsibilities for planning and carrying out a group project, and each learner would be expected to play a role in this process – for example coach, equipment manager or match organiser. Interestingly, although most teachers would claim 'personal and social development' to be an aim of physical education, judgements against such criteria have tended to be limited.

All three initiatives are still evident in some schools. However, it is probably true to say that there is *more* evidence of the perpetuation of the traditional skill-based approach to the teaching of, and success criteria in, physical education.

Criteria for success and the National Curriculum for Physical Education (NCPE)

The advent of an NCPE provided the first directive from government as to the nature of physical education and the criteria against which success was to be judged. The first NCPE document was produced in 1992, bringing with it more discussion about, and scrutiny of, the subject itself, of its value and of its aims, than perhaps at any time previously. It required the profession to consider such issues as 'educating through the physical,' and providing a 'balanced curriculum'. Each successive NCPE (Department of Education and the Welsh Office (DES/WO), 1992; Department for Education (DfE), 1995; Department for Education and Employment and the Qualifications and Curriculum Authority (DfEE/QCA), 1999; and CCA, 2007a) sought to develop:

- a more appropriate understanding of the purpose and value of physical education;
- effective, graded, norm-referenced assessment guidance against set criteria;
- approaches to bring coherence to work in the subject area.

The 1992 NCPE (DES/WO, 1992) identified three areas in relation to which learners' success was to be judged. These were in respect of 'planning, performing and evaluating'. The expectation was for teachers to arrive at one grade for each learner. This presented the teacher with a number of challenges. In particular, what are the criteria for, and means by which success can be judged in relation to planning and evaluating? Also, how can a single grade be arrived at across performances in a wide range of activity areas?

To arrive at one single grade to identify success in performance was made particularly challenging in the light of recommendations to provide a broad and balanced curriculum that covered a diverse range of activities to cater for the interests of all learners. A solution that was generally adopted was a system that gave learners a level grade in each activity, with the scores being averaged to arrive at a final assessment. The inadequacy of such a system is highlighted in the example of a learner who performs at a national level in one sport but is weak in other areas of work, being given a low grade or level. While this incongruity was recognised, as well as the issue that a norm-referenced, judgemental approach to assessment can have negative effects on some learners (Black and Wiliam, 1998), this 'averaging-out, levelling' system against set criteria was widely adopted as an acceptable, indeed, the 'right' way to make judgements. (Murdoch (2004) considers assessment in the NCPE 2000.)

It seems that the processes of planning and evaluating have been an ongoing source of uncertainty based on a conceptual lack of understanding of the terms and their potential value in learning in physical education. First, they have often been taken as separate, almost unrelated entities, each requiring a judgement. Judging success in planning would tend to be based on a learner's ability to devise, for example, sequences in gymnastics, pieces in dance or new forms of games. Assessment of learners' ability to 'evaluate' aspects of movement and performance was resolved in the minds of many teachers by asking learners to identify for themselves and for others 'one thing that is good and one thing that needs improving'. A fundamental problem with these examples is that they do not demonstrate *progression* in the processes of planning and evaluating. If these processes are broken down into their fundamental sequential constituent parts (for example, being able to say what they see, describe what they see, and propose differences that could be made) and these constituents are addressed in the planning and teaching of lessons, then learners *will ultimately* become more able to evaluate, rendering the common belief that some are 'good at performing but not at evaluating' and vice versa as inappropriate.

Q2

The notion of averaging out levels or grades provided a solution in respect of performance across a range of activities and has been erroneously, but widely, accepted. This averaging of grades was also seen by some schools as the answer when the 1999 NCPE (DfEE/QCA, 1999) moved from three foci to four strands and in 2007 when five elements were identified.

In the 1999 NCPE (DfEE/QCA, 1999) strands were:

- acquiring and developing skills;
- selecting and applying skills, tactics and compositional ideas;
- evaluating and improving;
- knowledge and understanding of fitness and health.

The 2007 NCPE (QCA, 2007a) identified five key processes:

- developing skills in physical activity;
- making and applying decisions;
- developing physical and mental capacity;
- evaluating and improving;
- making choices about healthy, active lifestyles.

Again, recognising the speed at which schools are expected to respond to these developments and the understandable reluctance to change currently manageable systems, it is not surprising that the fundamental outcome was a conceptual misunderstanding. There has been a tendency to make judgements against *each* of the above processes whereas it is the *relationship between* these processes that is important. Learners who *progressively* develop ability in relation to the processes of selecting, applying and evaluating *will* acquire and enhance their skills.

Process-focused judgements – a different starting point

It would seem the case that most attention in judging success in physical education has focused on the product or the observable physical performance. However, it is by developing the progressive processes of learning that greater success of the desired 'product' can be achieved by all. The NCPE has provided guidance on how judgements should be made in the creation of level descriptors. However, the language for each descriptor is somewhat repetitive and relates to both product and process, and this has created a widespread lack of clarity of progressions from one level descriptor to the next. In an attempt to address this issue an assessment project was undertaken by the Advisory Service Kent (ASK, 2007) and their teachers, to work towards establishing integrity in the making of judgements in physical education by the identification of process words for each level descriptor. By extracting the progressive process words, such as describe and copy, describe differences and select from these differences, and using them as key drivers for planning and teaching, it became evident that these were instrumental in ensuring all learners made good progress in the acquiring and developing of skills, whatever the curriculum or aspect of physical education. Moreover, it became easier to differentiate tasks and, subsequently, learners became more confident and more motivated through success.

There was the view that a progressive thinking and learning cycle of choosing, doing and then reviewing could become the focus for our judgement of success in physical education, rather than always making a judgement on the performance outcome. A process aim of this nature would be valuable in that, if achieved, it could facilitate learners in taking responsibility for their involvement in physical activity outside and beyond school. Successful employment of these process tools would foster reflection and appropriate decision-making. The point being made here is that high quality performance is different from top level performance and whilst not everyone can achieve the latter, everyone can achieve the former through a process-led approach to teaching. The skills-based approach only works for some; a process-led approach can work for all and give us what we all really hope for our learners, that is high quality performance which inspires and motivates learners to dig deeper, achieve more and choose to be active beyond their school years. The message would not be one that indicates that effective physical performance is not important, but one that respects all individuals at whatever level they are working. With this perspective, success would be judged on the ability to reach individual potential, via confident involvement in the process of learning, rather than performing at the highest level. Assessment would be ipsative rather than norm-referenced. An approach such as this, in which process skills are recognised, is closely aligned with the goal of physical education that is concerned with lifelong participation.

Q3

Participation in physical activity as a criterion for success in physical education

Among the range of criteria for success that have been proposed and used in respect of physical education, government has identified participation in physical activity as one of its key criteria for success. Teachers are encouraged to work towards increased participation in physical activity. A significant driver for this policy was to encourage those at school to be motivated to continue with physical activity beyond their schooling. Indeed 'life-long participation' is usually cited as an aim in the policies of physical education departments across the country. However, when the government funded PESSYP (2008-11) was introduced, outcomes had to be quantifiable. This was reflected in the Public Service Agreement (PSA) targets, the motive being to reduce costs through lowering demands on the National Health Service. The National Strategy for PE and School Sport was introduced in 2003 and a network of 450 school sport partnerships across England were created to ensure that the PSA targets were achieved. In the 2009/10 academic year there were 21,486 schools and 357 further education colleges within the PESSYP, arranged into partnership groups (Quick *et al.*, 2010). In the *PE and Sport Survey 2009/10* the main outcome was to confirm that in partnership schools a high proportion of learners were receiving two hours of curriculum physical education a week and a good proportion of learners, in a typical week, were participating in at least three hours of high-quality physical education and school sport, within the curriculum and in extra-curricular time (Quick *et al*, 2010). An approach that schools have used and continue to use to encourage participation by learners in the short and long term is to introduce them to a wide range of activities. Of course this has benefits in enabling learners to 'sample' a good many activities; however there is a worry that too little time spent on so many activities will never allow learners to get a real grasp of the activity, and may leave them uncertain as to whether the activity is for them.

Whilst participation may be one indicator of success in the short term, what will be the long-term benefit of this strategy? For example, will participation in schools remain high when much of the funding for school partnerships has been withdrawn, and to what extent will young people retain a positive attitude to physical activity throughout their lives, without oversight and encouragement from the teacher? Have the PESSYP strategies provided the platform from which young people themselves will invest in their own activity-led future?

Aims of physical education reviewed

It is clear from the chapter so far that identifying criteria for success in physical education is integrally related to the aims of the subject. The aims that have been identified include winning school teams, the effective performance of movement skills, examination success, enhanced health and fitness, ability to understand the nature of games and the number of hours during which learners are involved in organised physical activity.

In order to achieve any consensus as to how judgements should be made in physical education, clear aims need to be articulated and agreed. In spite of the overriding focus on the teaching of the various physical activities and sports, it is suggested that few in the physical education professional would argue against the following aims:

- that all learners should be *motivated to be physically active* and to understand why it is important to *remain active for life*;
- that all learners can and do *make appropriate choices*, not only about the activity in which they take part but also related to life habits such as eating, drinking and sleeping patterns, which will make participation more effective and rewarding;
- that all learners *set and review personal targets* for achieving success.

These aims have a very different feel about them, moving as they do beyond the enhancing of school kudos through successful sports teams or the demonstration of high-level physical skill as the benchmark for success. They also move beyond any simple number-crunching of participation figures. They focus on individuals and their experience in physical education. It is argued that these experiences must be positive for there to be a desire to continue with activity. All experiences in physical education must be meaningful, so that learners can make informed choices concerning the nature of their participation after schooling has been completed. And they should encourage learners to be realistic about their potential and able to set and review appropriate goals. There is a sense that if the learners themselves experience success, the subject will be successful in terms of the three criteria above.

Assuming some acceptance of the above aims, these provide a clear underpinning against which criteria for success could be identified in physical education. If these aims are regarded as worthwhile, it follows that they must be achievable. History, however, shows a profession that has pursued aims about which there is doubt if they are achievable by all learners. However, rather than questioning assumptions and beliefs, Kline (1998) suggests that a valuable approach is to ask the incisive question that challenges us to think in a different way and thus open up possibilities. The incisive question here is one that asks us to *consider what we would do differently if we knew for a fact that we could achieve what we really wanted*.

This would seem to be a valuable and realistic approach, highlighting, as it does, the feasibility of any aim the profession adopts. Clearly an aim has to be appropriate and based on the nature of the subject but very importantly it must be achievable, and we would add, assessable. The chapter will now look at how we might enable all learners to achieve success in respect of these aims and then consider the challenges this approach presents in respect to judging success.

Implications of a learner-centred approach to succeeding in physical education

Looking at the three aims set out above and considering them from the perspective of the learner experiencing success, what are the implications for the teacher? At its simplest, when planning and teaching, teachers need to accommodate the three interrelated elements of the learning situation: – the learner, the process of learning and the product of the learning.

Figure 6.1 shows their relationship. It is significant to appreciate, first, that the starting point is the learner; second, that the process is the bridge between the learner and the product; and finally, that in achieving the product the learner will have developed enhanced self-belief as well as acquiring movement skill.

Keeping in mind the elements of this diagram, how can we help learners to succeed in respect of the three aims identified?

Since each learner is at a different stage in their learning, it is particularly helpful for the teacher to set appropriately differentiated tasks, and provide sensitive feedback that will raise self-belief and self-esteem in all learners. Recognising that one critical look, one harsh comment in respect of one poor performance can be all it takes to threaten self-confidence, it follows that 'layers' of negative teacher attitude and assessment that draw attention to poor performances can result in a lack of motivation, and the avoidance of participation in physical activity, within and beyond the curriculum. The damage caused by a sense of humiliation can run very deep indeed. Since such feelings tend to result in a lack of motivation and avoidance of participation in curricular physical activity or in physical activity after learners leave school, teachers should guard against their development. It is very important that every teacher reflects on the extent to which any of their learners believe they are 'no good' at physical activity, that they are 'not the sporty type', and consider what they can do differently to counter these perceptions. Often a teacher can feel helpless to make a difference because the problems are deep, and conventional educational systems often conspire against making the necessary changes in working with learners. Teachers need to recognise that there *is* a key to unlock potential in each and every learner. This key is appropriate planning to cater for individuals, a positive ambience in lessons and personalised guidance and feedback.

It would not seem educationally acceptable for the profession to advocate a goal that is demonstrably out of reach of many and yet, not only do we still have those who underperform but many would see this as inevitable. Inevitable, that

Figure 6.1 The relationship between the learner, the process of learning and the product.

is, in a skill-focused, sport programme which takes the product of sport performance as the dominant success criteria. *This has probably been our biggest mistake throughout our history.* For the learner who has a natural inclination towards physical activity and sport or is motivated and inspired early on by a parent, teacher or through some other medium, then the physical activity itself can be the key driver. These learners move to a level of competence that creates a confidence and motivation to continue, to practise, to attend clubs out of school hours and to try new activities. If they progress far enough, coaches will help them to analyse their fitness and their diet in relation to their sport and help them to develop appropriate training programmes. For those learners who have less inclination towards physical activity it is clear that judgements of success based on norm-referenced high-quality outcomes for all is flawed. Success on these grounds is out of reach of many.

Having worked over the past few years with Year 11 learners who were underperforming in all areas of the curriculum, this fundamental flaw has increasingly come into sharp focus. These were not necessarily learners with statemented learning difficulties. These were young people who have come to believe that they 'are no good', that they are 'failures', that they will 'never be able to..'. This is the language that they use about themselves and with which teachers have tacitly agreed. By asking the learners themselves what it was that was preventing them from learning, the following responses were typical:

- working in large groups with the fear of getting things wrong, and others thinking they are stupid;
- fear of asking a question which might expose them as less able and might result in answers which they do not understand;
- the problem with absences over which they have no control, normally connected with a dysfunctional family life;
- some lack of support from teachers in helping them to 'catch up' in relation to work they have missed;
- personal emotional turmoil caused by unsettled family life so that they cannot settle down to learn anything.

Q4

The following factors have also been cited as unhelpful in promoting a positive attitude to physical education and physical activity in general:

- tasks persistently set at too high a level;
- little time given to really establish a skill or learn a game or sequence;
- little recognition of effort or improvement;
- infrequency of receiving positive encouraging feedback from the teacher;
- receiving no feedback from the teacher and therefore feeling ignored;
- spending time on activities that have no relevance to opportunities outside school.

Strategies for achieving success in physical education

Referring back to the incisive question. 'What, if we knew, without a shadow of doubt, that we could achieve confidence and success for all our learners, would we need to do differently?' The following provides a brief outline of an alternative approach that has been delivered to underperforming Year 11 learners.

In an attempt to overcome some of the key issues highlighted by the learners (see above) an NCFE Personal Exercise, Health and Nutrition Level 2 course (www.ncfe.org.uk) was delivered to a small group of learners (maximum of eight) over an initial five-day period, followed by their own two-week exercise and nutrition programme and a follow-up day for evaluation and review. The programme was designed to prepare learners to set personal targets for being active and eating healthily. These learners responded well to the intensive nature of the learning process, to the flexible and varied teaching strategies and to the absolute confidence that the teacher had in their *ability* to learn. The opportunity to 'dig deep' and 'linger longer' created an understanding not only of the subject but of themselves, resulting in life-changing outcomes. They changed from referring to themselves as failures to talking of resetting targets. They changed from saying they could not achieve to asking 'What else can I do?' These young people are now equipped with the knowledge, skills and understanding to maintain their health and well-being for life, through making and reviewing choices to be active, recognising the relationship between what they eat and what they do. Indeed it could be said that these young people are well on the way to being 'physically educated'. If this can be achieved in a short space of time with reluctant learners then what could be achieved if this programme, adapted appropriately, was delivered as 'core' to younger learners?

The value of a progressive process-led rather than product-led approach to teaching and assessing has already been discussed but it is important to reiterate that this call to change the focus of making judgements in physical education away from the product of skills and performance is not suggesting that the teaching of skills is not important. The message is that a product-led approach is counterproductive even to the aims of the product-led teacher, for it limits the potential of all learners to be successful and confident performers. What is needed is a review of the design of the curriculum and of delivery styles to meet the needs of all learners. In this way we could create a platform from which learners could make informed choices, based on what they do best rather than what they are 'no good at'.

Criteria for judging success in relation to the process aim

To return to the topic of the chapter, by what criteria should we judge success in respect of each of the aims? The following provides some preliminary suggestions in relation to each aim:

- Judging the success of Aim 1: that all learners should be *motivated to be physically active* and to understand why it is important to *remain active for life*. This judgement could be made on learner attendance in class and in activities beyond the curriculum. However, this aim is integrally linked to the process of personal target-setting. When learners learn to set, work on, and review their own targets in relation to any learning activity from an early age, then judgements could be made in terms of noting how difficulties have been overcome, defeat resisted and challenges accepted. Notions of failure would be eradicated. Evidence would be ongoing and could be recorded by learner and teacher at key discussion points. We could expect that such a focus over a learner's school years would provide a good indication that s/he is physically educated and equipped to make lifelong decisions for being active.
- Judging the success of Aim 2: that all learners *make appropriate choices* in every lesson and across all activities, would start with recording decisions, for example, between two simple skills and continue through to monitoring the making of choices related to life habits concerning physical activity, eating, drinking and sleeping patterns. This judgement would be made on the grounds of ongoing choices and could be recorded in the form of a personal diary.
- Judging the success of Aim 3: that all learners *set and review personal targets* for achieving success. This judgement would be dependent on the use of open tasks and questioning by the teacher. 'What might you do?' 'What might you do differently next time?' 'What other choices could you have made?' Ongoing records of targets met, of milestone achievements and of barriers overcome would be kept by the learners, with teacher encouragement and support.

These aims are, of course, interrelated and have the potential for all learners to be successful.

Q5

Conclusion

To conclude, any judgement regarding success should relate closely to our aims for physical education. For many years it could be said that we have been 'dancing to the tune' of policy-makers and many outside our profession. Many voices have steered us to perceive that a high-level performance product should be our aim, not least to foster winning school teams or feed into the elite scene at international level. Others have focused on the inclusion of theory in the form of examinations to substantiate our credibility. To satisfy performance tables, more BTEC courses have been offered and success has been judged on the number of GCSE A*–C passes or equivalents. To satisfy policy-makers, more activities have been offered, more sports coaches deployed and success has been judged on more learners participating in activities. These criteria for success have created an expectation that, we would argue, has been unquestioned for too long.

It is time for the profession as a whole and each physical education teacher individually to stand back and reflect on the unique contribution physical education provides for every learner. The success of every individual should be something we expect. Where success is not the outcome, then the challenge is to consider what *we* need to do differently to ensure that that each learner *does* become a successful learner, rather than to assume the problem lies with the learner. The challenge is to re-examine how we engage learners in the progressive processes of learning and modify our practice appropriately. The criteria for success in physical education should be understood as the experience of achievement on the part of each and every learner. Judgements regarding success should then require no moderation process, no tick boxes, no elaborate systems. Achievement of the criteria for success will be written on the faces of our learners, all of whom will be successful, both in our eyes and, more importantly, their own.

Questions for consideration

Q1 To what extent have you been influenced by any initiatives and previous developments in relation to how judgements are made concerning learner success? Can you describe any changes made and the impact they have had on specific learners?

Q2 To what extent do you/does your department teach learners to apply *progressive* processes towards being able to 'evaluate'?

Q3 What changes would you need to make in your teaching to facilitate ipsative process assessment as opposed to norm-referenced product assessment?

Q4 Do you teach any learners who feel they are 'no good' at physical education? What are the particular issues that these learners are meeting in the home, at school generally and in relation to PE? What could be done differently to help them to become more motivated and engaged?

Q5 To what extent do your learners set personal targets for being active? If not, what changes could be made to promote this challenge?

Further reading

Black, P., Harrison, C., Lee, C. and Marshall, B. (2003) *Assessment for Learning: Putting It into Practice*. Milton Keynes: Open University Press.
This provides clear guidance on engagement strategies that support learning.
Clarke, S. (2005) *Formative Assessment in the Secondary Classroom*. London: Hodder Murray.

This book provides guidance on how to develop clear learning objectives that separate the *process* from the context for learning.

Kirk, D. (2011) The crisis of content knowledge. *Physical Education Matters* 6(2): 34.
This short paper gives an insight into why physical education content has been resistant to change.

Talbot, M. (1995) The politics of sport and physical education, in S. Fleming, M. Talbot and A. Tomlinson (eds), *Policy and Politics in Sport, Physical Education and Leisure*. Hove: Leisure Studies Association, pp. 3–26.
This chapter highlights the need for everyone to understand the influence of political processes on sport and physical education.

The following physical education journals should support further reading. There are also many education journals which contain articles related to relevant topics across education more generally, which are useful to extend debate further. They may also contain physical education specific articles.

- *European Physical Education Review*
- *Journal of Teaching in Physical Education*
- *Quest*
- *Physical Education Matters*
- *Physical Education and Sport Pedagogy*
- *Sport, Education and Society.*

Part III

Teaching in physical education

Introduction to Part III

The three chapters in Part III – 'Rethinking teacher knowledge in physical education. What do physical education teachers need to know?', 'Why do physical education teachers adopt a particular way of teaching?' and 'Are physical education teachers reflective practitioners?' – all move the spotlight from the learners to the teachers. Chapter 7 addresses the topic of the range and content of the knowledge teachers need, while Chapter 8 asks why teachers tend to adopt and maintain certain teaching approaches. Finally Chapter 9 challenges you to look in depth at the concept of the reflective practitioner.

Chapter 7, 'Rethinking teacher knowledge in physical education: what do physical education teachers need to know?' considers what knowledge teachers need to be good physical education teachers. The chapter stresses that it is impossible to formulate a definitive knowledge base because the knowledge base will be different depending on the context and the definer's ideological position. The chapter seeks to navigate a path through several areas of debate, including: an overview of some perspectives on the characteristics of teacher knowledge and knowledge production; a summary of some of the main theories, ideas and concepts that have given physical education teacher education programmes direction; and four knowledge areas (content knowledge, pedagogical knowledge and pedagogical content knowledge, knowledge of pupils and self-knowledge and reflection). You are asked to consider and debate your views on each of the areas considered in the chapter.

Chapter 8, 'Why do physical education teachers adopt a particular way of teaching?' focuses on why teachers adopt a particular way of teaching and how this affects learners' learning. The chapter looks first at whether teaching is a rational activity. It then looks at four possible reasons why teachers choose particular teaching strategies. The last of these, because the teacher has a particular philosophy of physical education, is then considered in relation to the strong socialisation of physical education teachers which can result in routine action rather than deliberate decisions being made to support the intended learning of pupils. The chapter then considers the implications of teachers not always questioning why they teach as they do and concludes by encouraging you to reflect on why you teach the way you do and to ensure that the rationale behind your teaching is always in the interests of your learners' learning. Thus, the chapter argues that what has perhaps been taken for granted – or assumed that teachers do – is not always the case, and teachers need to give particular attention to 'taken for granted' assumptions.

Chapter 9, 'Are physical education teachers reflective practitioners?' presents an innovative framework that reveals the complex nature of reflective practice. You are asked first to examine three types of discourse to highlight the nature of different conversations used by teachers to interrogate their reflections, and then nine discrete but interrelated dimensions of reflective practice. This is followed by a short presentation of the characteristics of a professional and of an extended professional. You are then challenged to reflect on the extent to which physical education teachers are reflective practitioners and extended professionals.

Chapter 7

Rethinking teacher knowledge in physical education

What do physical education teachers need to know?

Daniel Tindall and Eimear Enright

Introduction

Debates about what makes a good physical education teacher and what knowledge is needed to be a good physical education teacher have flourished in the literature and within and beyond educational institutions for decades. This is in no small way connected to historical and sustained ideological debates about the contested nature of the meaning of physical education and its aims, content and pedagogy. There are no definitive answers to the unresolved question of what physical education teachers need to know and it is impossible to formulate a definitive knowledge base because the knowledge needed will be different depending on the context, course and each person's ideological position. Ideological differences have, however, supported helpful debate and discussion about the current nature and purposes of the knowledge base, and the necessity and reality of reconstructive thinking and acting in physical education initial teacher education (PE ITE).

This chapter seeks to navigate a path through several of these debates and provoke your (re)thinking around what physical education teachers need to know. We open the chapter with a brief overview of some different perspectives on the characteristics of teacher knowledge and knowledge production. We give a summary of some of the main theories, ideas and concepts that have given direction to PE ITE programmes. For the sake of clarity, we then divide our discussion into four knowledge areas: content knowledge (also referred to as subject matter knowledge); pedagogical knowledge and pedagogical content knowledge (where we pay special attention to knowledge of movement observation, a knowledge form which is arguably becoming a dying art); knowledge of pupils; and self-knowledge and reflection. These areas are neither mutually exclusive nor comprehensive. The selection of these four areas was informed by a number of different conceptualisations of the various content, forms and categories teacher knowledge assumes (Shulman, 1987; Feiman-Nemser, 1990; Grimmett and MacKinnon, 1992; Fernandez-Balboa, 1997; Cochran-Smith and Lytle, 1999; Rovegno, 2003).

Knowledge production

In a review of teachers' construction of knowledge Rovegno (2003) proffers four conceptions of the nature and characteristics of teacher knowledge. First, 'teacher knowledge as practical knowledge', meaning knowledge is orientated towards practice, enabling teachers to negotiate challenges that arise in particular situations. Second, 'teacher knowledge as personal knowledge', meaning knowledge informed by personal biography, values, knowledge and experiences in educational contexts. The third conception refers to 'teacher knowledge as complex', which reflects the idea that knowledge develops through experience in a world which is complex. As a result, at times teacher knowledge can include contradictory and incomplete elements. Rovegno's (2003) final conception 'teacher knowledge as situated' emphasises how knowledge emerges from, shapes and is shaped by practice.

Constructivist theories of learning have primarily guided research on how teachers create knowledge. Constructivist theories support the idea that teachers actively construct new knowledge based on their prior knowledge and experiences (Shuell, 1986; Rovegno, 2003; Rovegno and Dolly, 2006) and that physical education teachers' knowledge of their subject is socially constructed, acquired through interaction with other people, either formally or informally (Rovegno, 2003; Capel, 2007). Constructivist theories also posit that knowledge becomes more differentiated, organised and connected with development (Chen and Rovegno, 2000).

In literature on PE ITE there is some agreement on the characteristics of teacher knowledge and on how teachers construct knowledge; however, there is greater diversity when it comes to identifying what knowledge is most worthwhile for physical education teachers. PE ITE programmes and teacher educators often model and support very different answers to this key question (Tinning, 2006). Some programmes view student teachers as recipients of knowledge with little or no input in shaping their own professional development (traditional/craft orientation). Others focus on developing specific, observable teaching skills within contexts where the criterion for success has been made explicit (behaviouristic orientation). Content based on student teachers' self-perceived needs is reflected in programmes which seek development of self as key to effective teaching (personalistic orientation). Programmes that privilege the critical thinking skills orientation are grounded in the belief that all education is ideological and PE ITE has a key role to play in helping student teachers to recognise knowledge as socially constructed and in challenging taken-for-granted assumptions (critical orientation). Finally, programmes with an academic focus tend to be content-centred models of teacher education (academic orientation). These different orientations represent contrasting ideologies and philosophies about what PE ITE programmes should look like and therefore what physical education teachers need to know (Tinning, 2006). What is, at times, particularly confusing for student physical education teachers is that no PE ITE programme is absolutely faithful to just one of these orientations and, indeed, even if the explicit curricula of a particular programme were closely aligned to one of these orientations, the ideologies and teaching styles of individual teacher educators ensure variability. The ideological differences reflected in PE ITE programmes and individual teacher educators result in the privileging of different types of knowledge and different theories of learning. This is also likely to result in differences in what student physical education teachers ought to do and what they actually do and, hence, learn on a PE ITE course.

Q1

Content knowledge (CK)

Content knowledge has traditionally constituted the heart of academic study for future physical education teachers. However, while student teachers and qualified physical education teachers practising in schools are in general agreement in identifying content knowledge as the most important knowledge when it comes to teaching the subject (Capel and Blair, 2007), physical education teacher educators continue to disagree on what should constitute content knowledge in physical education. According to O'Sullivan (2003) some teacher educators believe that content knowledge required by student physical education teachers must align with what is currently being offered in the secondary school setting, focusing primarily on sport, games and fitness activities. This perspective receives strong support from both student teachers and practising physical education teachers. Capel and Blair (2007) found that the knowledge student physical education teachers identify as being most important focuses largely on the knowledge they believe they need to teach in schools; for example, the six areas of activity within the National Curriculum for Physical Education (NCPE) as well as other theoretical areas for examinations. Furthermore, student teachers privilege the acquisition of content knowledge in activities in which they have had limited prior experience as being important in their development. However, others contend that PE ITE ought to focus on the 'sub-disciplines' of physical education (sport psychology, exercise physiology, biomechanics, etc.) with teacher educators assisting student teachers to apply what O'Sullivan (2003) terms a 'foundational knowledge base' in order to help them learn the sports, games and fitness activities in context. Further, for Rossi and Cassidy (1999: 193), content knowledge in physical education is much more than just understanding the subject matter.

Q2

Pedagogical knowledge (PK) and pedagogical content knowledge (PCK)

Pedagogical knowledge is the understanding and implementation of teaching skills necessary for creating and putting into practice an effective learning environment. Teachers must know and be able to facilitate such an environment if pupils are to successfully use the content knowledge of physical education. Aspects of this form of knowledge include things such as class organisation and management (taking attendance, equipment set-up, grouping, transition time, etc.), discipline and behaviour management techniques (teacher movement and positioning), motivating pupils to participate, conveying instructions successfully and providing appropriate behavioural, corrective and skill feedback (Graber, 1995).

Pedagogical content knowledge is a teacher's ability to combine content knowledge and pedagogical knowledge in a way that fosters and supports pupils' learning. It is one of the most critical components in teaching expertise (Lund *et al.*, 2008; You, 2011). Shulman (1986: 9) refers to pedagogical content knowledge as, 'the ways of representing and formulating the subject that make it comprehensible to others' which 'includes an understanding of what makes learning of specific topics easy or difficult: the conceptions and preconceptions that students of different ages and backgrounds bring with them to the learning of those most frequently taught topics and lessons'. Pedagogical content knowledge is also conceptualised as a 'teacher's ability to make the content penetrable for pupils' (Hoyle and John, 1995: 65) and making sure that pupils are 'provided with the appropriate cues, feedback and instructional techniques specific to the content area being presented' (Graber, 1995: 169). Regardless of how it is viewed, the idea is to tie knowledge of pedagogy to content knowledge (O'Sullivan, 1996: 328).

Newer aspects of pedagogical content knowledge

While the more traditional views of 'teacher knowledge' have been addressed above (content knowledge, pedagogical knowledge and pedagogical content knowledge), other areas of knowledge have recently been identified as relevant to ITE programmes in physical education. Many in the field agree that particular 'non-traditional' aspects of pedagogical content knowledge, identified as important to future and serving physical education teachers, must be developed. Doing so will allow those individuals to feel more comfortable in using such knowledge to educate learners today. These aspects, the use of technology in physical education, the understanding and effective engagement of pupils with special educational needs and the skill of movement observation, are all essential areas of knowledge that must be learned and developed.

Knowledge of technology

In the past decade or so, the ability to use technology has gained momentum internationally as an important area of physical education teacher development

(McDiarmid and Clevenger-Bright, 2008). As it relates to pedagogical content knowledge in physical education, technology could involve, for example, computer-based audiovisual software packages and digital camera equipment to facilitate homework assignments such as qualitative skill analysis (movement observation tasks where pupils break down a sport skill or fitness exercise) or game analysis projects (recognising tactics and strategy during competition). It could also include the use of pedometers or heartrate monitors, worn for the duration of a class, to monitor activity; the use of handheld electronic devices (i.e. smart phones or tablet computers) that contain software to keep track of pupil attendance or assessment records. It might even include the use of podcasts containing things such as directions for homework assignments or explanations of content presented during class. The possibilities are endless. But what is not endless is the time required in an ITE course to expose student teachers to such technological knowledge.

Knowledge of pupils with special educational needs

Likewise, it is important to debate what is necessary for physical education teachers to know in relation to teaching pupils with special educational needs (SEN). Recent research has suggested that most teachers today have had no formal training (i.e. courses and workshops) in teaching pupils with SEN, or at best that any such training has been extremely limited (Morley *et al.*, 2005; Meegan and MacPhail, 2006). There may be limited time in many ITE programmes, perhaps one course or module, to prepare student teachers to plan and teach diverse populations – including pupils with special educational needs (Hardin, 2005). Research suggests that although these inclusive or adapted physical education courses improve the attitudes of student teachers, many are insufficient in providing practical information and teaching strategies to enable them to successfully teach pupils with special educational needs (Hodge and Jansma, 2000; Hardin, 2005; Morley *et al.*, 2005; Rust and Sinelnikov, 2010). As a result, many newly qualified physical education teachers feel unqualified to teach pupils with special educational needs. In response, those in teacher education recommend ITE courses provide two things in particular; more 'hands-on experience' for student teachers with diverse pupil populations and more realistic information about teaching pupils in an inclusive environment (Folsom-Meek *et al.*, 1999; Hodge and Jansma, 2000). Again, the question remains, how much time should be devoted to this area of knowledge?

Knowledge of movement observation

A key attribute needed by physical education teachers is the ability to observe, assess, interpret and ultimately improve the performance of pupils as they engage in motor skill development, skill practice, physical activity and game play. The capacity to analyse human movement is a critical aspect of physical education teacher knowledge, both content and pedagogical. It is unique to physical education and is an important part of learning to teach in physical education. According to O'Sullivan (1996: 327), 'It [analysis of human movement] ties together one's knowledge of content with knowledge of pedagogy and one's ability to detect errors with one's knowledge of the appropriate sequence of steps to help students improve their performance.' Conversely, the ability of student physical education teachers to critically examine human movement is becoming a topic of concern for teacher educators in recent years. Lounsbery and Coker (2008: 259) express this sentiment stating, 'The failure of pre-service teachers to consistently demonstrate the ability to accurately detect and correct movement errors is an obvious concern.' The question then becomes why is this happening? Are teacher educators failing to reinforce the importance of movement analysis? Is it being taught incorrectly or maybe not at all? Are student teachers not seeing the skill as valuable when compared to other aspects of professional growth (e.g. lesson planning, behaviour management, content knowledge development, curriculum and assessment, etc.)? Is movement observation a dying art? The purpose of this section is to paint a small picture of movement observation, enabling you to decide what its place should be in a PE ITE programme.

The capacity to analyse human movement is an important skill for physical education teachers in that it allows them to build pupils' skill, proficiency, success and confidence as they participate in physical activity and sport. By doing so, teachers can hope to develop a lifelong commitment in pupils to being physically active. Research has suggested that pupils who experience success in performing physical activity and sport are more likely to continue being active later into life (Tammelin *et al.*, 2003); however, many future and current physical education teachers lack the ability to observe and critique movement effectively in order to help pupils become more proficient, successful and hence confident (Imwold and Hoffman, 1983; Beveridge and Gangstead, 1988; Morrison and Reeve, 1988; Stroot and Oslin, 1993; Behets, 1996; Wilkinson, 1996). If teachers cannot recognise correct (or incorrect) movement patterns how will they be able to provide pupils with the appropriate feedback and practice opportunities needed to improve their performance and confidence? If pupils do not perceive themselves as progressing or becoming more competent in their performance, they may be less likely to participate in physical activities outside school or beyond the secondary level (Taylor *et al.*, 1999; Carroll and Loumidis, 2001). Thus, we argue that it is important for physical education teachers to recognise the importance of movement observation and how it can positively affect the learning experiences and behaviour patterns of pupils if they are serious about supporting pupils in leading active and healthy lives.

Movement observation has been expressed in many different ways throughout the various sub-disciplines of physical education. Terms such as *error identification/detection*, *qualitative assessment*, *skill analysis*, *movement analysis* and *clinical diagnosis* have been used in the areas of biomechanics, motor development, motor learning, sport psychology and sport pedagogy to describe the skill of recognising and understanding how the body manoeuvres during different physical activities and sport-oriented movements. Yet, some in our field believe these terms are neither accurate nor all-encompassing in describing the process of analysing movement (Morrison, 2004). Knudson and Morrison (2002) have approached the concept from a different perspective, coining the term *qualitative analysis of human movement*, combining the interdisciplinary contributions of all the sub-disciplines of kinesiology. Qualitative analysis is defined as 'the systematic observation and introspective judgement of the quality of human movement for the purpose of providing the most appropriate intervention to improve performance' (Knudson and Morrison, 2002: 4). We agree with this definition and approach and refer to, and use, this term throughout the remainder of this section.

Regardless of the terminology used, many in the field agree that qualitative analysis must serve as a key focal point to any PE ITE programme. According to Reeve (2000) PE ITE programmes have yet to thoroughly address competency in qualitative analysis. What is the reason behind this phenomenon? Lounsbery and Coker (2008: 259–60) cite the issues of time, background and interest of teacher educators and the lack of a unified approach to teaching as noteworthy obstacles that hamper the development and use of qualitative analysis skills by student physical education teachers. The first obstacle, time, is similar to discussions above regarding content knowledge, use of technology and special educational needs in physical education. The amount of time provided in a PE ITE programme to cover the knowledge student teachers need for teaching is very limited. Like learning the rules of a game, practising class organisation and management skills or the process of lesson planning, qualitative analysis is another essential form of knowledge that future teachers must be taught and learn to apply if they hope to become effective professionals in the field. Unlike coaches who spend a significant amount of time focusing on one particular sport, physical education teachers must study movement concepts as they apply to a variety of activities and sports (Williams and Tannehill, 1999). Given the range of content knowledge, pedagogical knowledge and pedagogical content knowledge, as well as other types of knowledge and school-based experiences student teachers undertake during their ITE, many may not have the opportunity to cultivate the range of knowledge necessary to teach the overall physical education curriculum.

A second obstacle to the development of qualitative analysis lies in the background and invested interest of teacher educators working on PE ITE programmes today (Lounsbery and Coker, 2008). In order for student teachers to develop the skill of qualitative analysis, teacher educators working in both university and school-based aspects of the programme must not only possess the necessary proficiency required in qualitative analysis, they must also work together to incorporate it throughout the entire PE ITE curriculum. Anything less only perpetuates the cycle of newly qualified teachers entering the profession who are unable to effectively observe and analyse pupils' movement patterns.

The last obstacle that has hindered the development of qualitative analysis competency in physical education is the lack of a unified teaching approach in PE ITE (Lounsbery and Coker, 2008). As mentioned previously, the many sub-disciplines of kinesiology have taken different approaches to the application of qualitative analysis within their own areas of study; thus creating a sometimes limited or incomplete view of the process involved (Knudson and Morrison, 2002; Morrison, 2004). It has been recommended that qualitative analysis opportunities should be embedded in activity-based, pedagogical-based and theory-based course work throughout the PE ITE curriculum (Pinheiro and Simon, 1992; Pinheiro, 2000). By building a more integrated approach into the curriculum, student teachers are provided with multiple opportunities to prac-tise and demonstrate their competency in qualitative analysis throughout the PE ITE programme, thus becoming more effective teachers of physical education. Throughout PE ITE it is important that student teachers are provided with the knowledge, opportunity, assistance and support to practise the skill of qualita-tive analysis in a variety of settings within both university- and school-based experiences. But given what we know about the importance of qualitative analy-sis, do future physical education teachers see it as significant to their growth as a professional? As the purpose of this book is to stir debate among those inter-ested in physical education teaching, the discussion now lies with you.

Q3

Knowledge of pupils

Capel and Blair (2007) argue that 'knowledgeable physical education teachers should take a pupil rather than subject-centred approach and place pupils' learn-ing at the heart of their teaching' (p. 8). Physical education teachers need to know their pupils in order to facilitate their learning, engagement and enjoy-ment. While this statement may not seem contentious, there are different ways of knowing and a longstanding, and to some degree, ongoing debate between competing images of pupils in schools. Thiessen (2007) has identified the most popular competing images as the *transmission image*, in which pupils are seen as unknowing neophytes who benefit from the wisdom passed onto them by knowledgeable teachers, and the *discovery-based image*, which advocates pupils as capable and active agents in their own development who benefit from nurtur-ing and enabling environments. These two images reflect particular theoretical perspectives on learning and on student teachers' and teachers' roles and responsibilities. The transmission image aligns most closely with the traditional, behaviouristic PE ITE programme orientation. The latter discovery-based image is informed by and aligns with constructivist principles to support pupil-learning (Piaget and Inhelder, 1969; Piaget, 1973; Vygotsky, 1986). This emphasises the importance of pupils actively constructing knowledge and understanding and recognises pupils as knowledgeable and collaborative actors whose insights into and expertise on their own ideas, comments and actions are critical to their education (Rovegno and Dolly, 2006). This image is supported by a personalistic and critical PE ITE programme orientation which has gained notable traction in physical education research, policy and practice. Some schools, curricula and pedagogical strategies are changing in an effort to become more pupil-centred. Rovegno and Dolly (2006) acknowledge that pupil/learner-centred education requires that teachers focus on what pupils know, believe and can do and bring to the classroom and then on how they understand, interpret, think and feel about the content being taught.

Teachers who have come to know and appreciate their pupils as problem-solvers, inquirers, meaning-makers, negotiators and capable agents will answer the key curriculum question 'What knowledge is of most worth?' (Ennis, 2003) in consultation with their pupils because they appreciate that learners have expertise that curriculum developers need to draw on if they are to create relevant and meaningful curricular experiences. On the other hand, teachers who consider pupils as passive recipients, apprentices, respondents and beneficiaries will often answer the key curriculum questions on behalf of the learners. They assume they know and understand pupils' needs and interests (Graham, 1995) and, while their answer might be well intentioned and reflect developmentally appropriate content and sequences, the resultant curricular experiences will often be more self-centred, more consistent with their own prior experiences and biographies than those of the pupils they claim to serve. Oliver and Oester-reich (2011) contend that there is currently little in PE ITE to assist student teachers in the process of how to authentically engage with, by listening and responding to, the needs and interests of the individual pupils in their classes. They suggest that teacher education needs to begin utilising models which allow student teachers to be pupil-centred and to challenge and transform their core principles about teaching and learning during their PE ITE experiences.

Q4

Self-knowledge and reflection

Ayers (1993: 129) has suggested that 'of all the knowledge teachers need to draw on, self-knowledge is the most important (and least attended to)'. Fernandez-Balboa (1997) supports this assertion, contending that teachers cannot be expected to know, understand and teach pupils unless they know and understand themselves first. One of the principal ways advocated for gaining self-knowledge is to engage in reflective practice. Teachers need to be able to reflect on why they teach, what they teach, who they teach and how they teach, in order to critically engage with their own biographies and the impact that the values, ideas, behaviours and knowledges they have absorbed during their own education and physical education experiences have on their teaching identities (Rossi and Cassidy, 1999).

Many student teachers are unaware of how to reflect and must be taught processes which support 'learning to reflect' in teaching (Hellison and Templin,

1991; Rovegno, 1992). Most physical education teacher educators would agree that reflecting upon one's own teaching performance and decisions made before, during and after teaching is an important skill for all teachers to learn. According to Tsangaridou and O'Sullivan (1997: 4) reflection is defined as 'the act of thinking about, analysing, assessing or altering educational meanings, intentions, beliefs, decisions, actions or products by focusing on the process of achieving them'. The notion of preparing student teachers to become reflective practitioners, as well as to become proficient in the technical skills of teaching, has increasingly become the focus of many ITE programmes (Valli, 1992; McDiarmid and Clevenger-Bright, 2008). The concepts of 'reflection', 'reflective teaching' and 'reflective teachers' are not however new phenomena. Tsangaridou and Siedentop (1995) offer an extensive literature review on reflection and how it relates to the teaching profession, examining its beginnings and evolution through the work of Dewey (1933), van Manen (1977), Schon (1983) and Zeichner and Tabachnick (1991) as well as various other theoretical perspectives.

There are many ways in which teacher educators engage student teachers in the practice of reflection (Tsangaridou and O'Sullivan, 1994); focusing their attention primarily on *what* things should be reflected upon, *how* one might go about reflecting and *when* reflection can or should occur. According to Ovens and Tinning (2009), what student teachers reflect upon and how they construct their reflections can occur in different experiences, settings or contexts contained in an ITE programme (lecture/course context, school-based experience or assignments), depending on who is asking for the reflection and for what purpose. A common example may be for student teachers to explore and reflect on why they entered the teaching profession in the first place. Internationally, research suggests that love of the subject (physical activity, sport, health, etc.) and love of children are the common reasons why young people are attracted to teaching physical education (Dewar, 1989; Doolittle *et al.*, 1993; Hutchinson 1993; O'Connor and Macdonald, 2002; Stroot and Whipple, 2003; Matanin and Collier, 2003; O'Sullivan *et al.*, 2009). Reflection in this area not only encourages the student teacher to recognise and assess the main reasons for entering the profession and how their biographies may influence their teaching, but also informs the teacher educator.

As a way to better structure student teachers reflections, Tsangaridou and O'Sullivan (1997: 4) proposed two useful conceptual frames *Micro reflection* and *macro reflection*. *Micro reflection* looks at what teachers reflect on in their day-to-day teaching and how this reflection may relate to their practice and educational values. Examples may include reflections on lesson planning and whether or not learning outcomes for pupils were achieved and appropriate; the way in which content was offered and if it was suitable for the level of the learner; or what the teacher would change if he or she could go back in time and do the lesson over again. *Macro reflection* looks at the degree to which teachers' reflections and educational values change over a period of time. This may occur as part of an in-class microteaching assignment or at the end of a school-based experience. *How* and *when* to reflect depend greatly on the setting or circumstance in which student teachers are asked to reflect (Ovens and Tinning, 2009). Assignments or projects incorporated within a course may require student teachers to examine audio and videotaped recordings or conduct live observations of themselves or peers as they teach classmates in a controlled practice setting (e.g. microteaching episodes). This form of reflection requires the use of systematic observation in which student teachers gather quantitative data in order to critically analyse their teaching performance (Stroot and Whipple, 2003). In so doing, student teachers can play, pause and rewind their teaching performances; collecting information on various teaching behaviours (e.g. movement patterns, logical progression of tasks, types of teaching cues and feedback offered to pupils, effectiveness of groupings and transitions, activity time, etc.) as well as pupil-oriented behaviours (time on task, opportunities to respond and practice, academic learning time, etc.). Some teacher educators may use a case study approach to spark thought, conversation and reflection as part of the coursework or school-based experience. Others may ask student teachers to keep a journal during their school-based experiences. This journal may contain things such as responses to periodic prompts centred on educational and non-educational issues that revolve in and around the school setting: what Tsangaridou and O'Sullivan (1997: 4) refer to as 'classroom and school realities in authentic settings'. Regardless of the method or approach, reflection is considered by most as key to supporting teachers in expressing their thoughts and ideas as they try to connect theory and practice. See Chapter 9 for more on reflective practice.

Q5

Summary

This chapter has attempted to synthesise and critically engage with some of the debates around what it is that physical education teachers need to know and be able to do. It supports the notion that there is no fixed or definitive knowledge base which student physical education teachers should, and do, develop in PE ITE. PE ITE programmes, student teachers and teachers in the field must be able to 'construct and question knowledge, critically connect education with the broader socio-cultural contexts and influences and act politically and ethically to transform and improve schools and the professions' (Fernandez-Balboa, 1997: 162). We hope that this chapter has supported you in critically reflecting on what you believe physical education teachers need to know and be able to do, argue your point of view with deeper theoretical knowledge and understanding and hence, to identify what knowledge you need to develop.

However, with only a limited amount of time in which to prepare student teachers there is little doubt that PE ITE programmes should be comprehensive, concise, focused and personalised (Darling-Hammond and Bransford, 2005). It is important that consideration is given to how all the salient areas of teacher knowledge are addressed in order to prepare student physical education teachers to be effective teachers.

Questions for consideration

Q1 What types of knowledge and theories of learning does/did your PE ITE programme and individual staff privilege?

Q2 What do you consider to be crucial content knowledge in physical education and why? Is it the rules, tactics, strategies and essential skills needed for pupils to participate in various sports, games and activities? Is it performance competence? Is it the knowledge required to plan, create and implement an effective learning environment for learners? Or is it all of these things? Are certain aspects of content knowledge more important than others? Why do you consider this to be the crucial content knowledge in physical education?

Q3 Is the capacity to analyse movement an important skill for a physical education teacher? Justify your answer.

Q4 How and why has your PE ITE experience supported you in becoming a pupil-centred teacher? How do you view the pupils in your gymnasium/classroom and what role do they play in curriculum design?

Q5 Learning to teach is a career-long process. How does engaging in reflective practice play a part in this career-long process?

Further reading

Capel, S. (2007) Moving beyond physical education subject knowledge to develop knowledgeable teachers of the subject. *Curriculum Journal* 18(4): 493–507.

This paper provides a useful introduction to the social construction of knowledge and argues that in PE ITE attention needs to be given not only to the knowledge, skills and competences that student teachers ought to develop but also to the social aspects of their learning and development and the context in which they learn. The author suggests that PE ITE needs to focus on the development of critical thinking skills in student teachers to enable them to become reflective practitioners able to challenge and, where appropriate, change the teaching of the subject.

Darling-Hammond, L. and Bransford, J. (eds) (2005) *Preparing Teachers for a Changing World: What Teachers Should Learn and Be Able To Do.* London: Jossey Bass.

This book examines the core concepts and central pedagogies that should be at the heart of any initial teacher education programme. Written for teacher educators, university and school system leaders, teachers, researchers and educational policymakers, the book addresses the key foundational knowledge for teaching and discusses how to implement that knowledge within the educational setting. Chapters focus on areas such subject matter knowledge, curriculum that attends to pupils' needs, the demands of the content, using technology in the classroom, and the social purposes of education in teaching specific subject matter to diverse pupils.

Morley, D., Bailey, R., Tan, J. and Cooke, B. (2005) Inclusive physical education: Teachers' views of including pupils with special educational needs and/or disabilities in physical education. *European Physical Education Review*, 11(1): 84–107.

This paper explores teachers' perceptions of including pupils with special educational needs and/or disabilities in mainstream secondary physical education. The paper concludes with a discussion of the implications of this research for teachers' professional development and school organisation, offering implications for the future practice of physical education teachers and teacher educators.

Tsangaridou, N. (2006) Teachers' knowledge, in D. Kirk, D. Macdonald and M. O'Sullivan (eds), *The Handbook of Physical Education*. London: Sage Publications, pp. 502–15.

In this chapter Niki Tsangaridou presents, summarises and discusses illustrative findings of the research on teachers' knowledge. The chapter is constructed around the types of knowledge teachers have; what teachers know; how this knowledge is acquired; and under what conditions teacher knowledge is demonstrated.

You, J. (2011) Portraying physical education: pedagogical content knowledge for the professional learning of physical educators. *Physical Educator*, 68(2): 98–113.

This paper attempts to redefine pedagogical content knowledge in physical education (PE-PCK) by identifying the components of PE-PCK through synthesising related literature on PCK in education and physical education. This paper will be meaningful to those in the teaching community as it provides practical insights that will guide teachers along the road toward professional learning in the development of PE-PCK.

The following physical education journals should support further reading. There are also many Education journals which contain articles related to relevant topics across education more generally, which are useful to extend debate further. They may also contain physical education specific articles.

- *European Physical Education Review*
- *Journal of Teaching in Physical Education*
- *Quest*
- *Physical Education Matters*
- *Physical Education and Sport Pedagogy*
- *Sport, Education and Society.*

Chapter 8

Why do physical education teachers adopt a particular way of teaching?

Susan Capel and Richard Blair

Introduction

The main function of teaching in schools is to achieve intended learning. Learning can be defined as a change in an individual's knowledge, skills, understanding, values, beliefs and/or attitudes brought about through particular experiences (Mazur, 1990).

The approach used most often to achieve intended learning is known as objectives-based planning and teaching. A specific state of affairs to be achieved in the foreseeable future is identified and longer-term aims (for schemes of work), medium-term objectives (for units of work) and shorter-term intended learning outcomes (for lessons) are set for learners to achieve. Aims, objectives and intended learning outcomes focus on what pupils should be learning and should be achieving. In the light of these desired outcomes teachers plan how they will teach. The intended learning outcomes are the rationale for the type of teaching adopted. In referring to the 'type of teaching' we mean all those aspects of the teaching situation that are created by the teacher. For example, the material to be covered, the teaching strategy to be used, the space and time available, the organisation of learner groups, and the development of an appropriate learner–teacher relationship. It is often assumed that what is taught, rather than how teaching is conducted, is the key to achieving intended learning outcomes. However, it is argued that in many instances how teaching is conducted is as, if not more, important in achieving intended learning outcomes than the material covered. In fact all aspects of teaching mentioned above influence learning and this makes teaching a highly complex activity.

This chapter explores this complexity in relation to why teachers teach the way they do, why they adopt a particular way of teaching, and how this affects learners' learning. The chapter looks first at whether teaching is a rational activity. It then looks at teaching strategies as a key to rational teaching and the advantages and disadvantages of using teaching strategies as the answer to rational teaching. The chapter then considers five possible reasons why teachers chose particular teaching strategies. The last of these, because the teacher has a particular philosophy of physical education and/or of teaching physical education, is then considered in relation to the strong socialisation of physical education teachers which can result in routine action rather than deliberate decisions being made to support the intended learning of pupils. The chapter then considers the impact of strong socialisation on teaching physical education and, in particular, the implications that teachers do not always question why they teach as they do. It concludes by encouraging you to reflect on why they teach the way they do and to ensure that the rationale behind their teaching is always in the interests of learners learning.

Teaching as a rational activity and can we identify what makes good teaching?

Is teaching, particularly physical education teaching, a rational activity? On the face of it there should be no debate. Teachers are employed to enable learners to learn and thus their actions should be carefully weighed to ensure that they are as effective as possible. After teaching a lesson teachers should evaluate their teaching and, on rational grounds relating to how effective it has been in promoting pupils learning, decide to continue or modify the way their teaching is conducted. Three issues arise in looking more closely at this question. First, is there a blueprint of effective teaching for teachers to refer to in their deliberations? Second, what guidance is there to support teachers' rational decision-making? And finally, is there any sense in which teaching is not rational (i.e. is not based on carefully thought-through procedures in every respect)?

This section looks at whether there is a blueprint for teachers to refer to in respect of effective teaching, the next section will propose the notion of teaching strategies as a valuable tool to support rational teaching and the following sections will question if there are situations that might cause a teacher to teach in ways that are not deliberately adopted in a premeditated way.

Debate about identifying the most effective way to teach is closely associated with the issue of whether teaching is an art or a science. Is teaching an art, comprising activities which cannot be learned, or a science, which is capable of being broken down into a series of tasks that can be mastered and are amenable to systematic evaluation? Teaching is a complex activity and, it is argued, is both an art and a science. There are certain essential skills, techniques and procedures that teachers need to master through practice that help them to be effective. These include, for example, the sequencing and packaging of the material to be covered into a series of progressive tasks, the time allocation for each lesson episode, the extent of the responsibility devolved to pupils, the nature of the communication between the teacher and pupils, the grouping of pupils, the focus of teacher feedback, the form and focus of assessment, the organisation of pupils and equipment in the space. However, there is no one correct way of teaching, no one specific set of skills, techniques and procedures that teachers must master and apply mechanically. Likewise, there is no consistency in the outcomes when these skills are combined in teaching. This is, in part, because every teacher is an individual and brings something of their unique personality to the job and their interactions with pupils and, in part, because pupils are all different and each day brings a new context in which teachers operate. It is also because of various factors which influence teachers (see below).

The considerable body of research that, over time, has looked at effective teaching can help to illustrate these points (see, for example, Brophy, 1979; Rosenshine, 1987). Within the effective teaching research there are a number of large, correlational research studies in both classrooms and physical education which have examined the relationship between the characteristics of teaching (the process) and the learning of pupils (the product), measured in terms of achieving intended learning outcomes. Such research did not result in the iden-tification of precisely what makes for effective learning; hence the focus has largely been replaced with propositional rules and principles to guide teachers and which they can apply to teaching. These rules and principles are those with which teachers are familiar: identifying intended learning outcomes; developing the content and planning learning experiences, teaching episodes/tasks and teaching strategies to enable learning outcomes to be achieved; organising, monitoring and managing the learning environment; and evaluating the effec-tiveness of the process. The rules and principles can be learned but, beyond that, different teachers may apply the rules and procedures in different ways, the same teacher will not apply the rules and principles mechanistically but will apply them in different ways at different times depending on the needs of the class and individuals, and the same rules and principles can perform different func-tions at different times.

Although teachers learn and practice the same rules and procedures, effective teachers are able to adapt the highly developed skills they possess to meet the demands of a specific learning setting. This adaptation is the art. It is based on the teacher's skill (awareness, emotional intelligence) of reading the cues that classes and individual pupils give and then making decisions which in reality are based on their philosophical, theoretical and pedagogical position. It requires intuition and inventiveness and is influenced strongly by the personality of the teacher.

In our opinion this is why it is important that teachers have some clarity regarding these perspectives as it will allow a clearer lens through which to read and interpret the cues. Learning how to teach can perhaps be seen as having a number of stages. In initial teacher education (ITE), we argue, the first stage should be about aligning philosophical (ontological), theoretical and pedagogical positions. This would allow student teachers to really consider what they believe and value and what teaching physical education actually means to them, giving them the awareness to challenge their socialisation.

In order to develop the art of teaching the first step is to learn the rules and procedures and master the basic skills, or constituents, of teaching, such as effective communication, safe practices and good observation. The second is to master ways of combining the constituents of teaching to work towards the achievement of specific intended learning outcomes. This aspect of teaching is called teaching strategies, being teaching that is specifically designed to promote identified learning. The third stage of learning how to teach is where an individual's personality begins to colour teaching, giving it a unique and distinctive nature. This is usually referred to as the teachers' teaching style. (See Capel and Whitehead (2010) for detailed discussion of teaching strategies and styles.) Terms that are commonly used to describe how a particular teacher teaches are 'teaching method' and 'teaching approach'. It is suggested that these concepts are interchangeable as both provide an overall description of the way a teacher teaches. Broadly they describe the cluster of teaching strategies employed by a teacher, coloured by their personality. Both terms therefore 'encompass both teaching strategies and teaching styles' (Whitehead with Blair, 2010: 156). In the remainder of this text we use the term *approach*, except where the word *method* has been used by other authors to whom we refer.

Teaching strategies as the key to rational teaching

Teaching strategies, defined as purposely designed episodes of teaching, would seem to be a significant element of rational teaching. The concept of teaching strategies in physical education has been usefully developed by Mosston and Ashworth (2002). Their work is relevant here as they claim that all teaching should be carefully selected and planned. An intended learning outcome is identified and this must be matched with a particular teaching strategy. Mosston and Ashworth's spectrum of teaching strategies (which they label 'styles') serves as a very valuable tool for student teachers in their ITE, providing them with a useful range of ways of conducting teaching. For further information about the spectrum, see Mosston and Ashworth (2002). These are also covered in other texts.

Other writers also consider teaching strategies across all subject areas, as the answer to how teachers should design their teaching. In the 1960s and 1970s, as a result of much analysis and research about teaching, recommendations about teaching were produced by, for example, Cox and Dyson (1975), Bennett (1976) and Galton and Croll (1980). Rink (2003) has also written on teaching strategies. The *Key Stage 3 National Strategy: Key Messages Pedagogy and Practice* (Qualifications and Curriculum Authority (QCA), 2003) identifies three teaching or pedagogic strategies each of which is related to a specific type of objective. These are set out in Table 8.1.

The classifications of teaching strategies identified in the table, and in other classifications, are broad guidelines for planning teaching to achieve a particular

Table 8.1 Teaching or pedagogic strategies related to a specific type of objective

Objective	Teaching strategy
To acquire new knowledge and skills	In a direct strategy the teacher tends to use whole class instruction and demonstration, after which pupils carry out individual tasks
To develop a concept or process	In an inductive strategy the teacher designs a structured set of directed steps which pupils use to collect and examine data
To use, consolidate or refine skills and understanding	In an exploratory strategy the teacher gives the pupils more freedom to collect, use and evaluate information

learning outcome; they provide guidance rather than detailed planning. None of these, and, in particular Mosston and Ashworth's spectrum as perhaps the most commonly used classification of teaching strategies in physical education, is a panacea. In some senses they are blunt instruments and do not take into account the many variables in the teaching situation, such as the age, characteristics and previous experience of the learners as well as research about how learning is achieved. Each group of learners is unique, as is each teacher. It is therefore well to remember that it is seldom appropriate to use one teaching strategy through-out a whole lesson and that with learners having different needs, a number of strategies could well be employed at any one time.

In order to make informed decisions about practice, it is important to understand that any teaching strategy makes some assumptions about how pupils learn and that particular processes are taking place that will lead to par-ticular types of learning. However, we cannot assume that a particular teach-ing strategy automatically results in a particular process of learning for all pupils. Thus, in order to be able to make deliberate choices about what to teach and how and when to teach it, it is important to evaluate how far the strategy is being effective. Did the learners achieve the intended learning out-comes? Were they engaged in the intended learning process? We use discovery or exploratory teaching strategies as an example here, based on the work of Stanley (1969) and Logsdon *et al.* (1977). These strategies are based on the assumption that movement responses that are more adaptable and transferable to the real world and/or other situations result from the creative engagement of pupils in the activity. Although research has shown that pupils who are more creative produce more varied responses (with more incorrect responses), pupils who are less creative primarily copy what other pupils are doing or come up with one or two responses that they adopt during the time given for the task. Hence, it is difficult and problematic to infer a particular learning process from the selection of a particular teaching strategy. Thus, in order to make informed decisions about teaching it is important to understand learning theories upon which different teaching strategies are based and the differences between them. (For further discussion of learning strategies refer to Light, 2008.)

Advantages and disadvantages of using teaching strategies as the answer to rational teaching

There is no doubt that thinking through how you are going to teach to achieve a particular learning outcome and thus selecting a particular strategy is an essential element of planning.

The understanding of the role of teaching strategies in relation to achieving intended learning outcomes is very important in that it alerts student and practising teachers to the close relationship between learning and teaching. For example this rational planning can help the teacher to:

- clarify the direction in which learning is to be guided;
- focus on important and worthwhile achievements;
- retain focus and be less likely to be side-tracked;
- provide clarity for both teacher and pupils about the criteria against which the work is to be judged;
- adopt fairer and more equitable assessment of pupil attainment.

However, there are dangers in adopting too rigid a planning regime that links all intended learning outcomes to specific strategies. These include a possible reluctance to respond appropriately to lesson events as they unfold, a resistance to modify the strategy to cater for individuals and an adherence to performance-oriented outcomes that are easy to measure in the short term.

We argue that classifications of teaching strategies should be viewed as tools from which teachers can select what is appropriate in order to help pupils achieve intended learning outcomes. One way of describing this is to consider classifications of teaching strategies as books on a shelf from which appropriate material can be selected according to what it is the teacher is trying to achieve. The book may guide specific planning or it may be referred to in the ongoing teaching situation as a result of a need to rethink how best to achieve an intended learning outcome within a lesson. These cautionary words should alert teachers to consider carefully how far it is wise to follow specific guidance on which strategies should be used. The teacher needs to be reflective in planning and flexible in the teaching situation.

Although work on teaching strategies assumes that the choice of teaching strategy appropriate for a specific situation is deliberate (i.e. teaching is a rational activity) and we argue that the use of teaching strategies is an essential element of rational teaching, research and literature suggest that teaching is less of a rational activity than the research on effective teaching would suggest it should be (and would be if teaching was purely evidence-based) (see, for example,

Lawson, 1983a, 1983b, 1986; Curtner-Smith, 1999, 2001; Capel, 2005). For Cassidy *et al.* (2009) teachers do not always make conscious decisions regarding the methods they adopt. Hence, teachers rarely use strategies as defined above. Rather, they experience and/or replicate a general approach to teaching and simply use this without questioning it. Why is this? We now consider factors which influence the way teachers teach.

Why do teachers teach the way they do?

This section is divided into five factors which influence the way teachers teach.

1 Because the teacher has a particular personality

The unique teaching style of each teacher is an outcome of their unique personality, for example introvert or extrovert. Thus, each teacher makes a personal interpretation of how a teaching approach or strategy is brought to life based on their personality. For example, two teachers may both use a command strategy, but this can manifest completely differently. The first may use a harsh, direct and aggressive tone, whilst the second may use a softer more supportive, encouraging pitch in their communication.

Q1

2 Because the teacher identifies specific intended learning outcomes

As clearly indicated above, different teaching strategies are needed to achieve different intended learning outcomes. This is succinctly put by Whitehead with Blair (2010: 156) who say 'A strategy is designed to serve an intended learning outcome and should be planned after the intended learning outcomes of the lesson have been identified'. They continue with some pertinent examples:

> A tightly controlled didactic approach, for example, does not foster creativity in dance, nor does an open-ended discovery method result in precision in learning specific techniques such as a swimming stroke or throwing the discus. Likewise, the development of co-operative skills in pupils cannot be achieved if they are always working alone and self-esteem cannot be developed if pupils are always engaged in competitive situations.

3 Because the teacher knows his/her pupils

Effective teachers know their pupils and so can select teaching strategies to meet their individual needs by using a range of different strategies to support learning. Such teachers differentiate work (by task and outcome) to meet the needs of each individual pupil. If taken more broadly, this is linked to personalised teaching and learning.

4 Because the teacher has a particular belief in the way learning occurs

There are different theories about how learning occurs. Three theories of learning are briefly mentioned below.

- Behavioural theories are primarily concerned with generating principles for behaviour and focus on the relationship between consequence and action using rewards and punishment to reinforce desired behaviour and extinguish less desired behaviour (e.g. Skinner's (1953) operant conditioning).
- Constructivist theories promote a view that we do not learn passively; rather, understanding and meaning is constructed and created through existing knowledge being synthesised and new knowledge generated through social interaction with others (see Bruner, 1966; Vygotsky, 1978). For Vygotsky (1978) key principles for effective learning to take place include social interaction with a more capable other, mixed ability groups and co-operative learning environments.
- Information processing theory argues that the learner actively selects, organises and integrates existing knowledge with incoming knowledge and experience to create new knowledge and understanding in an attempt to explain the process of learning (McInerney and McInerney, 2002: 74).

A teacher's belief in the way learning occurs (which may be implicit, see below) directly impacts on the intended learning outcomes selected, the content and how lessons are taught, the planned learning experiences, the teaching episodes and strategies adopted, the learning tasks designed, the learning environment created for pupils and hence both on what pupils learn and on their perceptions of physical education lessons. In turn, these impact on the medium-term objectives of units of work and longer-term aims of schemes of work.

Q2

5 Because the teacher has a particular philosophy of physical education (i.e. a clear goal and rationale for teaching physical education)

A teacher's personal philosophy is very important in relation to how and why they teach the way they do. Although a philosophy may be explicit, we believe that for a large majority of teachers it is implicit; a certain philosophy is held but is unquestioned. Research by Green (2000a) suggests that teachers simply *do* and are not actually philosophising very much about teaching physical education. Hence, a teacher may not be aware of what the impact of their teaching implies.

Some research looks at different philosophies. For example, Lawson (1983a, 1983b) referred to teachers either having a 'teaching orientation', whereby they are mainly concerned with teaching curricular physical education or a 'coaching orientation', whereby they have a desire to coach school sport and school teams in particular. These two orientations have implications for both how and what teachers teach. O'Sullivan (2005) concluded that the dominant view of student physical education teachers is that they perceive physical education to be skill-oriented and prefer coaching to teaching. Tsangaridou (2006a: 492) highlighted that teaching is viewed as a career contingency for coaching by many physical education teachers who therefore experience tensions in managing their dual roles of teacher and coach. For Green (2003), many physical education teachers with a strong sporting focus do not distinguish clearly between the roles of coach and teacher, either in theory or in practice, and many focus on coaching sports in teaching and coaching situations.

This philosophical orientation impacts both on what teachers choose to teach and the way they teach it; and hence on what pupils learn. According to Evans and Davies (1986), the sporting perspective and conservative beliefs of many in ITE and in physical education teaching result in a strong preference for, and therefore replication of, curricula largely based around sports and games, and mainly didactic teaching approaches (particularly those experienced at school and which 'worked for them'), in which the focus is largely on improving performance in traditional (British) team games (Sparkes, 1991).

Curtner-Smith's (1999) research on how teachers view the National Curriculum for Physical Education (NCPE) in England, highlights three broad interpretations of teachers; conservative, innovative and eclectic. Teachers holding a conservative interpretation value the development of successful school teams and sporting achievements and use teaching methods aligned theoretically to a behaviourist orientation which are mainly teacher-centred and based largely on one-way didactic communication of knowledge from expert to novice, i.e. command and practice methods aimed at teaching skills and strategies for games through a series of discrete part practices developed by the teacher. The predominance of teacher-centred command and practice methods in physical education lessons has also been highlighted in research by Penney and Evans (1995). This approach limits how and what pupils learn in physical education. For example, it supports the acquisition of skill and motor development, but it could prevent pupils developing their knowledge, understanding and skill in other key domains such as affective cognitive, and social.

At the other extreme, teachers holding an innovative interpretation have more of a constructivist orientation which supports motor development and also an environment where the affective, cognitive and social domains are developed. Such teachers value and teach a range of non-traditional activities and attempt to decentralise their role in the overall learning environment and adopt more child-centred methods such as convergent and divergent discovery, learner-initiated methods and self-paced problem-solving. Communication is multi-directional, with asking and answering questions central. The teacher supports pupils in the production of knowledge, understanding and skill through interaction with others, learning tasks and the overall environment based on a relationship of 'I have knowledge, you have knowledge, let's develop new knowledge'.

Teachers with an eclectic, or non-traditional, background incorporate elements of both conservative (e.g. they focus almost exclusively on improving pupils' performance of activities and employ mainly direct teaching styles) and innovative positions (e.g. they teach a wide range of activities to provide opportunities for all pupils to develop a leisure interest) and place significantly higher priority on the learning process value orientation than teachers with a traditional activity background.

We argue that a teacher's own philosophy is particularly important in determining why they teach the way they do because the dominant teaching approach originates in the dominant philosophy of the individual teacher. It is also perhaps the most entrenched as a result of socialisation of physical education teachers. We consider work on socialisation next.

Q3
Q4

Socialisation of physical education teachers and its impact on teaching physical education

Lawson (1986) identified three stages of teacher socialisation. The first stage, acculturation, starts at birth and continues through childhood and adolescence, when there is a heavy influence by those who have an immediate impact on our day-to-day existence, such as, parents, teachers and significant others. It comprises influential experiences and the predispositions these engender, including experiences in physical education and sport (both in and out of school); success in education and in sport; love of and valuing of sport; interactions with and positive influences of physical education teachers, coaches and others working in physical activity and sport contexts with whom they come into contact (see, for example, O'Bryant *et al.*, 2000). Capel (2010) discusses how student teachers have been at school for at least 11 years before they make a final decision to enter physical education ITE, probably because they had some success in physical education lessons or extra-curricular sport or physical activity at school. Positive experiences lead to identification with and attachment to sport, both important influences on the decision to become a physical education teacher, and on the knowledge, ideas and attitudes with which student physical education teachers enter their ITE course, including understanding of what it means to be a physical education teacher and orientation to physical education and sport (see Lawson's (1983a, 1983b) teaching and coaching orientations discussed above, p. 128). In turn, they become prospective teachers holding particular values and beliefs about the nature and purposes of the subject, including both the content and how it should be taught (Behets and Vergauwen, 2006;

Tsangaridou, 2006b). As Green (2000a, 2005b) highlights, physical education teachers are a self-selecting group. For many physical education teachers, this career path is an opportunity to continue being involved in an area of their life in which they have previously been successful.

The second stage of socialisation, professional socialisation, is the time spent on an undergraduate degree and physical education ITE; the processes through which student teachers are required to meet the official requirements of teaching physical education as well as being initiated into the profession. Because student physical education teachers on secondary ITE courses in England spend a large part of their time in schools, experiences in school generally, and teaching experiences particularly, are identified as most important and influential in developing their knowledge, beliefs and practices (see, for example, Velija et al., 2009).

As the school-based part of the course is situation specific, and student physical education teachers work with a mentor and other established teachers in school, the mentor and other teachers are very influential in student physical education teachers' development as teachers (Gower and Capel, 2004; Behets and Vergauwen, 2006). Booth (1993: 194) found that mentors are focused upon 'the immediate, practical issues of subject-specific teaching and classroom management and control'; that is, they view their role primarily as passing on to student teachers practical advice about the day-to-day demands of teaching physical education. Thus, mentors provide advice and guidance to student teachers on their development as teachers and on their teaching, including content, teaching methods, management, organisation, reflection on and evaluation of lessons. In this process, mentors pass on their values and beliefs about the aims and purposes of physical education and how it is taught. For Parker (1995), teachers' beliefs of effective teaching were expressed through a hierarchy of pedagogical practices, including organisation, management, discipline and control.

Both formal and informal aspects of an ITE course are important socialising influences on student physical education teachers' development of knowledge. Indeed, 'the informal social structure [of school placements] may, in certain situations, be more powerful than the formal structure. Success in teaching may depend on accurate perceptions of what is accepted as "good" and where the power lies' (Wendt and Bain, 1985: 25). For Stroot and Whipple (2003), the informal social structure, including informal interactions with mentors, is particularly influential on student physical education teachers' perceptions and practices. For Green (2003), as student physical education teachers interact both professionally and socially with mentors and other physical education teachers who share a background comprising largely positive experiences of sports, particularly team games (both in traditional physical education lessons and experiences outside), and who are also interested in and enjoy physical activity and sport, they tend to have an unquestioning view as to what is taught in physical education and how it is taught, rather than seeing the possibility of alternative models. Thus, student physical education teachers' existing values, beliefs and knowledge about physical education, particularly the role of sports and games and how they are taught, are reinforced rather than challenged during ITE. This results in student physical education teachers being absorbed and initiated into physical education teaching, including what is considered 'good' or 'effective' practice. Hence, many physical education teachers see content and teaching approaches as 'self-evident' and 'unproblematic' (Thomson, 1999), resulting in what Penney and Evans (2005: 21) called 'the taken-for-granted routines in physical education'. Zeichner and Tabachnik (1983) refer to an 'institutional press', whereby pedagogical practices are often passed unquestioned from one generation to the next. This unquestioned practice is often routine (Dewey, 1933). Likewise, according to Siedentop and Tannehill (2000) it isn't bad teaching that we have to worry about in physical education but rather non-teaching, by which they mean teaching that is conducted without thought.

For Green (2003), student physical education teachers have presuppositions and preoccupations and use a particular lens or prism as a result of their sporting orientations which result in their assimilating rather than challenging what they are taught. As a result, student physical education teachers are selective in what they learn on school placement because they see the world through a particular lens and only pick up what they want to hear. Matanin and Collier (2003) found that student physical education teachers on a four-year course only absorbed that part of their ITE course concerned with content, teaching effectiveness and the role of planning, whilst they were less likely to take on board content covering classroom management and the purposes of physical education. Generally, student physical education teachers have more difficulty in making a connection between the knowledge covered in their university-based work (with the exception of that part designed to develop content knowledge in specific activities) and the knowledge they believe essential for teaching, perhaps because they cannot see its immediate relevance (Graber, 1995). Graber also found that where university-based work influenced their beliefs about physical education one particular teacher educator was identified as being mainly responsible.

Thus research has shown that, as a result of values and beliefs already largely established before entry to ITE, the practices with which they are linked and the importance of school-based work and the mentor, ITE has little impact on beliefs and practices (Placek et al., 1995). This reinforces the status quo and, soon after qualifying to teach, the impact of teacher education tends to be 'washed out' (Zeichner and Tabachnik, 1981: 7; see also Stroot and Ko, 2006; Tsangaridou, 2006b); what Evans et al. (1996: 169) describe as physical education teachers being 'neither shaken nor stirred by training'. As a result, physical education teachers teach how they were taught, or as a direct consequence of watching or being mentored by other teachers, unless they experience a critical intervention by a credible educator who holds alternative views.

The third stage comprises organisational socialisation, the learning of attitudes and behaviours 'on the job' which encompasses the impact on a teacher's values and beliefs through contact with the culture and environment of the workplace. Green (2003) describes this process as being characterised by new-comers being absorbed into physical education departments and physical educa-tion teaching by consecutive generations of physical education teachers.

For Lawson (1983a, 1983b, 1986) the formative experiences in physical edu-cation and sport are particularly influential in the socialisation of physical educa-tion teachers and hence acculturation is the most powerful stage. Organisational socialisation is the second most influential, with the least significant stage being professional socialisation; unless a student teacher meets an innovative educator whose opinion and views they respect and see as credible. As a result, decisions future teachers make about teaching are influenced by factors long before they learn how to teach. For Tinning *et al.* (1993), the combination of past experi-ence, personal values, beliefs and learning orientation impact on the establish-ment of a personalised style of communication and teaching and the choice of teaching strategies. For Schempp and Graber (1992: 333), the beliefs with which student physical education teachers enter ITE have 'a distinct and trace-able influence on an individual's future decisions, practices, and ideologies as a teacher' which, according to Placek *et al.* (1995: 247), have 'a long-lasting impact on school programmes'. This approach to learning how to teach can be closely aligned with an apprenticeship model where much learning occurs 'in the school' or 'on the job' (Wenger, 1998).

What are the implications of teachers not always questioning *why* they teach as they do?

Physical education teachers have considerable influence on the pupils they teach so it is important that physical education lessons meet the needs of all pupils and are meaningful to them. The literature on philosophy, values and beliefs and socialisation of physical education teachers suggests that physical education as currently taught may not be achieving this (see, for example, Green, 2003; 2005b; Capel, 2005). It suggests that teachers may be concentrating more on their teaching rather than on pupils' learning. It also suggests that the focus is on learning motor and performance skills rather than on planning and evaluat-ing, preparation for lifelong participation, and other objectives.

We have spent considerable time focusing on personal philosophies, values and beliefs and socialisation as we believe these are the most influential factors in what pupils learn in physical education because they are the most powerful factors influencing teachers' teaching of physical education. We argue that the strong socialisation evident in physical education, which results in many student and practising physical education teachers being entrenched and unquestioning in their philosophy, is exacerbated by many student physical education teachers adopting a surface approach to learning as opposed to a deep or transformative learning orientation, which results in lack of reflection (if you are interested in additional reading on approaches to learning and learning orientations see, for example, Entwistle, 1990; 1993).

The result of this is that student and practising physical education teachers do not think critically about what pupils are learning, what they themselves are doing, what and why they teach as they do and what the implications of this are. Thus, they are not reflexive (engaging in activities in which they analyse the circular relationship between how their teaching (the cause) affects pupils' learning (the effect)). This, in turn, prevents them from engaging in reflective practice, i.e. continuous learning which is required to develop practice (and pupils' learning) and which Bolton (2010: xix) refers to as 'paying critical attention to the practical values and theories which inform everyday actions, by examining practice reflectively and reflexively. This leads to developmental insight.' Authors such as Siedentop and Tannehill (2000) and Tinning *et al.* (2001) have critiqued the lack of reflective teaching and learning in physical education.

Without being critical and reflexive and adopting reflective practice, teachers are unlikely to change and develop their teaching to enhance pupils' learning. Indeed, it is generally recognised that, despite there being a number of developmental initiatives and changes in recent years, there has been little change in the teaching of the subject (Capel and Blair, 2007). We argue that the traditional content and teaching approaches are contributing to the alienation of many young people from physical education and therefore physical activity. This is illustrated in four ways below:

1 Teaching approaches and strategies selected are not appropriate to achieve a range of intended learning outcomes

The way many teachers were taught themselves probably followed an approach in which the skills were taught first and then applied in the activity setting with a fairly rigid format of warm-up, skill development, whole activity, conclusion (Kinchin, 2010). This is therefore likely to be the favoured approach to teaching adopted by many physical education teachers. It has several implications in relation to intended learning outcomes. First, these tend to focus on performance outcomes (i.e. skills and tactics) with less focus on planning and evaluating outcomes, both of which serve to improve performance. Second, the lesson format may not always be the most appropriate for achieving a broader range of intended learning outcomes, including affective, cognitive and social outcomes. In relation to dance, it might not encourage creativity. Likewise, in games it might not enable pupils to learn how to solve problems they experience in an authentic game situation. On some occasions it might be more appropriate to encourage pupil problem-solving (e.g. do I dribble, pass or shoot?) which might require a different format to the lesson. Rarely, we argue, are pupils put in situations where they are required to make such decisions; and hence they do not experience the essential features of participating in a game.

2 Teaching approaches and strategies do not take account of the learning needs of the class and hence are demotivating

It is important that all teaching is underpinned by the learning needs of the class and individuals. Differentiation for individuals can be by outcome or task. However, where a teacher does not question the teaching strategies used, it is less likely that the needs of each individual pupil are considered and, hence, less likely that work is differentiated appropriately. The learning of all pupils is therefore likely to be compromised, so the most able are less likely to be stretched and the less able are less likely to achieve the outcome. This is likely to be demotivating for pupils.

3 Teaching approaches and strategies focus on performance rather than learning

Intended learning outcomes tend to measure the product of learning, the performance, rather than the learning itself. Performance outcomes (whether skills or behavioural; physical, affective, cognitive or social) focus on readily observable outcomes (i.e. what pupils can do), rather than, for example, in the case of behavioural outcomes, the development of attitudes and changes in long-term dispositions and potential. Hence, teachers measure pupils' performance against stated outcomes. They do not measure what they have learned that is not assessed, what they have learned in a broader sense or what they cannot control (Swann, 1999: 59). Further, performance is not synonymous with the process of learning; therefore learning is inferred in this approach. In order to measure learning, teachers need to be able to adjust their lessons to be able to take account of the open-ended nature of learning to enable both them and the pupils to discover and address the unexpected and undesirable consequences of action. This is very difficult because learning is often an unconscious process with autonomous activity, is complex and is not linear. Each learner must take responsibility for their learning and be active in the process; learning will not occur as a result of coercion. Learning may not be able to be measured in an objectives-based approach to teaching. Indeed, 'Gagne emphasises that we cannot control learning, but we can increase the probability that certain kinds of learning behaviour will occur' (Joyce *et al.*, 2002: 166).

Q5

4 Teachers blame learners on their lack of progress rather than reflecting on their own teaching

If teachers adopt an unquestioning approach to their teaching, they are likely to see any lack of progress as the fault of learners (e.g. through lack of effort or motivation) rather than caused by what and how they teach not being appropriate.

Q6

What do we need to do so that teaching strategies are adopted to achieve intended learning outcomes, not as ends in themselves?

First, we turn back to the implications of the five factors which we identified as influencing the way we teach (see pp. 126–9).

We contend that ITE cannot influence a teacher's personality. However, this is not to say that personality should be ignored in ITE. It is important that (student) teachers are aware of their personality and understand how it impacts on their preferred teaching style and, in turn, how this impacts on pupils' learning. Such an understanding should enable (student) teachers to consider and learn how to use alternative styles when the need arises. For example, a teacher with an extrovert personality and loud voice may, on occasion, find that a quieter approach works better with some pupils and/or in some situations. There is no one right way of teaching, but any way should be used rationally in the interests of learning. Hence, it is important that in ITE student teachers are 'taught' about the art of teaching and this should be developed along with the science of teaching.

We also contend that the other four factors should be influenced directly during ITE. It is easy to see where principles such as identifying specific intended learning outcomes, the importance of knowing pupils individually and theories about the way learning occurs are taught in the university-based parts of ITE courses. However, it is more difficult to understand how what is taught in the university-based part of the course is put into practice on school-based placements and why, and for many why they are not, put into practice. For example, student teachers may have been taught about setting appropriate intended learning outcomes which address affective, cognitive and social development as well as motor development (and within motor development addressing planning and evaluating as well as skill development and performance). However, there may be many reasons why they do not always include such learning outcomes in their lessons on school placement. These include:

- student teachers' own development;
- whether they are ready to move beyond the immediate, practical day-to-day concerns of teaching (ranging from issues about themselves as teachers and the material they are teaching to considerations about pupils' learning);
- the particular views of student teachers regarding the way learning occurs which is not changed by being taught alternative theories;
- the difficulties inherent in school-based placements, such as the relatively short time spent in a school, making it difficult to get to know pupils individually and hence difficult to plan for their individual needs.

However, we contend that perhaps the two most important, and interrelated, reasons are the strong influence of school-based placements, and particularly of the mentor, and the fifth factor identified above – that the teacher has a particular philosophy of physical education, a clear goal and rationale for teaching physical education, which is not challenged or changed at any time in their teaching career, before, during and after ITE. For us, the worry is that (student) teachers do not reflect on their personal philosophy; hence, in essence, their philosophical, theoretical and pedagogical views and practice do not match – there is a difference between their rhetoric and the reality of their practice. As a result, some would be alarmed that what they preach is certainly not being realised in how they teach.

So, what does this suggest? That we need to enable student teachers to reflect on, critically evaluate and be reflexive about their own philosophies, values and beliefs. In order to achieve this, we contend that a student teacher's past experiences, philosophical roots, values, beliefs and approaches to learning need to be made explicit and challenged so that they can deliberately plan physical education lessons that are meaningful for all pupils and address affective, cognitive and social as well as motor outcomes.

This should mean that all aspects of teaching are planned to support pupils' learning. This requires deliberate rather than routine action – what Siedentop and Tannehill (2000) call non-teaching, or teaching that is conducted without thought. This needs teachers to take a problem-based approach to planning and evaluation in which they understand, take into account and build on what the pupils (as learners) bring to the situation in terms of past experiences, knowledge, skills and understanding, values and attitudes. In order that deliberate action becomes the norm, teachers need to develop the ability to critically reflect on the current environment in which they are working and take deliberate action to create meaningful, inspiring learning tasks which build from pupils' past experience(s) and support all pupils in achieving the intended learning outcomes of each lesson. This requires a reflective approach to teaching which challenges and embraces student teachers' own past experience, philosophy, values and beliefs, allowing them to make clearer decisions on how they would like to teach their physical education lessons to enhance pupils' learning. In this approach, teachers will deliberately combine theoretical understanding with knowledge and experiences to enable pupils to achieve intended learning outcomes.

Such understanding and engagement should enable student teachers to identify appropriate intended learning outcomes; develop the content and plan learning experiences, teaching episodes and tasks and teaching strategies to enable learning outcomes to be achieved; organise, monitor and manage the learning environment to encourage pupils' learning and motivate them to learn (chapter 9 looks at reflective practice). It should also enable student teachers to make informed contributions to debates about what have been described as methods 'wars' in physical education, where advocates of one teaching method attempt to show that their way of teaching is far better than other teaching methods and therefore should be adopted for all teaching in physical education (see, for example, Rink, 2001). The most recent conflict in the literature has positioned more traditional, or direct, teaching methods against methods based on more constructivist and socially based learning theories (see, for example,

Light, 2008). We argue that one method is not better or worse than another and should not be used at all costs (see also, for example, Rink, 2001); rather the method should be selected according to the planned intended learning outcomes but there should also be flexibility.

At present, we argue, not enough emphasis is placed on structuring student teachers' learning experiences in many ITE courses, within both the university-based part of the course and the school-based placements, to encourage and support the development of critical thinking and reflexivity. It is also difficult for student teachers to do this on a course where they are required to meet a set of standards. Their highest priority, and hence their focus, is on achieving the relevant standards and qualifying as a teacher. As a result, most student teachers focus on the immediate day-to-day concerns of teaching and many select content or copy methods from their mentor or other teachers. However, what is important is that we try to find mechanisms to encourage critical thinking and reflexivity on ITE courses. This requires us to work not only with student teachers but also with mentors and other teachers in schools to encourage critical thinking and reflexivity. Further, it is important that once student teachers have achieved an acceptable level of competence in ITE, they are pushed onto considering how they can develop their teaching to better enhance pupils' learning. Without a consistent message being received from tutors, mentors and other teachers, student teachers will continue to prioritise those aspects of the course which they perceive are most important in enabling them to meet the standards and pass the course.

Thus, a priority in ITE and into teaching should be improving student teachers' ability to think critically, be reflexive and engage in reflective practice to enable them to make deliberate, informed decisions about all aspects of their teaching to enhance pupils' learning. We recognise the difficulties in doing this and challenging the strength of socialisation over a long period of time. For this to have a chance of being effective requires teacher educators to consider their own teaching approaches. Rather than lecturing, they need to use different styles, including encouraging discussion and debate, which require student teachers to become independent, reflective learners. It also requires university tutors, mentors and other physical education teachers in schools with whom student teachers come into contact to critically evaluate, reflect on and be reflexive about their own philosophies, values and beliefs in order to be able to support student teachers in this task.

We also argue that what occurs in ITE is only a start. Hopefully, by structuring student teachers' learning to encourage them to challenge their philosophies, values and beliefs, understand why they hold these views and, hence, why they teach the way they do and the impact of this on pupils' learning, and what they need to do to focus on pupils' learning and to plan all aspects of their teaching to achieve intended learning outcomes, student teachers will graduate with open minds willing to continue learning. However, they need continuing professional development opportunities in their first and subsequent years to encourage continued critical thinking, reflexion and engagement in reflective practice.

Summary

This chapter explores the complexity of the relationship between teachers teaching and pupils learning. The chapter first looks at whether teaching is a rational activity. It then looks at five possible reasons why teachers choose particular teaching strategies and hence teach the way they do. The last of these, the teacher's particular philosophy of physical education and personal values and beliefs, is then considered in relation to the strong socialisation of physical education teachers. This can result in routine action rather than deliberate decisions being made to support the intended learning of pupils. As a result, the intended learning outcomes teachers select for their classes and, in turn, the content and learning experiences, teaching episodes/tasks and teaching strategies planned and the learning environment they create to support pupils to achieve the intended learning outcomes may not maximise pupils' learning. The chapter then considers some implications of teachers teaching the way they do and what we need to do to encourage and support teachers to reflect on why they teach the way they do and enable them to make deliberate decisions to focus on and enhance pupils' learning. We argue that it is important that teachers focus on pupil learning, rather than on their teaching. It is hoped that by reading this chapter (student) teachers will give careful consideration to the reasons why they teach the way they do and the consequences of pedagogical choices made on pupil learning and enable them to make deliberate decisions to select teaching strategies that enable pupils to achieve specific intended learning outcomes.

Questions for consideration

Q1 Reflect on your own personality. What are your dominant personality traits? How do these impact on your own teaching (and hence on pupils' own learning)?

Q2 Reflect on how you plan lessons and, in particular, whether and to what extent the intended learning outcomes you plan contribute to the medium-term objectives of the unit of work and longer-term aims of the scheme of work?

Q3 How, and why, does the NCPE (2007) impact your teaching approach?

Q4 What is your philosophy of physical education and teaching? What do physical education and teaching physical education mean to you? What are your beliefs about how physical education should be taught?

Q5 How certain can we be that our teaching brings about certain kinds of learning? How can you increase the probability that certain kinds of learning will occur?

Q6 Reflect on the relationship between your own teaching and pupils' learning. How much is lack of progress the result of the content and/or teaching approach/strategies adopted and how much is it the fault of learners, e.g. through lack of effort or motivation?

Further reading

Capel, S. (2007) Moving beyond physical education subject knowledge to develop knowledgeable teachers of the subject. *Curriculum Journal*, 18(4): 493–507.

This paper looks at social aspects of learning in physical education which has implications for the development of knowledge for teaching. It argues that attention needs to be given to the knowledge, skills and competencies that student teachers ought to develop, to the social aspects of learning and development and the context in which student teachers learn, to the ability to think critically in order to challenge the strong socialisation which shapes the values and beliefs of physical education teachers.

Mosston, M. and Ashworth, S. (2002) *Teaching Physical Education*, 5th edn. San Francisco: Benjamin Cummings.

This book provides a detailed look at each of their teaching styles.

Rink, J. (2001) Investigating the assumptions of pedagogy. *Journal of Teaching in Physical Education* 20: 112–28.

This article discusses the relationship between learning theory and teaching methodology from the perspective of the research and the teacher.

The following physical education journals should support further reading. There are also many education journals which contain articles related to relevant topics across education more generally, which are useful to extend debate further. They may also contain physical education specific articles.

- *European Physical Education Review*
- *Journal of Teaching in Physical Education*
- *Quest*
- *Physical Education Matters*
- *Physical Education and Sport Pedagogy*
- *Sport, Education and Society.*

Chapter 9

Are physical education teachers reflective practitioners?

Paula Zwozdiak-Myers

Introduction

Reflective practice is in the foreground of key drivers advanced by governments and education departments worldwide not only to raise educational standards and maximise the learning potential of pupils but for accountability of teachers in relation to evidence-based outcomes against prescribed performance criteria. The broad consensus arising from recent large-scale surveys is that *teacher quality* is the 'single most important school variable influencing student achievement' (OECD, 2005a: 2) and characteristics which mark teachers at different stages in their careers should be built on a concept of teaching 'as praxis in which theory, practice and the ability to reflect critically on one's own and others' practice illuminate each other' (European Trade Union Committee for Education (ETUCE), 2008: 26). This highlights the need for physical education teachers to become very active agents in analysing their own practice and the importance of observing and tracking professional performance and pupil outcomes through self-monitoring (Webster and Schempp, 2008) in order to develop strategies for professional maintenance and growth.

Numerous claims have been advanced concerning the values inherent in reflective practice, yet to engage in debate as to whether physical education teachers are reflective practitioners, we need to clarify what we mean by this phenomenon. Underpinned by work advanced by eminent scholars, researchers and practitioners within the field, and discussed more fully elsewhere (Zwozdiak-Myers, 2012), to which you should refer for further detailed explanation, in this chapter reflective practice is defined as:

> a disposition to enquiry incorporating the *process* through which student, early career and experienced teachers structure or restructure actions, beliefs, knowledge and theories that inform teaching for the purpose of professional development.

> (Zwozdiak-Myers, 2012: 5)

Reference to reflective practice as incorporating a *process* embraces a multitude of theories concerning the nature of reflective activity and its translation into professional practice. These have been captured and used in a framework developed by the author to exemplify the complex, multi-dimensional nature of reflective practice as shown in Figure 9.1. Each dimension provides a specific focal point that physical education teachers can draw upon to guide, structure and interrogate their own teaching. Although presented in a sequential manner the initial catalyst for reflective practice can originate from any dimension and each is inextricably linked and related to others in multifarious ways.

A common thread permeating through many concepts and theories related to reflective practice is that the types of discourse or reflective conversations[1] teachers engage in may be indicative of their development from *surface* to *deep* to *transformative learning* (Moon, 1999); progressive stages of *epistemological cognition* (Baxter Magolda, 1999; Moon, 2005); and, different stages of *reflective reasoning* (King and Kitchener, 1994). Three broad types of discourse synthesised from the literature have been superimposed onto Figure 9.1, giving rise to the 9×3 framework of qualitative distinctions in reflective practice presented in Figure 9.2.

An exploration of how physical education teachers may exemplify qualitative distinctions in reflective practice through the types of discourse they engage in are briefly outlined below. This is followed by an exposition of some key processes embedded within the nine dimensions of reflective practice. You are encouraged to consider how the different types of reflective conversation are enacted in and through their own teaching in relation to each dimension of

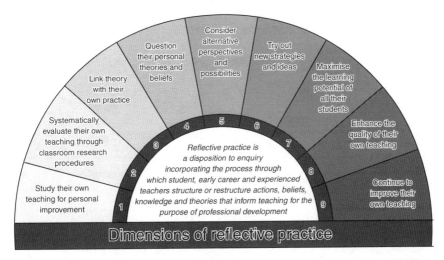

Figure 9.1 Dimensions of reflective practice (source: Zwozdiak-Myers, 2012).

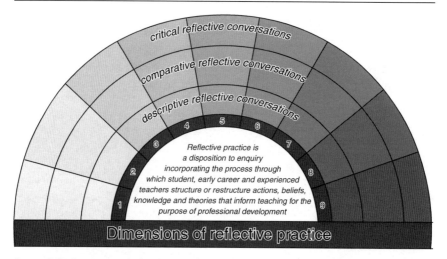

Figure 9.2 Qualitative distinctions in reflective practice (source; Zwozdiak-Myers, 2012).

reflective practice. The concluding section of this chapter invites you to consider how the constituent components of this framework relate to the pursuit of becoming an extended professional.

Qualitative distinctions in reflective practice

Descriptive reflective conversations

This type of discourse is based on concrete experience as physical education teachers examine and frame aspects of their own practice. It involves returning to experience and providing a detailed personal account of that experience to search for patterns and trends that may emerge in response to such questions as: What was taught? How was it taught? Did pupils achieve the intended learning outcomes? What teaching strategies were effective, or ineffective? How do I know? What does this mean? How does this make me feel? How might I do things differently next time?

Different types of question involve different patterns of thinking. For example, 'How was it taught?' requires a reflective process analysis of the approach that has been followed. 'How does this make me feel?' appeals to the affective aspect of a teacher's practice and discourse arising from this question may reveal insights into their disposition to enquiry. 'How might I do things differently?' requires a reflective self-evaluation of a particular type of performance using criteria against which professional judgements can be made.

Comparative reflective conversations

Comparative discourse is evident when physical education teachers relate personal assumptions, beliefs, theories, values and conceptions of teaching to that of others, e.g when teachers reframe the focus of their reflection in light of multiple perspectives, alternative views and possibilities, research findings from literature and their own engagement with prior experiences. This type of discourse is essentially 'a deliberation among choices of competing versions of good teaching' (Grimmett *et al.*, 1990) and involves moral, ethical and value commitments in response to such questions as: What alternative strategies might I use in my teaching? What are the advantages/disadvantages of using particular strategies for diverse learners? How might colleagues and/or pupils explain what is happening in my lesson? What research enables me to gain further insights?

Teachers come to recognise that knowledge claims contain elements of uncertainty, which those who hold these assumptions may attribute to missing information or methods of obtaining evidence. Teachers can expect to have an opinion, to think through issues and express these in a valid manner. They also consider colleagues may have useful contributions to make. However, the idea of judging some perspectives as more or less effective than others tends to be overlooked. Although teachers may use evidence, they do not necessarily understand how evidence entails a conclusion, particularly in light of the acknowledged uncertainty, and thus tend to view judgements as highly idiosyncratic.

This type of discourse has resonance with *transitional knowing* (Baxter Magolda, 1999; Moon, 2005) and *quasi-reflective reasoning* (King and Kitchener, 1994).

Critical reflective conversations

This type of discourse is characterised by the acceptance that knowledge claims cannot be made with certainty and teachers make judgements that are 'most reasonable' and about which they are 'relatively certain' based on the evaluation of available data. Teachers actively construct decisions and evaluate knowledge claims in terms of the context in which they were generated to determine their validity. They are also willing to re-evaluate the adequacy of their judgements as new data and methodologies become available.

Critical reflective conversations are evident when physical education teachers ask searching questions about their teaching that consider the implications behind alternative perspectives and demonstrate a willingness to suspend judgement until these avenues are fully explored. They analyse the wider cultural, social and political contexts, challenge their assumptions and question their practice in relation to ideological and equity issues in response to such questions as: What are the implications of using particular strategies in my teaching when viewed from alternative perspectives? Why select this particular strategy for this particular group of pupils rather than an alternative? How does my choice of objectives, learning outcomes and teaching strategies reflect the cultural, ethical, ideological, moral, political and social purposes of schooling? Critical thinking[2] underpins this type of discourse, which has resonance with *contextual knowing* (Baxter Magolda, 1999; Moon, 2005) and *reflective reasoning* (King and Kitchener, 1994).

QI

The nine dimensions of reflective practice are considered next.

Dimensions of reflective practice

I Study your own teaching for personal improvement

An understanding of *reflection*, how it may be structured and used to guide practice, lies at the heart of self-study and professional development planning for personal improvement. Through the development of skills such as keen observation, logical reasoning and analysis, reflection can become a powerful agent of understanding 'self' as physical education teachers recount not only what they observe in a given context but also their emotions, feelings, ideas and thoughts as to future possibilities. Dewey (1933: 12) associates reflection with the kind of thinking that involves turning a subject over in the mind to give it serious consideration and thought, 'a state of doubt, hesitation, perplexity, mental difficulty, in which thinking originates, and an act of searching, hunting, inquiring, to find material that will resolve the doubt, settle and dispose of the perplexity'.

Kolb (1984) integrates reflection within his four-stage cycle of experiential learning: immediate or *concrete experiences* (1) provide the basis for *observations and reflections* (2) which are distilled and assimilated into *abstract concepts* (3) from which new possibilities and implications for action can be drawn and tested through *active experimentation* (4) which in turn serves as a guide to create new experiences. The learner shifts from actor to observer, from direct involvement to analytical detachment, which creates a new form of experience to reflect on and conceptualise. Learning style assumes significance here as it has been used to describe individual differences based on a learner's preference for using different phases of Kolb's learning cycle: we develop a preferred way of selecting among the four learning modes due to the demands of our immediate environment, particular life experiences and hereditary make-up. We resolve the tension between being active or reflective and being concrete or abstract in patterned and characteristic ways (Kolb and Kolb, 2005). This line of argument would suggest that some physical education teachers are naturally more or less reflective than others, which in turn, could have implications for how they structure and use reflection to improve their own practice.

2 Systematically evaluate your own teaching through classroom research procedures

Stenhouse (1983) argues that the purpose of educational research is to develop thoughtful reflection in order to strengthen the professional judgement of teachers. Although physical education teachers may draw on a number of strategies and procedures to evaluate their teaching, action research is commonly used for the purpose of systematically reflecting on experience so as 'to understand it and create meaning out of that understanding' (Hopkins, 2002: 5). Since action research begins with everyday experience and is concerned with the development of living knowledge, the process of enquiry is, in many ways, just as important as specific practical outcomes (Reason and Bradbury, 2001). This incorporates the analysis and evaluation of a particular experience, occurrence or situation after the event through *reflection on action* (Schon, 1987), which involves a critical self-reflective spiral of cycles 'of planning, acting, observing, reflecting then re-planning, further action, further observation and further reflection' (Carr and Kemmis, 1986: 162).

This step-by-step process is ideally monitored 'over varying periods of time and by a variety of mechanisms' (Cohen *et al.*, 2007: 192) such as case studies, interviews, reflective diaries or journals and questionnaires, so that successful elements of teaching can be identified, built upon and retained and less successful elements discarded or modified in light of the teachers' reflections. Research instruments designed to gather data must be fit for purpose, analysed appropriately by drawing on criteria pertinent to qualitative and/or quantitative research, and administered in light of the ethical principles and procedures which underpin research involving human participants (British Educational Research Association (BERA), 2011). Good action research emerges over time 'in an evolutionary and developmental process' as physical education teachers develop the skills of enquiry and as 'communities of enquiry develop within communities of practice' (Reason and Bradbury, 2001: 2).

3 Link theory with your own practice

Theories associated with learning to teach emerge from at least two perspectives: *espoused theories* (propositional or explicit knowledge) – those viewed by a profession to guide action and encompass the formal philosophy of the profession – and *theories-in-use* (procedural knowledge and tacit knowing) – those patterns of behaviour learned and developed in the day-to-day work of the professional (Argyris and Schon, 1974). This gives rise to debate as to whether there may be a gap between the propositional knowledge and theory, which purport to underpin professional activity, and the reality of how a professional behaves in practice.

Schon (1987) recognises professionals must acquire a body of specialised knowledge yet argues that such knowledge cannot simply be applied in a rule-governed way to guide practice. At the heart of his discourse is the emphasis placed on *professional artistry*: thus the repertoire of approaches and strategies physical education teachers gain from experience provide *exemplars, images* and *metaphors* they can draw upon to frame each new teaching situation. *Framing a situation* involves interpreting it one way as opposed to other possible ways and *intelligent action* can be shown in the capacity of teachers to respond effectively in particular situations.

Schon (1987: 25) describes intelligent action as *knowing in action*, which may be inherent, intangible, intuitive, spontaneous and tacit, yet it 'works' in practice. He aligns this to *reflection in action* (p. 28), which occurs when teachers encounter an unknown situation or when a surprise occurrence in the learning environment triggers it off. Interpreting and providing solutions to complex, situational problems happens during an action as events unfold by 'thinking on your feet' and 'keeping your wits about you'.

Q2

4 Question personal theories and beliefs

Although there are different meanings about beliefs in the literature, in cognitively oriented research, conceptions tend to focus on the acquisition of knowledge, organisation of information and justification of knowledge claims in relation to what individuals believe about the degree to which information is true (Schommer, 1994). This perspective, which primarily focuses on the nature of intellectual growth and relationship between personal epistemology and learning, is particularly relevant here.

The study of personal theories and beliefs is essential in coming to understand both the complexity of teachers' knowledge and what constitutes effective teaching as all teachers have personal theories and beliefs about themselves as teachers, their teaching, the nature of knowledge, how learning takes place and their roles and responsibilities within the classroom. Although findings from research into teachers' personal theories and beliefs yield discordant messages, some consensus has been reached over several issues:

- Student teachers enter teacher education programmes with pre-existing theories and beliefs based on their own experiences as pupils in schools (e.g. Pajares, 1992; Richardson, 1996).
- Personal theories and beliefs are often robust and resistant to change (e.g. Kagan, 1992; Richardson, 1996). Accommodating new information and adjusting existing beliefs under familiar circumstances can be nearly impossible as student teachers have often made commitments to prior beliefs and see little reason to adjust them (Pajares, 1992).
- Personal theories and beliefs can act as filters, which *allow in* or *filter out* new knowledge that is deemed either compatible or incompatible with current theories and beliefs (e.g. Weinstein, 1990; Pajares, 1992). When left unattended, new ideas are simply incorporated into old frameworks.

- Personal theories and beliefs are implicit and tacit which makes them difficult to articulate (e.g. Pajares, 1992).
- Teachers are unable to change personal theories and beliefs they are unaware of and are often unwilling to confront those they are aware of unless they see good reason to do so (Leinhardt, 1990) (some reasons for teachers finding it difficult to change their theories and beliefs are included in Chapter 8).

Thus, physical education teachers need to question personal theories and beliefs to establish their origins and legitimacy. Failure to periodically re-examine personal theories and beliefs for their validity, particularly in the light of new information, can lead to mindless teaching or habitual behaviour (Mezirow, 1990) which may be inappropriate in changed contexts.

5 Consider alternative perspectives and possibilities

Although questions of significance to teaching and learning can involve private, inner conversations with self, Freire (1972) argues the need for practitioners to adopt a *reflective posture*, one that enters the public arena and examines personal experience through conversations with others. Bruner (1996) asserts that we construct ourselves through narrative (language) and by telling stories of our lives can make sense of our lives. The knower is inextricably linked to the known and knowledge-making is recognised as an active, creative, interpretive process, in which the telling and retelling of stories provide a framework for the construction of 'professional knowledge' (Beattie, 2000) in teaching.

Schon's (1987) models of *coaching reflective practice* (e.g. Hall of Mirrors, Joint Experimentation and Follow Me) are designed to show student and early career teachers how a particular setting appears through the eyes of experienced practitioners and how they frame problems of practice. Pendlebury (1995) uses the metaphor *dialogical other* to describe how a conversation between a student teacher and significant other (e.g. a professional colleague, peer or mentor), who assumes the role of *critical friend* (Gore, 1993) can be structured in a supportive way. Implicit within such discourse is recognition that several possible meanings can be associated with any course of action in relation to a particular teaching group within a particular context. At the core of such learning is the physical education teacher's propensity to recognise the importance of working with experience, as the context which shapes the experience also shapes the kind of learning from experience that is possible (Boud and Miller, 1996).

Open-mindedness[3] underpins this dimension, which Dewey (1933) refers to as the willingness to consider more than one side of an argument and fully embrace and attend to alternative possibilities. This requires an active desire to listen to more than one side and recognise that formerly held views and beliefs could be misconceived. Valli's (1992) characterisation of *deliberative reflection*, which involves consolidating several sources of information from a range of perceived experts as the teacher weighs up competing claims to give good reason for the decisions they make is pertinent here, as well as Brookfield's (1995) notion of *hunting assumptions* through a range of perspectives and lenses such as those of pupils and colleagues and in the theoretical literature.

Q3

6 Try out new strategies and ideas

Moon (1999) presents the view that learners approach their studies with a cognitive structure, a flexible network of ideas and knowledge, shaped by prior learning. This provides the framework within which teachers locate new ideas, and will, if deep learning is to occur, be challenged and modified (transformed) in the process. She associates the development of new understandings, insights and increased awareness with *deep* as opposed to *surface* learning. *Transformative learning* describes situations where physical education teachers are prepared to abandon preconceptions and re-examine their fundamental assumptions about themselves, their subject matter and the nature of knowledge.

To enable capacity building within the personal, interpersonal and organisational structures of twenty-first-century schools, teachers must be able to determine the relevance of new knowledge, be flexible, creative and adaptive to change, be innately curious and capable of 'asking intelligent questions about the world in which they live and work' (Australian Government Quality Teacher Programme (AGQTP), 2008: 7). Failure to experiment with alternative strategies and being guided by the disposition to accept the most commonly held view of resolving a problem in a routine almost thoughtless way is one distinction Dewey (1933) draws between *routine* and *reflective action*. Hargreaves (2003: 16) also cautions that teachers who do not keep learning 'by more than trial and error are a liability to their pupils'.

Thus, physical education teachers exemplify an active approach to professional learning when they seek and integrate new strategies and ideas into their own practice and take ownership of their teaching as they *appropriate* new knowledge (Boud *et al.*, 1985). In turn, this should give them the degree of autonomy needed to make professional judgements in response to both major educational trends and their own unique situations.

7 Maximise the learning potential of all pupils

The principles of entitlement and inclusion lie at the core of this dimension, which requires physical education teachers to ensure all pupils can access the curriculum by 'setting suitable learning challenges; responding to pupils' diverse learning needs; overcoming potential barriers to learning; and, devising assessment appropriate for individual pupils and groups of pupils' (Qualifications and Curriculum Authority (QCA), 2008). Personalised learning is an important strand of action in meeting statutory equalities duties (United Nations Educational, Scientific and

Cultural Organisation (UNESCO), 1994; Department for Education and Skills (DfES), 2005) as pupils' chances of success should not be limited by their disability, ethnicity, gender or socio-economic status. Therefore, tailoring provision is a matter not only of social justice but also of moral purpose. (Chapter 10 addresses issues of inclusion on physical education.)

All teachers are now expected to engage with a pedagogy of personalised learning underpinned by the principles of progression, differentiation, relevance and assessment for learning: 'High expectations of progress apply equally to children and young people working above, at, or below age-related expectations, including those who have been identified as having special educational needs' (Department for Children, Schools and Families (DCSF), 2008: 7). Teachers also need to prepare pupils for a society and economy in which they are expected to become 'self-directed learners, able and motivated to keep learning over a lifetime' (OECD, 2005a: 2).

Against this backdrop, the major challenge is how to cater simultaneously for a range of learners within one class, particularly as physical education teachers are increasingly called upon to engage with a diverse multicultural group of pupils with different aspirations, learning styles and needs.

Q4

8 Enhance the quality of your own teaching

Over the years, a wealth of literature has emerged in pursuit of trying to capture the essential ingredients of effective teaching. The phrase *pedagogic expertise* (Pollard, 2010: 5) has been used to capture:

- *the art of teaching* – responsive, creative and intuitive capacities;
- *the craft of teaching* – mastery of a full repertoire of skills and practices;
- *the science of teaching* – research-informed decision-making.

and combines the complementary needs for personal capacities, professional skills and collectively created knowledge, firmly underpinned by ethical principles and moral commitment. This particular framework considers *educational aims, learning contexts, classroom processes* and *learning outcomes* in relation to *curriculum, pedagogy* and *assessment*, and questions are posed within this construct to exemplify the high levels of reflective expertise teachers need in order to make evidence-informed judgements. It reflects current national and international initiatives (OECD, 2005a; Barber and Mourshed, 2007) that aim to build a professional knowledge base about what constitutes effective teaching and learning through combining teacher expertise and research (e.g. James and Pollard, 2006; Hattie, 2009).

The quality of teaching however is determined not only by the quality of teachers, although clearly this is critical, but also by the environment in which they work (OECD, 2005a). Capable teachers are not necessarily going to reach their potential in settings that do not provide appropriate support or sufficient challenge and reward. Although physical education teachers may be highly motivated by the intrinsic benefits of teaching – for example, working with pupils and helping them to develop and make a contribution to society – system structures and school workplaces must enable teachers to focus on these tasks.

Reynolds (1995) suggests the *touchstone* criteria for evaluating different educational policies or practices should be their impact on pupil learning outcomes. Therefore, the choice of these outcomes is crucial, as they become the criteria for judging school and teacher effectiveness. To focus on a narrow range of outcomes, which take no account of pupil and teacher backgrounds, individual or collective efficacy, motivation, or cultural, economic, organisational and social contexts would thus seem to provide only partial indicators of what we understand and mean by teacher quality.

Q5

9 Continue to improve your own teaching

There is widespread agreement that initial teacher education cannot provide student teachers with all the knowledge, skills and understanding required to handle various tasks and meet the strong demands of educational reform and social change throughout their professional career (AGQTP, 2008: Barber and Mourshed, 2007). Becoming a teacher is increasingly acknowledged to be a gradual process, which means that teacher education must be seen as 'a career-long process placed within the context of lifelong learning' (OECD, 2005a: 44). This implies that continuing professional development (CPD) needs to be built into a physical education teacher's career trajectory from the outset.

The development of new skills, initiatives, teaching methods and ways of working require practice, feedback and training *in situ* as well as time available outside the classroom (ETUCE, 2008). Some recent examples of effective CPD provision include:

- collaborative learning with colleagues within and across schools, rated as a 'highly important form of CPD' (Day *et al.*, 2006: xiv);
- building and making accessible cumulative knowledge across the profession by strengthening the connections 'between research and practice and encouraging schools to develop as learning organisations' (OECD, 2005a: 47);
- 'dialogue and innovation around quality teaching and learning [to reinvigorate] jaded mid to late career teachers' (AGQTP, 2008: 7);
- encouraging latent leadership potential to facilitate further 'change and improvement in the groups, faculties and schools concerned' (AGQTP, 2008: 7).

Day *et al.* (2006: xiv–xv) found that limited time provision for teachers to prepare to work and plan collaboratively and reflect collectively with colleagues on their practice was the main dissatisfaction 'for over 75 per cent of the teachers' and 70 per cent of teachers across all professional life phases perceived 'heavy workload, a lack of time and financial constraints were important inhibitors in their pursuit of professional development'. What becomes evident is that physical education teachers must exercise a degree of autonomy in response to tensions that may arise between personal, professional and situational priorities in the quest to continue to improve their own teaching, particularly since 'professional obsolescence' could enfold all except those 'engaged in lifelong learning' (Knight, 2002: 230). (Chapter 13 addresses continuing professional development, based on considering teachers as learners.)

Q6

Becoming an extended professional

When physical education teachers actively engage with the multi-dimensional framework presented in this chapter, they exhibit not only the qualities of reflective practitioners but also those associated with striving towards becoming extended professionals. The work of early theorists into the nature of the teacher as a professional highlights several distinctions between *restricted* and *extended* professionals. For example, characteristics used by Hoyle (1974) to describe restricted professionals include: a high level of skill in classroom practice; an ability to understand, establish and enjoy positive working relationships with children by adopting a child-centred approach; the use of personal perceptions of change in pupil behaviour and achievement to evaluate performance; and, short-term practical course attendance. Characteristics he used to describe extended professionals incorporate all those associated with restricted professionals and in addition:

- contextualising classroom practice by relating it to the wider contexts of school, community and society;
- participating in a wide range of professional development activities such as conferences, subject panels and in-service education and training;
- having an active concern to link theory and practice;
- engaging in peer observation and small-scale collaborative research studies.

Stenhouse (1975: 143–4) takes this debate further and argues that the outstanding hallmark of extended professionals is their capacity and commitment to engage in autonomous self-development through systematic self-study, reflection and research. He associates five key attributes with extended professionals, particularly in relation to the teacher as researcher, notably:

- a commitment to question their practice as the basis for teacher development;
- a willingness to reflect critically and systematically on their own practice;
- a concern to question and to test theory in practice;
- an appreciation of the benefit of having their teaching observed by others and of discussing their teaching with others in an open and honest manner; and
- the commitment and skills to study their own teaching and in so doing develop the art of self-study.

The above characteristics and key attributes of extended professionals signpost how reflective practice as a disposition to enquiry within the definition of the framework presented in this chapter has been interpreted. One vital ingredient in the pursuit of becoming an extended professional is that of commitment, which may be viewed as both a cognitive (intellectual) and an affective (emotional) endeavour that has an important influence on pupils' affective, behavioural, cognitive and social development.

As Rosenholtz (1989) argues, teachers committed to their work have an enduring belief they can make a difference to the achievements and learning lives of pupils (agency and efficacy) through who they are (their identity), what they know (their knowledge, skills, strategies) and how they teach (their attitudes, beliefs and personal and professional values embedded in and expressed through their behaviour in practice settings). However, to sustain commitment involves the personal and professional investment of emotional labour, emotional understanding and intellectual energy (Denzin, 1984), which requires resilience: the capacity to take a series of purposeful actions over time and emotional resilience to successfully grow and develop, particularly in the face of adverse circumstances. These factors are inextricably linked to a physical education teacher's disposition to enquiry in the pursuit of becoming both a reflective practitioner and an extended professional.

Summary

This chapter presents an innovative framework to exemplify how the complex, multi-dimensional nature of reflective practice can be defined and structured to guide and support the professional development of student and practising physical education teachers. Three types of discourse, descriptive, comparative and critical reflective conversations, have been explored to highlight qualitative distinctions exhibited by professionals in their reflective practice. Some key processes associated with the nature of reflective activity and its translation into professional practice have been identified and situated within nine discrete yet interrelated dimensions of reflective practice. The concluding section briefly explores how this framework has resonance with the characteristics and attributes associated with becoming an extended professional.

From this platform, as well as the fundamental assertion that learning to teach is a gradual process, physical education teachers are encouraged to engage with the constituent components of this framework so that reflective practice may become integral to their way of working as they adopt the stance of a *critical being* (Barnett, 1997) – one who thinks critically as a way of life and is willing to act upon personal insights and new understandings to continuously enhance their own pedagogic expertise. In so doing, the extent to which physical education teachers are indeed reflective practitioners can be recognised and more fully understood.

Questions for consideration

Q1 Critically consider the types of discourse you engage in with self and others to improve aspects of your own practice. Are some types of discourse more or less prevalent than others?

Q2 Differentiate clearly between *reflection in action* and *reflection on action* in teaching physical education. Focusing on one lesson you have taught recently, consider the nature of your reflection in action and consider how this influenced your reflection on action.

Q3 Critically consider the value of observing other teachers at work and of other teachers watching your work. In what ways might you make each of these situations the most profitable?

Q4 Critically consider how far you can accommodate the needs of all learners in your classes. What are the benefits to the learner and to you as the teacher, in knowing your pupils really well?

Q5 Focusing on one unit of work you have recently taught, consider the nature and appropriateness of criteria drawn upon to judge the effectiveness and quality of your teaching. Are these criteria unique to physical education or the same as those used by teachers in other subject areas?

Q6 To what extent are the dimensions of reflective practice enacted in and through your own teaching of physical education? Are some dimensions more or less prevalent than others?

Notes

1 The terms *discourse* and *reflective conversation* are used interchangeably here to denote ways of thinking and speaking about teaching as well as of practising teaching (Fairclough, 1998).

2 Critical thinking, as defined by Moon (2005: 12), is the capacity to work with 'complex ideas whereby a person can make effective provision of evidence to justify a reasonable judgement. The evidence, and therefore the judgement, will pay appropriate attention to the context of the judgement'. The fully developed capacity to think critically relies on an understanding of 'knowledge as constructed and related to its context (relativistic)', which is not possible if knowledge is viewed only in an 'absolute manner (knowledge as a series of facts)' (Moon, 2005: 12).

3 *Open-mindedness* is one of three reflective attitudes Dewey (1933) considers to be both prerequisite and integral to reflective action: the other two are *responsibility* and *wholeheartedness*.

Further reading

Borko, H. (2004) Professional development and teacher learning: Mapping the terrain. *Educational Researcher* 33(8): 3–15.

This article maps the terrain of research on teacher professional development and provides an overview of what we have learned about effective professional development programmes and their impact on teacher learning. Important directions and strategies for extending our knowledge into some areas are suggested.

ETUCE (European Trade Union Committee for Education) (2008) *Teacher Education in Europe: An ETUCE Policy Paper*. Brussels: ETUCE.
This policy paper involving 46 participating countries, sets out the ETUCE's vision on teacher education for today's society and explores how a highly qualified profession can ensure a good balance between the professional autonomy of teachers and their public and social accountability.

Kelchtermans, G. (2009) Who I am in how I teach is the message: Self-understanding, vulnerability and reflection. *Teachers and Teaching: Theory and Practice* 15(2): 257–72. Inspired by research into teacher thinking and a narrative-biographical approach to teaching and teacher development, the author argues that the person of the teacher is an essential element in what constitutes professional teaching; and, the 'scholarship of teachers' may be characterised by personal commitment and vulnerability, which have consequences for the kind of reflective attitudes and skills professional teachers should master.

Zwozdiak-Myers, P. (2012) *The Teacher's Reflective Practice Handbook: Becoming an Extended Professional Through Capturing Evidence-Informed Practice*. Abingdon: Routledge.
This book offers an innovative multi-dimensional framework of reflective practice and an accessible guide to facilitate student and practising physical education teachers' reflective practice through a range of reflective tasks, challenging questions, links to online resources, exemplification material and further reading. Underpinned by key theoretical concepts and contemporary research within the field it is an essential source of advice, guidance and ideas for you to build a meaningful, personally relevant portfolio of evidence-informed practice.

The following physical education journals should support further reading. There are also many education journals which contain articles related to relevant topics across education more generally, which are useful to extend debate further. They may also contain physical education specific articles.

- *European Physical Education Review*
- *Journal of Teaching in Physical Education*
- *Quest*
- *Physical Education Matters*
- *Physical Education and Sport Pedagogy*
- *Sport, Education and Society.*

Part IV

The key players in physical education

Introduction to Part IV

Part IV can be seen to move on from the earlier Parts, and asks you to reflect on how different constituencies should or do affect your work in physical education. Chapter 10, 'Who is physical education for?' challenges you to reflect if all your learners are given the opportunity to thrive in physical education, while Chapter 11, 'Who should teach physical education in curriculum and extra-curricular time?' argues that PE teachers cannot be replaced by coaches in teaching curricular PE and in delivering extra-curricular provision, although coaches do have a role to play. Chapter 12, 'What are the public perceptions of physical education?' alerts you to perceptions of our work from those outside the profession.

Chapter 10, 'Who is physical education for?' addresses issues that will be familiar to many of you – inclusion and equity in physical education. The chapter acknowledges that this is not a new question, but articulates the view that there is a need to continue and, indeed, seek to extend the debate. The chapter shares the range of views that exist in relation to aspects of inclusion and equity. It focuses first on gender, then on ability, and finally on social class – this last being an issue that has all too often been marginalised in debates and research in physical education. It extends previous discussion to interrelated influences, including intersections between gender, class, culture and ethnicity. The authors emphasise that there are no simple or straightforward answers to the questions being addressed in this chapter. The intention is to prompt engagement with the complexities associated with equity and inclusion in physical education and encourage renewed thinking about the challenges and opportunities that physical educators in various arenas face in relation to these issues. Hence, deliberately provocative and challenging questions are posed about various issues and about the ways in which they may typically be perceived and approached by policy-makers, teachers, teacher educators and/or researchers.

Chapter 11, 'Who should teach physical education in curriculum and extra-curricular time?' discusses the role of teachers and coaches in teaching curricular PE and in delivering extra-curricular physical activity/sport in

England. It includes two research-based vignettes to illustrate the points made. The chapter starts by looking at similarities and differences between curricular PE and extra-curricular physical activity/sport provision. It then looks at qualifications of teachers and coaches for working in schools before considering who should or can teach curricular PE and extra-curricular physical activities/sports. It is argued that PE teachers cannot be replaced by coaches in teaching curricular PE and in delivering extra-curricular provision, although coaches do have a role to play. Thus, the chapter takes a particular perspective on the issue and you are encouraged to debate whether you agree or disagree with the argument presented.

Chapter 12, 'What are the public perceptions of physical education?' aims to alert you to how physical education is viewed by those outside the profession, setting out aspects of the underlying current of opinion that often go unrecognised. The chapter works to raise awareness and to challenge you to consider how far both you and policy-makers should take public perceptions into account. It is proposed that there are at least two major sources of the perceptions that come to form public opinion. The first is an individual's own direct experience of physical education in one or more roles, such as pupil and parent. The other is ways that physical education is presented by the media such as film, video clips on YouTube, the press and television. You are asked to examine your own practice in respect of how far your own experiences have shaped your views on physical education and if and how you should address expectations and pressures from the general public.

Chapter 10

Who is physical education for?

Dawn Penney and John Evans

Introduction

In many respects debate about the question 'Who is physical education for?' is not new. Historically, various issues relating to inclusion and equity have provided momentum and focus for research and professional debates in the UK and internationally. Matters such as gender, class, ethnicity and ability remain both pertinent and challenging for physical education policy and practice to address. Inequalities in, for example, post-school participation rates in sport and active leisure, and unacceptable forms of communication including sexist, racist and elitist language and attitudes, continue to prevail in physical education, as in education generally. This is despite considerable efforts over many years to address these things. This chapter reflects the view that there is a need to continue debates about inclusion and equity in physical education and, furthermore, to seek to extend them.

What knowledge, skills and understandings are considered of value in physical education and *how* they are addressed, will always and inevitably have implications for (or will define) *whose* learning needs and interests are provided for or, in contrast, neglected or overlooked. Thus, questions should be posed of curriculum, pedagogy and assessment from an equity perspective, and none of these aspects of physical education should be considered neutral or independent of the other. A concern with equity recognises that notions of difference are inherently tied to social and cultural values. It prompts us to engage critically with the values and value structures that physical education curriculum, pedagogy and assessment act to reaffirm (see also Hay and Penney, 2011). Our emphasis is, therefore, that decisions about curriculum structure, principles and content, teaching contexts and approaches, and choices about assessment tasks and methods, all have fundamental implications for 'who will learn what' in physical education – about movement, physical activity, sport and health, but also, about the individuals, abilities and bodies that are valued in physical education, sport and society.

Throughout our discussion we reaffirm that many factors, including political ideologies, institutional histories and traditions, physical resources and many

people (policy-makers, teachers, coaches, parents and pupils themselves) are
influential in shaping learning opportunities, experiences and outcomes in physical education. There are no simple or straightforward answers to the questions
being addressed in this chapter. The intention is to prompt engagement with
the complexities associated with equity and inclusion in physical education and
encourage renewed thinking about the challenges and opportunities that physical educators in various arenas face in relation to these issues. In each of the
sections that follow, the starting point for debate is an issue that will be familiar
to many physical educators. We pose deliberately provocative and challenging
questions about various issues and about the ways in which they may typically
be perceived and approached by policy-makers, teachers, teacher educators and/
or researchers.

We begin by focusing on the issue of gender, but in addressing this, extend
discussion to consider intersections (Flintoff *et al.*, 2008) between gender,
class, culture and ethnicity. We then turn attention to ability in physical education, and consider the significance of the ways in which ability is conceptualised and enacted in physical education from an equity perspective. Our
discussion explores the abilities that are recognised and rewarded in physical
education, or in contrast, marginalised and overlooked (Evans, 2004; Penney
and lisahunter, 2006) and the implications of particular abilities being privileged over others. Once again, we draw attention to linkages with other equity
issues and reaffirm that multiple, interrelated influences, rather than single
issues, ultimately define whether or not physical education connects with any
individual pupil's learning needs and interests. The third main section of the
chapter brings to the fore social class as an issue that has, with a few excep-
tions (such as Evans and Davies, 2008), all too often been marginalised in
debates and research in physical education. We explore critically ways in which
class is embedded and embodied in contemporary physical education curriculum, pedagogy and assessment and how school systems and societies can be
seen to reaffirm and legitimate class-based differences in educational opportunities and attainment.

Gender issues

Do we have a physical education curriculum devised 'by men for boys'?

As indicated above, we recognise that questions such as this are provocative. In
distinguishing boys' interests from girls' and simultaneously pointing to gender-
based power-relations at play in policy and curriculum development, the
question is a potentially useful starting point for lively debate. At the same time
it may be seriously limiting, encouraging either broad (sweeping) generalisations
or, worse still, reductive essentialising of male and female characteristics (suggesting that boys and girls have certain natural and/or essential predispositions

by virtue of gender) that we wish to challenge rather than appear to legitimate. Further questions help to counter this risk and provide some insight into the directions that we wish to pursue in the discussion that follows.

- *Which* men and *which* boys are we really talking about here?
- Are *all* girls inherently disadvantaged in physical education?
- What *masculinities* and *femininities* are expressed in and legitimated by physical education curriculum and/or pedagogy?
- Is it gender issues that make *the* difference in terms of individual experiences, opportunities and achievements in physical education?

Research within and beyond physical education has repeatedly highlighted that policy development associated with curriculum change or reform is a complex, political and contested process in which not all interests are accorded equal value or given hearing and not everyone has the same opportunities to provide input to or influence decision-making (Ball, 1990; Penney and Evans, 1999). Who has authority in official curriculum development is undoubtedly significant in relation to the understandings of physical education and views about curriculum aims, structure and content, that will inform new proposals. However, how such policies are then mediated in schools is of equal if not more importance. It would be foolish to imply – as our opening question does – that all men (either within or outside schools) have equal power or authority in policy and curriculum development, or that they all take a common stance towards education and physical education, or share the same educational and political principles on these issues. It is similarly inappropriate to imply that men have solely led recent curriculum reform in physical education within the UK or internationally. Indeed we might note the influence that, for example, the largely female-led Association for Physical Education has had on the development of physical education in the UK over time and in recent years. We would also be remiss not to note Baroness Sue Campbell's role in (re)shaping political thinking about physical education and school sport in the UK in recent years.

Q1

The issue may be less about gender per se than the principles and pedagogies being advocated amidst curriculum developments and whether they further equality and equity for boys and girls. With others (Azzarito and Solomon, 2005; Flintoff, 2008; Flintoff *et al.*, 2008), we have stressed the need for debate and research concerning gender and physical education to be underpinned by conceptualisations of gender that simultaneously recognise the significance of differences *within and between* gender groups (Penney and Evans, 2002). In emphasising this dual concern, we acknowledge a reality that all teachers will be able to relate to; namely that pupils are differently positioned in physical education not only by virtue of gender, but rather, in relation to multiple issues and identities. Gender, alongside and in conjunction with, for example, ability, body shape, ethnicity and class, will shape experiences of physical education and meanings gained from it. So does gender *really* matter in physical education? And if so, in what way? There is a subtle balance to be achieved in arguing for attention to be directed to gender as a critical issue in equity debates in physical education, while also emphasising the potential flaws in considering it in isolation from other influences.

So, let's return to our opening question: *Do we have a physical education curriculum devised 'by men for boys'*? Is it that simple a matter?

It's not a girl/girl's issue

If physical education is devised by men for boys, then why do so many males dislike physical education and/or choose not to continue to be involved in physical activity and/or sport after school? Research and literature in education point quite clearly to certain boys' identities and subjectivities being seriously overlooked and inherently disadvantaged by education systems and the educational process in the UK and elsewhere (see for example, Martino *et al.*, 2005; 2009). Dominant social expectations of masculinity shape and limit boys' experiences of schooling – not in a uniform way, but differentially, as gender, class, culture, sexuality, religious identities, social values and structures intersect. Experiences of physical education thus need to be similarly acknowledged as far from the same for all boys. There is then, a clear case for more research in physical education that critically explores how boys from different backgrounds and with different dispositions relative to the curriculum, experience physical education; how those experiences affect their view of their bodies and their perception of ability; and how these effects are played out in terms of engagement in school and post-school physical activity.

Questions of tradition

The issue to which our opening question perhaps more accurately alludes, is one focusing on gendered *traditions* of the physical education curriculum and, therefore, the gendered understandings about movement forms, sporting contexts, bodies, performance and participation that are either reflected in official texts and school curricula, or challenged by them. David Kirk's work (Kirk, 1992; 2002b) has vividly illustrated ways in which particular thinking about girls and boys, men and women, their bodies and the forms of movement that physical education should engage them in, has been expressed in physical education curricula over time. Today's curriculum is no different in this respect; official texts and the 'pedagogical texts' that pupils experience as physical education in schools, are an expression of the social construction of knowledge – in this case, physical education – and as such they are never arbitrary or value-free. Curriculum frameworks, the prescribed teaching and learning *content* of physical education (i.e. particular knowledge, skills and understandings) and/or the *contexts* for learning (often sport-based) that are stipulated as required or optional aspects of the physical education curriculum, are historically and culturally specific takes on what physical education 'is' and what should be taught and learnt in the name of physical education. Inherent in any physical education curriculum are particular understandings of masculinity and femininity and, more specifically, the masculinities and femininities that can legitimately be expressed by boys and girls in physical education. That said, it is vital to acknowledge that the curriculum and pedagogies of physical education always carry multiple meanings and expectations. Thus, we need to also guard against essentialising policy or pedagogy and avoid reading either as merely unproblematic expressions of some caricatured 'male' or 'female' (or middle-class) centric view.

We therefore prompt renewed critical reflection about what learning is deemed core or peripheral in physical education and the activities and experiences that teachers, boys and girls from various social and cultural backgrounds and their parents, might expect to feature in physical education. What gender identities are being implicitly acknowledged, celebrated, marginalised and/or denied by virtue of how the physical education curriculum is typically conceptualised, perceived and enacted in schools today? Do, for example, contemporary discourses of health, slimness and slenderness now pervade thinking and practices within and beyond physical education (in families, sport, the media, youth culture and society) so that relatively few girls and equally few boys feel that their bodies meet 'new' gendered ideals? Do particular curriculum requirements accentuate such perceptions and pressures?

Q2

Research in physical education in recent years has pursued answers to some of these questions. We do, for example, have far clearer insights into the gendered identities that male and female physical education teachers may feel obliged to express and the masculinities, femininities, sexualities, cultural and religious identities that they and, in turn, pupils may feel unable to express in physical education (Brown and Rich, 2002; Clarke, 2002; Dagkas and Benn, 2006; Evans *et al.*, 2008). Benn and colleagues (Benn *et al.*, 2011) have highlighted the dynamic between gender and cultural and religious interests and values in physical education curricula, teaching and learning. In so doing, they have clearly demonstrated that designing curricula and learning experiences that will generate feelings of inclusion and worth amongst all girls and all boys is by no means an easy task. It requires us to think about pupils as *individuals*, who are differently disposed culturally and come to physical education with many and varied gendered identities. It also calls for more widespread recognition that the knowledge and activities that policy-makers and teachers deem 'important' in physical education reflect and legitimate particular social and cultural values and interests. Individual pupils, girls and boys, come to physical education differently positioned by virtue of their culture and their class, to relate to, access and enjoy the social, physical and cultural capitals that are made available to them in physical education. We then need to ask: Do the official curriculum and the enacted curriculum equally enable all pupils to develop such capital in and through experiences of physical education? Whose interests in physical activity, movement and sport and, more specifically, which girls' and which boys' interests do official texts and physical education curricula in schools reflect and connect with?

In considering these issues, we also need to bear in mind that the 'landscape' of physical education in the UK and internationally, is now characterised by complexity. The discourse of 'physical education and school sport' that has been explicit in many recent policy initiatives in England particularly, has been fundamentally tied to new modes of provision that encompass multiple school and community sites and that operate pre-, post- and in parallel with curriculum provision. It is also a discourse that is directly linked with new providers of physical education, physical activity and/or sport within and beyond the curriculum (see also Chapter 11 'Who should teach physical education in curriculum and extra-curricular time?'). In parallel, 'physical education' delivered in different forms – privately and through new technologies and websites (e.g. wiki games and fitness programmes) – and through popular pedagogies, multiply (confuse and/or liberate) the messages that pupils receive about what is to count as valuable physical education knowledge, how it can be accessed and by whom. The sections that follow reflect that amidst changes in structures and societies, there is still a need to address longstanding inequities that appear to have become normalised in much physical education in schools, and that remain seemingly highly resistant to change.

Questioning ability in physical education

Ability in physical education is a matter that still seems to be frequently overlooked, or only partially explored in equity debates. Yet it is central to the question we pose as to whose learning needs and interests are served in and by physical education in schools? (see also Chapter 6, 'What is success in physical education and how can this best be achieved?')

Is physical education really for all, or is it just for the 'gifted and talented'?

At one level this question may prompt us to recall our own personal experiences of physical education and to reflect on who (we think) really felt a part of the learning experience. Ask yourselves which pupils came away from the lesson feeling a positive sense of learning and belonging in physical education? And which pupils left physical education with a sense of both the competence and confidence to pursue opportunities for participation in physical activity, movement and/or sport beyond the curriculum and outside of school? Were some pupils left with feelings of inadequacy and/or embarrassment such that their preference will be to avoid all further involvement in physical education, physical activity and/or sport?

The question of inclusion does, therefore, set us thinking about how ability is defined and, more particularly, how pupils with different abilities will feel in physical education and what they will variously gain from it. Are we still in a situation whereby we are offering 'more of the same to the more able' in physical education (Penney and Harris, 1997)? Or have definitions of physical 'ability' widened in recent years to make physical education more accommodating to more pupils? There are lively lines of debate that might arise here about, for example, how well pupils who are labelled by teachers, peers and/or themselves as of 'low ability' are served by physical education curricula that privilege particular sports or physical activities – and in turn therefore, accord value and status to particular knowledge, skills and understandings. But before engaging with issues such as this, there is a need to step back and in the first instance, explore some of the assumptions or accepted norms that are in danger of going unquestioned. Hence, returning to the question posed in opening this section, we ask:

- What exactly is our (or policy-makers') vision of 'gifted and talented' in physical education?
- What (and therefore whose) abilities are recognised and rewarded in this vision – and in physical education curricula and lessons?
- Does our recognition of ability come down to 'a question of sport' (i.e., of being able to perform at a high level in particular high status sports) and therefore, particular cultural practice and values? And/or does body size and shape influence our feelings and our 'reading' of particular pupils' abilities or potential in physical education?

Once again, we emphasise that judgements about the respective worth or value of particular knowledge, skills and understandings in physical education are not neutral – and there are various ways in which ability in physical education can be conceptualised. But who is to decide these things? Internationally, curriculum writers have grappled with the question of 'what it is to be physically educated', what knowledge, skills and understandings will therefore be articulated in official texts, and how levels of achievement in physical education will be described. Reading various curriculum texts, we might suggest that in one sense, stated visions of the 'physically educated pupil' and the scope of the learning that is incorporated in curriculum frameworks for physical education, point to diverse knowledge, skills and understanding being valued. For example, knowledge and understandings associated with health and wellbeing and skills associated with cooperation and communication, are integral to many curricula in the UK as elsewhere (e.g. Department of Education, Tasmania, 2008; Learning and Teaching Scotland, n.d.). Yet, research such as that reported by Hay and lisahunter (2006) clearly calls into question the breadth of learning that informs everyday thinking about 'ability' in physical education, from both teacher and pupil perspectives. Pedagogical interactions appear likely to be shaped by notably narrow conceptualisations of ability in physical education and further-more, by particular perceptions about which pupils, by virtue of gender and/or ethnicity and/or body shape, have the potential to develop and demonstrate particular (acceptable and valued) abilities in physical education (Evans, 2004; Hay and lisahunter, 2006; Hay and Macdonald, 2010).

Q3

Why is this so? Why do we see a continuing disjuncture between official good intentions and the practice and lived experiences of physical education, espe-cially if teachers are versed (through their teacher education) in the language of equity and physical education? Teachers and pupils will inevitably read abilities 'into' and 'from' bodies – as the body imposes itself on culture and culture (in the form of the curriculum and attendant pedagogies) on the body. Even before anyone has moved in a first physical education lesson with a new class or new teacher, judgements about the 'abilities' and potential that individual pupils have and furthermore, are capable of developing, are being made. As Evans (2004) has previously discussed, contemporary dominant discourses of both sport and health have pervaded thinking in and about physical education and, more particularly, about ability in physical education. Amidst this reductionism;

> Education and 'educability' are defined only in relation to the values, ideals and mores that prevail in schools and other social fields, when consideration should be given to the ways in which 'abilities' are configured, recognized, nurtured and rejected within and across the physical cultures of communi-ties, societies and schools.
>
> (Evans, 2004: 99)

Gender, culture and social class are all integral to the processes of configuring, rec-ognising, nurturing and rejecting the abilities to which Evans (2004) refers. All will inform how pupils perceive their own and others' abilities within and beyond phys-ical education and also the choices and opportunities that they variously recognise, and feel able or inclined to take up to develop their abilities (Evans, 2004). Phys-ical education teachers and the physical education curriculum can serve to either reaffirm dominant gender, cultural and/or class discourses and values in these terms, or challenge established understandings and perceptions about 'who and what is valued' in physical education, and 'what learning can be achieved, by whom'. Below we explore these issues further in focusing specifically on social class. Before doing so, we take another tack in our discussion of ability.

Can pupils with special educational needs thrive in physical education?

There are many responses that might be made to this question, including 'Yes, as much as any pupil can' and the perhaps inevitable, 'It depends...'. Both responses reflect a point that we reaffirm throughout the chapter, that no single aspect of a person's identity can be considered in isolation and nor can we generalise about pupils who share one characteristic. In this sense, 'it depends' prompts us to consider the different ways in which pupils with particular special educational needs might be positioned in and by physical education, and how their curriculum experiences and what they achieve in and through physical education, could vary. As Barton (1993: 45) stressed many years ago:

> Terms such as 'the disabled' [or now, those with special educational needs] are a catch-all and give the impression of sameness. But the difficulties of and responses to being disabled are influenced by class, race, gender and age factors. These can cushion or compound the experience of discrimination and oppression.

Our cautious response also brings to the fore the many factors that may influence the opportunities and achievements of pupils with special educational needs in physical education. These include the facilities and physical resources available to support teaching and learning in physical education, teachers' experience and expertise in working with pupils with special educational needs (and furthermore, *specific* special educational needs) in physical education, teacher–pupil ratios, and so on. Decisions about curriculum design, teachers' pedagogical skills, and the adequacy of teacher education, will all play a part in shaping the likelihood that all pupils – in this instance, pupils with various special educational needs – will 'thrive' in physical education.

In implying a high degree of opportunity, given certain physical and human resources, for this outcome to be achieved we are, however, in danger of again glossing over some important underlying issues. We need to revisit questions of how physical education is being conceptualised, what knowledge, skills and understandings are being foregrounded in official and pedagogical texts and how success and achievement, therefore, are destined to be defined. What official curriculum texts, produced by government agencies and schools, have to say in relation to how the curriculum is intended to provide for the distinct learning needs of pupils with special educational needs, and/or their silences on this matter, are important to pursue. Haycock and Smith's (2010) recent research calls into question (certainly from teachers' perspectives), the adequacy and appropriateness of the statutory National Curriculum for Physical Education (NCPE) criteria for assessment of young disabled people and those with special educational needs. Yet it also raises questions about how statutory requirements are interpreted and implemented in particular political and educational contexts. Furthermore, as Barton (2009) highlighted, there is a need to consider whether the investments and changes required to enable 'commendable' visions to be realised have been made, and the ways in which wider social values and norms come into play, to inform and limit views of acceptable and ideal bodies in physical education.

Does it all change when it is 'high stakes'? In senior secondary schooling, who is physical education for?

In this final part of our discussion of ability, we focus specifically on senior secondary schooling and examination courses in physical education. Internationally, the development of examination courses in physical education has made explicit the differential value accorded to various knowledge, skills and understandings in physical education. The academic status and standing of physical education as a school subject and discipline of study may well have been enhanced as a consequence of developing examination courses. Yet these developments are not without cost for the subject if we consider the forms of knowledge that are privileged in assessment requirements (Green, 2005a). In some instances, the final assessment for examination physical education courses comprises *only* a written examination. In other cases, courses have a weighting for (1) theoretical and (2) practical components, with assessment of the latter involving a formal examination and/or externally moderated school-based assessment. Moves towards forms of assessment and examination that reflect and legitimate integration of different knowledges and knowledge forms in physical education remain relatively underdeveloped (see, for example, Thorburn, 2007). Established hierarchies of knowledge in schooling, and specifically in senior secondary schooling, have proved incredibly resistant to change and attempts at reform have provided a clear reminder that the hierarchy not only serves to accord different value to different knowledges (and those who provide it); it also serves as a gate-keeper for who can succeed in 'high stakes' schooling.

Assessment arrangements in senior secondary and examination physical education courses thus send strong messages about who physical education, in this arena, 'is for', or more accurately, who *certain versions* of physical education are for. Internationally, physical education course options for pupils in senior secondary schooling have often mirrored the choices that schooling as a whole for this age range presents, vocational or academic. The former is characterised by the extent to which it focuses on and accords value to practical or applied knowledge, skills and understandings. Education systems within and beyond the UK have historically distinguished vocational education and vocational qualifications as not merely of a different order to academic courses, but as also of inherently lesser value. This lower status label has similarly been tagged to vocational courses in physical education, sport and/or recreation, and those pupils who follow such courses.

As we discuss further below, the label is inherently class-based, carrying messages about who, in terms of social class, can access particular sorts of education and who is capable of developing particular knowledge, skills and understandings in physical education. We thus need to consider assessment as a cultural practice, asking amongst other things, what are the key socio-cultural influences impacting assessment, testing and pupil learning in physical education classrooms? How does failure to account for embodied differences and cultural variations among pupils influence and affect assessment validity? What is required to achieve cultural validity in physical education assessment? If these matters remain overlooked, then assessment and testing in physical education will continue to have a negative impact on pupils who are not predisposed by class or culture to meet its expectations.

A physical education for the middle classes?

In focusing on social class, we begin by again cautioning against broad general-isations. As we have stressed, it is essential to acknowledge the diversity within any group, while also considering the significance of the characteristics that position them in that group. In considering social class, therefore, the interplay of class with gender, culture, ethnicity, sexuality and ability needs to be ever-present in critical analysis and commentary; 'Class, like gender and 'race', is not enacted straightforwardly in schools and classrooms' (Evans, 2004: 101).

Again we also offer a series of questions as an opening for debate and as a way of problematising certain issues.

- What social and cultural values are legitimated by contemporary physical education curricula and how?
- Do opportunities in physical education come down to money? To what extent should we be concerned with the 'political economy' of physical education?
- How are pupils from very different social backgrounds positioned by, amidst and in relation to, contemporary school systems, and more specifi-cally, structures designed to support physical education?
- Can physical education seriously challenge social hierarchies? Who has access to what as a result of physical education and schooling?

Dominant discourses in and of physical education are inherently classed. In this respect, physical education is no different from the curriculum as a whole; the knowledge, skills and understandings it privileges have (and carry) different meaning for pupils from different class backgrounds. Bringing social class to the fore of discussion and analysis in physical education thus prompts us to recog-nise and critically engage with enduring inequities in physical education, school-ing, sport, leisure and society and to see physical education as part of the wider politics of schooling. As Evans and Davies (2008) have noted, physical educa-tion curriculum and pedagogy and body pedagogies serve to endorse particular class interests and identities. Furthermore, pupils come to physical education and schools differently positioned (by virtue of social class and the resources, including social, physical and cultural capital, that they have access to and can acquire) to successfully navigate the 'meanings and message systems' of physical education (p. 208). Evans and Davies (2008) thus direct our attention to the structural conditions of schooling and society that differentially shape opportunities to successfully engage in physical education but also, to 'be fit' and 'stay healthy'. They therefore ask;

> Does PEH [physical education and health] connect with the physical cultures and class conditions that regulate people's lives, does it offer children and young people the 'ability' in the form of confidence, competence and control of their bodies' potential to deal with them effectively; or, merely help reproduce the patterns of success and failure (whether defined in levels of participation or achievement levels), along class lines that stubbornly persist in and out of schools?
>
> (Evans and Davies, 2008: 210)

Q4

The 'class lines' that Evans and Davies (2008) refer to come into play pre-school and in parallel with schooling, such that pupils are variously positioned not merely to access opportunities for learning and participation, but more importantly, to develop, maintain and extend those skills and dispositions that are recognised as 'ability' in physical education (Evans and Davies, 2010). In these terms, the middle classes can be regarded as having a pedagogic edge and advantage (p. 780).

Even though central government, some local authorities and schools in the UK have invested heavily in recent years to increase opportunities for children to engage in 'free' or reasonably priced physical activity and sport in and outside school, for those families who have the inclination but not the resources to engage consistently with any of these things, 'success' is not an option; for them the gap remains unbridgeable. They can display neither 'the right' forms of embodiment for participation and 'health' nor the skills to perform in sport, and so are likely to be defined as 'lacking ability' for success in school PE and sport (Evans and Davies, 2010: 780–1).

Summary

In 2008 Evans and Davies encouraged physical educators to think about

> What forms of activism can or should PEH [physical education and health] teachers engage in across the curriculum, in wider structures and processes of schooling (play times, meal times, etc.) and in the wider community, if their chosen project is effecting education and social change?
>
> (Evans and Davies, 2008: 210)

This chapter has highlighted that questions of equity in physical education are far from simple, and prospective answers to longstanding and systemic inequities are difficult to formulate. It has emphasised a need to explore critically some of the conceptualisations and understandings that underpin thinking and practice in physical education – relating to the knowledge, skills and understandings that are or should be central to the subject, what we recognise as ability and how we think about issues of gender, class, ethnicity and culture in physical education. All of these considerations, we argue, impact upon *who physical education is for*. We have not attempted to underplay the challenges that face those teachers who do choose to make 'effecting education and social change' their project. In all arenas of education – teaching, teacher education, research and policy-making – it is always difficult to go against the widely expected 'run of play'. We hope, however, that this chapter will stimulate further debate about doing just that.

Questions for consideration

Q1 Is gender a helpful or adequate starting point for teachers to consider in relation to equity in physical education?

Q2 What gender ideals do you see various pupils seemingly aspiring to, or feeling that they will be judged by? Do experiences in physical education serve to reaffirm or challenge the ideals?

Q3 What abilities do pupils from different social and cultural backgrounds bring to physical education? To what extent does the curriculum then connect with their abilities?

Q4 How does social class impact upon pupils' learning opportunities pre-school and how do those differences then play out in experiences of physical education in schools?

Further reading

Flintoff, A. and Scraton, S. (2006) Girls and physical education, in D. Kirk, D. Macdonald and M. O'Sullivan (eds.), *The Handbook of Physical Education*. London: Sage, pp. 767–83.

This chapter provides a very clear and succinct historical overview of the issues pertaining to girls and physical education. Discussion addresses key concepts and theoretical development, gender power relations, difference and embodiment, curriculum, teachers and teacher education, teaching styles and approaches, girls' perceptions and experience of physical education, and future research directions.

Penney, D. (ed.) (2002) *Gender and Physical Education: Contemporary Issues and Future Directions*. London: Routledge.

This edited collection offers a critical commentary on understandings of gender and equity in physical education and an analysis of physical education policies and practices from a variety of gender perspectives. Chapters bring curriculum history, sexuality, race and religion, health, and pedagogy in teacher education to the fore of debate about how gender equity can be advanced in physical education.

Sport, Education and Society (2006). Special Issue: 'Ability', curriculum and pedagogy.

This special issue comprises a set of papers generated in response to challenging questions about how ability and talent are conceptualised in physical education, and how particular understandings of ability are expressed and enacted in curriculum and pedagogy. The collection sought to respond to issues raised by Evans (2004). It offers a range of theoretical perspectives and empirical insights pertinent to considering ability in physical education.

Wellard, I. (ed.) (2007) *Rethinking Gender and Youth Sport*. Abingdon: Routledge.

This text focuses on themes around the body, competence, ability and school physical education, cultural change and diversity, gendered spaces, human rights and wellbeing, in seeking to broaden debates about gender, youth sport and physical activity. It challenges the inference in much literature that physical education and sport are destined to be a positive for boys and suggests that concepts other than gender may offer useful alternative starting points for debates and research.

The following physical education journals should support further reading. There are also many Education journals which contain articles related to relevant topics across education more generally, which are useful to extend debate further. They may also contain physical education specific articles.

- *European Physical Education Review*
- *Journal of Teaching in Physical Education*
- *Quest*
- *Physical Education Matters*
- *Physical Education and Sport Pedagogy*
- *Sport, Education and Society.*

Chapter 11

Who should teach physical education in curriculum and extra-curricular time?

Richard Blair and Susan Capel

Introduction

In many countries there are two aspects of physical education provision; a compulsory part that occurs in curriculum time and a non-compulsory part that occurs outside curriculum time. In England, physical education in curriculum time is statutory and delivered through the National Curriculum for Physical Education (NCPE) (Qualifications and Curriculum Authority (QCA), 2007a), whilst the non-compulsory part is delivered in what is known as extra-curricular physical activity/sport. Penney and Harris (1997: 42) define extra-curricular provision as 'activities outside the formal physical education curriculum, most often after school and at lunch times, but also in some schools, at weekends and/or before school by physical education teachers'.

Curricular physical education lessons in England have traditionally been taught by qualified teachers. In primary schools it has been taught largely by generalist primary teachers, although there have been some specialist physical education teachers working in primary schools (Chedzoy, 2000; Faulkner *et al.*, 2004; Wright, 2004; Garrett and Wrench, 2007; Sloan, 2010). In secondary schools curricular physical education has traditionally been taught by specialist physical education teachers, although some teachers of other subjects with an interest (and/or with qualifications) in a specific activity have taught games lessons, particularly in public schools (Sports Coach UK, 2004; see also Chapter 1). In recent years, however, physical education in primary and secondary schools has also been taught by people other than the class or specialist teacher (Sports Coach UK, 2004, 2007; Stewart, 2006; Blair and Capel, 2008, 2011; Griggs, 2008; Lavin *et al.*, 2008; North, 2009; Sloan, 2011). This is mirrored in extra-curricular provision. Sport England (2003b) report that two thirds (68 per cent) of secondary schools use outside agencies to help deliver sport outside curriculum time.

This change has been due, at least in part, to the 1997–2008 Labour government's Physical Education School Sport Club Links (PESSCL) strategy (DfES/DCMS, 2004), which developed into the Physical Education School

Sport and Young People (PESSYP) strategy from 2008 onwards Department for Education and Skills (DfES)/Department for Culture, Media and Sports (DCMS, 2008). The PESSCL and PESSYP strategies were explicitly aimed at supporting a range of education, sport and community agendas through a network of interconnected partnership arrangements that encouraged different organisations to work towards collective outcomes (Phillpots, 2010). Additionally, the Workforce Remodelling Act (DfES, 2003b), with the introduction of planning, preparation and assessment (PPA) time in 2005, has also influenced this change. (PPA time allows for all teachers to have 10 per cent of their timetable away from pupils to plan lessons, prepare resources and assess pupils work.)

Sports Coach UK (2004) report there were around 514,000 people operating as school sports coaches helping coach in schools, with a large percentage of these being unpaid. These include around: 70,000 specialist physical education teachers acting in the role of a sports coach, 250,000 non-specialist teachers; 67,000 adults other than teachers; and 85,000 external coaches. Further, Sports Coach UK (2007) suggest that the most frequent coaching environment for a full-time coach is a school. This is also supported by North (2009) who reports that there are 100,000 coaches working in schools and 90,000 working exclusively in this environment.

Football has the largest number of qualified coaches, at 142,000 (Sports Coach UK, 2004). Sports Coach UK (2007a) also report that 32 per cent of all coaches are football coaches, with the next highest being swimming with 12 per cent of coaches. Blair and Capel (2009) report that coaches from 85 per cent of football league clubs (Championship, League 1 and League 2) in England are working in schools in PPA time. Thus, we can see that the inclusion by Penney and Harris of the words 'by physical education teachers' in their definition of extra-curricular activity (see p. 171) is immediately problematic and challenging because extra-curricular provision is not necessarily delivered by physical education teachers (indeed, nor is curricular physical education).

This chapter discusses the role of teachers and coaches in teaching physical education in England. It argues that physical education teachers cannot be replaced by coaches in teaching curricular physical education and in extra-curricular provision, although coaches do have a role to play. First, we look at similarities and differences between curricular physical education and extra-curricular physical activity and sport provision.

Similarities and differences between curricular and extra-curricular provision

A national curriculum (NC) was introduced in England as a result of the Education Reform Act, 1988 (ERA, 1988). The NCPE was introduced in 1992 (Department of Education and Science/Welsh Office (DES/WO),

1992). Since then, the NCPE has been revised three times: 1995 (Department for Education (DfE), 1995); 1999 (Department for Education and Employment/Qualifications and Curriculum Authority (DfEE/QCA), 1999); and 2007 (QCA, 2007a).These revisions have resulted in significant changes to curriculum requirements. Curricular physical education has established aims and purpose that are operationalised by a clear learning process, providing direction on what, in NCPE 2007, are called key concepts, key processes and the range and content through which physical education should be taught (QCA, 2007a). The NCPE is designed to provide a broad and balanced curriculum for pupils. Physical education also makes a contribution to the broader education of pupils, including meeting the overall aims of the NC, that of developing successful learners, confident individuals and responsible citizens (QCA, 2007a).

The NCPE, as well as academic rhetoric (Penney and Harris, 1997; Green, 2000b, 2005b), are clear there should be a difference between pupils' experiences in curricular physical education and in extra-curricular provision. If we look at the meaning of the word 'extra' (outside or beyond an area or scope), it explicitly implies that the activity is outside or in addition to something, in this case, as a prefix attached to curricular physical education lessons. What is the purpose of extra-curricular provision? Is it just something extra, something beyond the scope and time limitations of the curriculum? This might be further refined as we seek to understand if extra-curricular provision is able to provide the fundamental or 'extra' link between curricular experience and young people's involvement in physical activity and sport as a lifelong participant (Penney and Harris, 1997; Whitehead, 2010a).

Physical education teachers frequently use the term extra-curricular physical education (Green, 2005b), whilst government agencies refer to extra-curricular sport (Sport England, 2003a, 2003b). Are they the same or different? Daley (2002) and Sport England (2003b) both highlight that extra-curricular provision is almost always directed towards competitive team games. This is supported by Green (2000b) who commented that extra-curricular practice, dominated by performance-orientated sport, especially team games, is generally conventional and conservative in nature and remains independent from developments such as the NCPE. Here we start to get a sense of the often ill-defined or well-disguised aim(s) and purpose of extra-curricular provision. Extra-curricular activities, unlike the NCPE, are not bound by any specific aims, purpose, pedagogical processes or the need for broad and balanced content.

We argue that there should be both similarities and differences between curricular physical education and extra-curricular provision. However we are firm in our belief that they should both have an educational role, and hence, there should be a pedagogical focus that provides a connection between the two aspects of provision. Thus, for example, in our view, extra-curricular provision has the potential to support NCPE key concepts of; competence (physical), performance, creativity and healthy and active lifestyle (QCA, 2007a). Additionally, we would like to think that physical education in both curricular and extra-curricular contexts supports pupils in developing the overall aims of the NC, that of developing successful learners, confident individuals and responsible citizens (QCA, 2007a).

QI

It is unlikely that curricular physical education and extra-curricular physical activity/sport will be planned and executed effectively if those delivering this provision do not have the necessary qualifications, knowledge, skill and understanding to undertake this role. Hence, it is unlikely that an aim of lifelong participation will be achieved by most pupils. Unless we are clear about what it is we are trying to achieve through all aspects of provision, identifying suitably experienced and qualified adults to support it is a very difficult proposition. In the next section we look at the qualifications, knowledge, skill and understanding of physical education teachers and coaches.

Qualifications of teachers and coaches in curricular physical education and extra-curricular provision

Due to the statutory requirements outlined by the NC and the NCPE it appears, at first glance, that identifying who should work in curricular physical education lessons should be straightforward. In order to deliver physical education lessons that cater for the learning needs, abilities and motivations of all pupils, teachers undertake a specialist course of education to satisfactorily meet standards to gain qualified teacher status (QTS). There is a specific, graduate level of knowledge, skill and understanding required; they therefore have considerable specialist knowledge, skill and understanding across a range of areas in order to support pupils' learning. This knowledge can be categorised in a number of ways; for example, in England initial teacher education is founded on a competency-based conceptualisation of knowledge organised into standards which are the minimum legal requirement of what student teachers must demonstrate they know, understand and are able to do to qualify as a teacher (see Teaching Agency www.education.gov.uk/publications/standard/publicationDetails/page1/TDA0600). These standards apply equally to primary generalist teachers delivering physical education and secondary specialist physical education teachers. Other countries conceptualise knowledge for teaching in different ways, some of which identify competencies or standards. Further, there are academic conceptualisations of knowledge for teaching (several of these are described by Hoyle and John (1995); see also the seven knowledge bases identified by Shulman (1999)).

The British Association of Advisers and Lecturers in physical education (Baalpe, now the Association for Physical Education (afPE)) stated (2005: 29):

Anyone teaching PE needs to be competent (i.e. to have the knowledge, skills, understanding and expertise necessary to plan, deliver and evaluate the pupils' work in a context of appropriate challenge and a safe working environment). At least some of the components of this are identified in the requirements for undertaking 'specified work' (as identified by DfES (2003b)).

Baalpe (2005: 4) identified 'specified work' as part or all of:

- planning and preparing lessons and courses for pupils;
- delivering lessons to pupils, including distance learning or computer-aided techniques;
- assessing the development, progress and attainment of pupils;
- reporting on the development, progress and attainment of pupils.

Thus, coaches working in schools should be expected to meet the requirements to carry out 'specified work'. Planning, preparing and delivering lessons require those working in schools to have knowledge of the aims, purposes and requirements of the curriculum; both physical education specific content and the contribution physical education makes to the broader education of pupils, as well as short- and medium-term planning. It also requires them to have knowledge of pedagogy and reflection (Blair and Capel, 2008) which, it is argued, support the role of the professional educator who is critically aware of the consequence of choices in planning, delivery and evaluation (see Schon, 1983; Gilbert and Trudel, 1999; Leach and Moon, 1999; Jones *et al.*, 2004; Attard and Armour, 2006; Jones, 2006; Trudel and Gilbert, 2006; Cassidy *et al.*, 2009). Although these are important in being able to work effectively in schools, they are missing in current coaching qualifications.

Although some coaches who are employed in schools to cover both curricular physical education and extra-curricular provision might be qualified as teachers (sportcoach UK, 2004), the majority are not. Rather, they are qualified through national governing body (NGB) awards in specific sport(s), mainly at levels 1, 2 and 3 (Blair and Capel, 2008). For the largest NGB, the Football Association (FA) level 1 and 2 courses are open entry (i.e. no formal qualifications are required for entry) and the level 3 qualification can only be accessed after the first two levels have been completed. All three levels comprise theory and practical, including a final practical assessment, covering mainly technical, tactical, physical and at the higher levels psychological content knowledge for coaching.

Results of our empirical work (Blair and Capel, 2008, 2011) agree with literature critical of large-scale coach education programmes, in which content is decontextualised and delivered in a vacuum; participants coach others on the course rather than a group of young people (e.g. Douge and Hastie, 1993; Abraham and Collins, 1998; Gilbert and Trudel, 1999; Cassidy *et al.*, 2009).

This is further supported by Nelson and Cushion (2006) who question the term 'coach education' and argue it lacks conceptual clarity, highlighting that the term 'education' is misleading and that many courses more closely resemble 'training' or, in extreme cases, indoctrination.

We acknowledge that the FA have made a significant step in the right direction by developing age-appropriate modules, specifically aimed at working with children (FA Learning, 2008, 2009, 2010). However, given the well-established fact that coaches work in schools (North, 2009), it would seem appropriate for all NGBs to consider how they support their coaches regarding what and how pupils experience physical education and extra-curricular physical activity and sport at school. Some very basic mathematics informs us that children spend roughly six hours a day, five days a week, for 39 weeks a year at school. We are not suggesting that coaches need to know and understand the NCPE in the same detail as a physical education teacher, as we are not suggesting that coaches work in the same way as physical education teachers in curriculum time. However, we would pose the question why any full- or part-time coach or parent volunteer, working with children in whatever context, curricular, extra-curricular or club setting, in a role aimed at supporting a pupil's education, would not be interested and would not benefit from knowledge and understanding of what and how they are learning during this time and hence would benefit from having an awareness of the NC and the NCPE, its core aims and how it is structured as a process of learning.

We argue that coaches who have learnt to coach through NGB awards and through their own experiences are unlikely to have the background, experience or knowledge, skill and understanding in relation to working within the NCPE. Formal coach education courses do not adequately prepare coaches for working with pupils in the NCPE (in terms of content) or delivering extra-curricular provision (depending on the view of extra-curricular provision outlined above) or indeed for working with young people inside and outside school in terms of pedagogy and reflective practice. Therefore, if coaches are to work with young people and, in particular with pupils in schools during curricular physical education and/or extra-curricular physical activity and sport, we argue that NGBs have a responsibility to educate coaches, through formal or non-formal coach education (Trudel et al., 2010) in order that they have the required knowledge, skill and understanding.

Some of these issues are highlighted in vignette 1 below which describes two coaches, both qualified through NGB awards, working in curricular physical education time in one primary school. Note: The content of this vignette (and vignette 2 below) is constructed from empirical evidence; however, its structure has been organised by the authors (see Sparkes, 2002). The writing style was chosen to help guide you while engaging interest and creating relevance, meaning and reflectivity (Miles and Huberman, 1994). You are encouraged to reflect on similarities and differences with your outlook, views and experience (Sparkes, 1991). Pseudonyms are used throughout the vignette.

Vignette 1: Sports coaches working in curricular physical education time in a primary school

Frank and Steven work as full-time football coaches for a community sports trust (CST) at a professional football club. It is the first time either of them has worked at the Red School.

Before the lesson

Frank and Steven arrive at the school a few minutes in advance of the first lesson and Frank speaks to the receptionist, 'we're here from the CST to coach the football teams.' Steven interrupts. 'No we're not, we're here to cover PPA time.' The receptionist asks them to sign in and then the duty pupil takes them to Mrs Lennon's room.

On the way Steven asks 'Do you know anything about the National Curriculum?' 'No' replies Frank [in a less than enthusiastic manner]. 'Do you?' 'Not really, I can't remember doing anything about working in schools on the last coaching course I did.'

Mrs Lennon sends the two coaches straight outside to the playground with the keys to the physical education shed. 'Did she tell us how many will be in the first class?' 'I can't remember but they're year 3s.' 'How old are they?' 'I'm not sure, around six or seven, I think.' 'What should we do with them?' 'I don't mind, dribbling and first touch?' 'Yeh that's fine, you start and I'll follow your lead.' 'Ok, I'll start with Space Invaders.'

Before the two coaches have finished organising their space a class of excited pupils comes running around the corner. They are followed by an anxious looking women shouting 'Children, children please slow down, come back, I will tell Mrs Lennon, come back.' The two coaches look at each other. 'This should be fun' says Frank.

The woman introduces herself as Vicky, a teaching assistant (TA). 'As there's two of you I'll just pop back into school for a quick cup of tea. You don't mind do you? Only I didn't get one this morning because I had to supervise this lot getting changed. I'll be back at the end of the lesson. Good luck!' Frank asks 'Er, OK. How many of them are there?' The TA scans the class, who by now are running around the playground with an adventurous few heading for the climbing stations. 'There's usually 31, but I think at least two are away. Oh and it's Jordan's first day back. She was suspended for three days for swearing at Mrs Clegg, the headteacher, she's the one in the all pink tracksuit.'

Frank: 'You get the kids in and I'll quickly finish setting up the area, then we'll get going as quick as we can, how long have we got?' 'About forty five minutes now.'

The lesson begins

'My name is Frank and (pointing) that is Steven. Do your best and enjoy it, have fun, any questions ask us. Everyone happy with that?'

'Everyone stand up and make your way over here.' One of the boys asks Frank if they can play a match today, 'No we can't play a match today, we've got to concentrate on dribbling and stuff like that, OK.'

'Everyone start to come round and see me and Steven please.' (As Frank is walking backwards he bumps into one of the pupils) 'Oh, where have you come from? Everyone come in, stand there.' Another pupil asks Steven if they are playing a match. 'No we won't be playing a match because we won't have time.'

'How are you all doing? Alright?... Before we get started, as Frank has said, we need to listen carefully, it is very important to listen. The first game we're going to play is called Space Invaders' (the pupils cheer). 'Has anyone played Space Invaders before? Put your hands up. If me or Frank pass you a yellow or blue bib put it on you are the Space Invaders. Then get a football. It is very important not to kick the ball about, OK, so stand there, put your foot on the football and wait until we say go, OK. If you don't have a bib you will be aliens, so you need to stand in the middle of the pitch. Can everyone see the pitch we have marked out with all the cones?' The pupils start talking about aliens and cones and are generally quite excited. Steven says 'Listen up guys' and Frank adds 'We've got the bibs here, so if you would like to be a spaceman put your hands up'. The organisation of the pupils into spacemen and aliens is quite hectic and chaotic. Frank says 'That's it, go and get a football over there ... if you need any help putting on your bibs come and see us.' Frank and Steven both ask the pupils to stand still and put their foot on the ball. Steven: 'Those of you with a yellow or blue bib come down here please.' (Steven signals with his hands for the pupils to move towards him.) 'Everyone needs to stand along this white line and put their foot on the football like this. Aliens go and stand in the middle.'

Frank and Steven spend about 30 seconds repeating their instructions about where to stand and for the pupils to stand still and put their foot on the ball. Frank: 'OK everyone, quieten down please.' (He puts a finger to his mouth and shhhs.) 'I'm going to explain the rules of the game. When I say spacemen are you ready, you've got to shout really loud "yehhhhh".' (Frank is quite animated.) 'Try and scream the whole school down OK. When I shout aliens are you ready you've got to make a weird alien noise' (the pupils start shouting 'yehhh'). 'No listen, listen. What noises do you think aliens make?' Both the coach and the pupils start making loud 'wowing' noises. Frank is also waving his arms and hands about. 'When I say, 3, 2, 1, go, the spacemen are going to dribble their ball after you. Me and Steven are going to demonstrate the best way to do it. Say I'm a spaceman and Steven is an alien, I've got to dribble the ball after Steven. You've got to control using both feet, keep looking up. Don't try and shoot when you are miles away from the player. It's best to shoot from here. Try and get to about this close. As soon as you hit him he's got to roll over and die.' To the aliens: 'If the ball hits you on the knee or below, you are out of the game. You've got to go and stand to the side.' Frank passes the ball to hit Steven on the foot, Steven falls to the floor screaming 'wawawa' and rolls over three times. At this point the pupils starting running around the playing area...

Straight after the lesson...

'That went ok didn't it?' 'Yeh, I thought so.' 'Should we just do the same with the other four classes?' 'Yeh it seemed to work quite well.' 'We might need to make the area a bit bigger for the older ones.'

Four classes later...

'I just didn't have the energy for that last class.' 'Me neither.' 'I can't believe how those two kids reacted, it was only a game.' 'It was a good job Mrs Clegg was looking out of her window.' 'I remember being sent to stand outside the headteacher's door when I was at school.'

Before we consider vignette 1, what do you identify as the key points? Although vignette 1 only gives a brief overview of two coaches working in curricular physical education time, it highlights some key points and themes found by Blair and Capel (2008). These include: the coaches' unprofessional outlook (arriving late, no prior planning), a narrow pedagogy i.e. an overreliance on one method of communication (Mosston and Ashworth, 2002) and non-reflective practice; their lack of knowledge regarding the NCPE (there had been no input about NCPE on any coaching course attended); the content of the lesson which was focused on entertainment at the expense of education, and hence did not meet requirements of the NCPE and was inappropriate for a curricular physical education lesson (and we would argue even as part of extra-curricular provision); lack of induction or proactive support or guidance by the school and teachers as to what to teach and how it would fit in with a larger scheme of work.

Headteachers who employ coaches to cover PPA time perhaps identify physical education as relatively easy to cover because coaches are available at a relatively low cost and are willing to work in schools (Blair and Capel, 2008, 2011; Hutchings *et al.*, 2009; North, 2009; Ofsted, 2009). They may also assume that because coaches have a recognised qualification (NGB awards) they are qualified to work with pupils in schools and/or to teach curricular physical education. Further, the coaches in this vignette were just left to 'get on with it'. This presents an important question in relation to the Workforce Remodelling Act 2003 (DfES, 2003b), which had dual outcomes, to address teachers' workload and at the same time raise educational standards. Blair and Capel (2008) suggest that using coaches to cover physical education lessons only supports one of the dual aims of workforce remodelling: teachers' workload. We need to reflect on a key point: raising educational standards. By employing coaches who are not competent against the definition of specified work to deliver physical education lessons, and whose focus is on content rather than pedagogy, educational standards are not being raised as differentiated lessons are not being planned, prepared and delivered to pupils (Blair and Capel, 2008). Further, by employing football coaches, the sport in which there are the largest number of coaches (Sports Coach UK, 2004), the school provides coaches with knowledge and understanding of football but not other activities, hence, there are also questions concerning the breadth and range of content. Although this situation may be occurring inadvertently, we ask whether headteachers would allow such a situation to occur in English, mathematics or science?

There is, perhaps, an immediate temptation to lay the responsibility for the unacceptable practice highlighted in vignette 1 with the coaches and NGBs. We would discourage this mode of thinking and indeed any move to promote a 'blame culture' towards any specific group. Rather we would encourage all partners, schools, teachers, coaches and NGBs, to engage and work collaboratively in order to produce the optimum outcome for all concerned (Sloan, 2010). We believe that possible answers to our question 'who should work in curriculum and extra-curricular time?' are complex and heavily reliant on the moral responsibility of schools and teachers to make decisions on deployment of staff based on raising educational standards, and for coaches and NGBs to give careful consideration to the knowledge required for working with children and young people both in and out of schools. This is discussed in further detail in the next section.

Who should or who can teach curricular physical education and extra-curricular provision?

We argue that different people might be best placed to deliver in different contexts and at different times. We start by looking at extra-curricular provision.

To look at this aspect of provision, it is perhaps helpful to reflect on often ill-defined aim(s) and purpose(s) of extra-curricular provision. We argue that part of the reason is that aims and purposes of extra-curricular provision are context specific, different at different stages of the education system, primary and secondary, as well as highly localised and bespoke to individual schools. It is important to differentiate between working with school sports teams and working with pupils who are undertaking extra-curricular physical activity for enjoyment, to increase their skill or for health reasons. However, even with sports teams, the purpose will differ between contexts and schools. In some contexts, sports teams may, quite reasonably, be focused on success as measured through progression in competitions; in others success may be defined by taking part and enjoying competition. In some schools there may be different teams with different foci. Our view is that both are equally valuable for different pupils and in different contexts.

Q2

Taking into consideration different aims and purposes of extra-curricular physical activity and sport in school, and given our own backgrounds as teachers, we boldly suggest that, theoretically at least, it seems reasonable that, in the case of school teams whose success is measured by progression in competitions, a coach may be at least equally well, if not better, placed to work with those pupils who have committed themselves to representing their school in sporting competition. In theory, a coach may have a more advanced level of content knowledge relating to the specific sport than many physical education teachers (although we recognise that many physical education teachers may be equally well qualified). The point about sport coaches being equally well or better placed to work with competitive school teams can be developed furthered by considering the value of utilising coaches from minority sports such as korfball, softball, cycling, ultimate frisbee or even fishing. We can see a great deal of value in utilising a coach's specific content knowledge, passion and enthusiasm to inspire and teach pupils the fine detail of sporting activities that otherwise they might not get the opportunity to experience, or indeed the opportunity to excel in. This approach has the potential to allow pupils to choose from a wider range and content for extra-curricular sports teams.

We do not, however, make the same argument for extra-curricular physical activities and sport designed for fun and recreation or for intra-mural activities. Hence, it is important to be clear about the aims and purposes of specific extra-curricular provision. This is illustrated by the results of a pilot project called 'Move It', in which coaches from local sports clubs were employed to lead a range of extra-curricular physical activity and sport for all pupils in years 7, 8 and 9 (ages 11–14 years) in four schools in one London borough over a four-year period from 2004 to 2007 (see Brown, 2011). The rationale for employing the coaches in this project was to give pupils the chance to be coached by people with considerable knowledge of the specific activity which was seen as being motivational for pupils participating in the activities. Results showed, however, that this was not a particularly successful strategy for a number of reasons, including the approach taken by the coaches was not appropriate to the pupils taking part in 'Move It'. Many of the pupils had not participated in the activities previously and their major priority was to have fun. However, coaches were more used to working with young people who chose to attend the activity to improve their performance; the coaches did not have the pedagogical skills to motivate and manage the behaviour of a range of young people who were not self-motivated to improve their performance for competitive reasons but only wanted to participate for fun. Indeed, older pupils in the schools taking the Community Sports Leaders Award, became heavily involved in the programme, with much greater success. Thus, because the programme's aims and purpose were not clearly identified the coaches employed were placed in a context in which they had no real experience and for which they had no preparation. In hindsight, the employment of coaches was inappropriate in this context. Thus, it is important that the aims of the activity are clear to enable the most appropriate people to contribute in the most appropriate way.

We also argue that coaches may have a role in working within curricular physical education time in certain circumstances, despite our concerns over current coach education and the employment of coaches being able to meet the dual aims of the Workforce Remodelling Act (DfES, 2003b). We should state immediately that our view regarding coaches working in schools is dependent on a willingness by school senior managers and teachers to think strategically about how coaches are deployed in curricular physical education lessons; that they are clear how and where the coaches' contribution fits into a pupil's entire curriculum physical education experience; and that they provide guidance and support to achieve this. In our view, schools have a considerable responsibility when employing coaches to work in curricular physical education and extra-curricular provision; they should be sure that the coaches can deliver what is required and be able to work effectively with young people.

We are certainly not arguing that coaches should replace physical education teachers. Indeed, in our view the class teacher should still have responsibility for the class and utilise a different set of knowledge, skill and understanding from those a coach brings to a pupil's educational experience. In many respects, the class teacher will have a greater responsibility for constructing theoretically and peda-gogically progressive lessons that build on an understanding of the relationship between pupil, teacher, learning tasks and learning environment (Leach and Moon, 1999; Wright, 2002). The teacher has responsibility for preparing pupils for the period (say a half-term) during which they would work with the coach.

Thus, we argue that a responsible physical education department with clear five- or six-year curriculum plans that demonstrably show how pupil progression will be achieved could use coaches in a planned and structured way in some aspects of provision. It would be incumbent on any school employing a coach to work in curriculum time to ensure that the coach's delivery fits into the medium- and long-term curriculum planning of the physical education department. For example, a korfball (or other sport) coach might be hired by a school to deliver, say, a six-week unit of outwitting opponents through korfball. There are clearly transferable skills and understanding utilised to outwit opponents in korfball that are similar to other invasion games, for example, keeping the ball, exploiting and creating available space and creating uncertainty (Grehaigne *et al.*, 2005).

Consider the potential motivational value for pupils in having a specialist coach who possesses an intricate, detailed understanding of korfball or another specific area of activity or sport. To us, this seems a potential opportunity to inspire young people to intentionally practise in order to refine their skill and understanding with the aim of developing successful performance, to enter their imagination and to encourage them to be physically and cognitively active. However, we must stress that in our view this only works if the coach is used as a supportive mechanism in the appropriate context (for example, for a specific period of, say, six weeks deliv-ering a specific aspect of the curriculum at a specific time) and does not take responsibility for medium- and long-term delivery to one specific class of pupils. Additionally, the context in which the coach is being asked to work should be appropriate for their skills. By this we mean the coach should have a clear under-standing of the expectations regarding behaviour and there should be established routines and procedures that they are able to follow.

This approach seems to us to have potential for broad benefits for a pupil's education as it opens up pathways for pupils, teachers and coaches to work together (Sloan, 2010) and to develop exciting and innovative opportunities for pupils to increase independence and take personal responsibility for their learn-ing and behaviour. We would argue that it might outweigh any potential dis-advantages of coaches working in schools.

Q3

However, although we see possibilities of utilising the services of a sports coach in curriculum time (financial implications aside), here we must make our views very clear: the coach must be qualified to undertake specific work which requires them to have knowledge, skills and an understanding of:

- the aims, purpose and requirements of the NC and NCPE (i.e. they have an awareness of how their input will fit into the longer term learning of the pupils they work with);
- inclusive pedagogy and its underpinning theories;
- reflective practice;
- planning in the short and medium terms.

Our empirical investigations (Blair and Capel, 2008, 2011) lead us to conclude that this would need to be addressed through a formal and/or non-formal coach education programme that has at its core an understanding of how educational concepts inform sports coaching (Jones, 2006).

Vignette 2 shows how coaches with appropriate training are well placed to teach aspects of curricular physical education within their limited range of content. See under vignette 1 for the writing of the vignette. We again meet Frank and Steven and are introduced to Wayne, another full-time football coach working for the same CST at a professional football club. The data forming the content of this vignette was collected from coaches after they had taken part in a 22-month continuing professional development (CPD) programme aimed at developing their knowledge, skill and understanding of pedagogy, NCPE and the purpose of planning, in the short- and medium-terms (see Blair and Capel, 2008, 2011), for further information.

Vignette 2: Working in schools, some reality

Frank and Steven have just returned to the CST offices after a morning covering PPA time in the Red School. They enter the kitchen where they meet Wayne.

'Where have you two been?' 'We've had a right morning at the Red School.' Frank laughs, 'Tell Wayne about your morning Steven.'

'The teacher comes out with the first group. I say "How many have you got?" and she tells me and say's "good luck". She doesn't say anything to me, I don't get a register and some of them are wearing jeans and school shoes. At the end she asks "Were they good? Is there anything I need to know?" There's one year 4 class I have, I've only ever seen the teacher once and I don't even think that was the teacher. She doesn't come out and say "You've got 26 today, someone's off ill or they're not very switched on today or whatever." The class just comes out, it's like "oh right there here". Then at the end of it nobody picks them up, they just go to play time.'

Seeing that Steven is quite uptight as he talks about his morning Wayne smiles and asks Steven if he felt the school could improve its communication. 'Yeah, I think it needs to be improved and be better. I'm feeling more frustrated than usual today because of my year 3 class. The group came out and I think I had 32. They're all different sizes. When I started a warm up game and some of them just weren't getting to grips with it, I asked one of them what year they were in and he said year 1. I had 7 year 1s in the group. Obviously a teacher wasn't in. Then 20 minutes into the session the teacher comes out and says "I need to collect some of the year 1s." They go and I'm left with the year 3s again. I carry on and then some year 4s come out and join in. No one had spoken a word to me.' 'That must have played havoc with your planning.' 'Exactly, you can't expect me to do a good quality job. I'd planned my session for the number of pupils I knew I had, then halfway through some go (I didn't know they were going to be there so I adapted it to having them in) and you're like "right that's fine I can go back to what I planned." Then another group come out so you then have to explain to them what you're doing etc. It's a bit of a nightmare and that's what wound me up more than anything.'

Frank brought the teas over 'I've only just started this season so I don't really know the school. Has any of the teachers ever observed you coach?' 'No. Any observation of sessions has purely been by chance...' Wayne interrupts: 'Schools like having coaches in because the teachers get their PPA time.' 'Yeah and teachers don't seem to want to know about or teach physical education. Do you think that because we've had the input from the CPD programme we are more aware of some of these issues?' Steven replied quickly, 'I do, I think that sending a coach into a school to cover PPA time without this type of input is like putting a sticking plaster over a broken leg.'

Vignette 2 highlights the complexity of the situation in one school. Before we consider the vignette, what do you identify as the key points? The coaches have been prepared for working in curricular physical education time in primary schools through a non-formal CPD coach education programme which has developed their knowledge, skill and understanding. However, they are working in a context of an uncoordinated approach to deploying coaches in curricular physical education lessons, and hence the school, teacher and coaches do not have a shared understanding of the aims and purpose of curricular physical education, what the coaches should be doing and how that should contribute to the pupils' entire curriculum physical education experience. Further, the coaches are not guided and supported in their work in school. We are not apportioning blame for the situation to any one party; however, the vignette reinforces the importance of all parties taking responsibility and working in partnership to achieve a successful outcome where all concerned, pupils, teachers, coaches and school, derive mutual benefit (Sloan, 2010).

Summary: so ... who should teach curricular physical education and take extra-curricular physical activity/sport?

Ultimately, who should teach curricular physical education and take extra-curricular physical activity/sport is your decision. We have attempted to offer some points for your consideration, discussion, debate and reflection.

Our view is that teachers should be teaching in curricular physical education and extra-curricular time. However, theoretically, we believe that coaches can, in the right contexts and circumstances and where they are allowed to work collaboratively with teachers, also work in curricular physical education and extra-curricular time (Sloan, 2010; Blair and Capel, 2011). We make this statement without an explicit understanding of specific local contexts and circumstances and therefore encourage careful consideration regarding how a specific context and circumstance might impact on the purpose and then use of a sports coach. As we have stated, we are clear that there are several aspects of coach education that, in our opinion, should be developed through embracing educational concepts (Jones, 2006) to enable coaches to be prepared to work in schools. We are also clear that coaches bring different set(s) of knowledge to pupils' education. However, they do need to develop knowledge of areas such as the NC, NCPE and pedagogical content knowledge (Blair and Capel, 2008, 2011) and should not be expected to take on sole responsibility for the medium- and long-term education of any single class of pupils. What they do have is detailed, intricate knowledge and understanding of a specific sport or activity that can be experienced by pupils as part of a medium- and long-term curriculum plan which is led by the physical education teacher. However, in order to meet requirements for range and content in curricular physical education lessons, rather than working with one set of coaches it is likely that coaches covering a range of sports will need to be employed. Finally, being confident that you are using coaches in a supportive context, as we have outlined, and that you are clear about the aims and purpose of that context and therefore the rationale for why you are utilising a coach, has in our view the ingredients for successful outcomes for all concerned. On a positive note we get a sense that things are moving in the right direction but there is still a considerable way to go.

Q4
Q5

Questions for consideration

Q1 How far do you agree with the view that extra-curricular provision should be educational and support the curricular work in physical education (and in England the work in the NCPE)? How does your view compare with the reality of the context in which you work? Is coaching a school team viewed as an educational experience for the pupils and/or the teacher/coach? Consider why your work context operates as it does and, if appropriate, what changes you consider are needed (Chapter 8 looks at socialisation which might be helpful in addressing this question).

Q2   What is your view of the aims and purposes of extra-curricular activities? What is your experience?

Q3   Who should teach curricular physical education and take extra-curricular physical activity/sport? What are your arguments for and against and what conclusions do you reach from the discussion in this chapter? Are there any issues not raised in this chapter which should be considered in relation to your specific context?

Q4   Should NGBs support coaches to develop the knowledge, skill and understanding to work in schools? How could they do this?

Q5   Should coaches who cannot demonstrate their knowledge, skill and understanding against the definition of specified work be allowed to work in school curriculum or extra-curricular time? Should headteachers be more accountable for the deployment of coaches in curricular and extra-curricular coaching?

Further reading

Blair, R. and Capel, S. (2008) Intended or unintended? Issues arising from the implementation of the UK Government' 2003 Schools Workforce Remodelling Act. *Perspectives in Education* 26(2): 105–25.

This article reports the findings from the initial context data collected from a group of community football coaches who were working in PPA time or just about to start working in PPA time.

Blair, R. and Capel, S. (2011) Primary physical education, coaches and continuing professional development. *Sport, Education and Society* 16(4): 485–506.

This article reports the findings from the first 12 months of a CPD programme aimed at developing community football coaches' knowledge, skill and understanding of working within the NC and specifically the NCPE covering PPA time in primary schools.

Jones, R.L. (2006) How can educational concepts inform sports coaching? in R.L. Jones (ed.), *The Sports Coach as Educator: Reconceptualising Sports Coaching*. London: Routledge, pp. 3–13.

This chapter looks at coaching as a pedagogical process and argues that coaching and teaching are not as dissimilar as tradition may have led us to believe. The text argues that there is a need to develop more realistic coach education aimed at addressing the complex nature of a coach's role.

Sloan, S. (2010) The continuing development of primary sector physical education: Working together to raise quality of provision. *European Physical Education Review* 16(3): 267–81.

This article discusses reasons why primary schools find it difficult to provide quality physical education and school sport. It examines why primary class teachers have concerns about teaching physical education.

Trudel, P. and Gilbert, W. (2006) Coaching and coach education. In D. Kirk, M. O'Sullivan and D. McDonald (eds), *Handbook of Physical Education*. London: Sage, pp. 516–39.

This chapter provides a comprehensive overview of coaching and coach education.

Trudel, P., Gilbert, W. and Werthner, P. (2010) Coach education effectiveness, in J. Lyle and C. Cushion (eds), *Sport Coaching Professionalisation and Practice*. London: Elsevier, pp. 135–52.
This chapter provides a detailed discussion on the effectiveness of coach education. It divides coach education into three main categories; small-scale coach education, university-based coach education and large-scale coach education programmes.

The following physical education journals should support further reading. There are also many education journals which contain articles related to relevant topics across education more generally, which are useful to extend debate further. They may also contain physical education specific articles.

- *European Physical Education Review*
- *Journal of Teaching in Physical Education*
- *Quest*
- *Physical Education Matters*
- *Physical Education and Sport Pedagogy*
- *Sport, Education and Society*.

Chapter 12

What are the public perceptions of physical education?

Helen Ives and David Kirk

Introduction

Public perceptions of physical education would appear to be divided. In a telephone survey of public attitudes to physical education in the USA in 2000, 81 per cent of adults were reported to agree that physical education should be compulsory, and another 64 per cent strongly agreed that 'physical education helps children prepare to become active, healthy adults' (Opinion Research Corporation, 2000: 2). In stark contrast, a posting on the *Guardian* comments webpage in November 2010 stated

> school PE is nothing but licensed bullying and the sooner it is entirely voluntary the better for those pupils who have no interest in being forced to charge about a muddy field in the company of a bunch of 'sporting heartie'.
>
> (noteverpc, *Guardian*, 28 November 2010)[1]

The existence of such extremes may be commonplace in public opinion generally, but it is nonetheless informative to learn that the same school subject or, at least, a subject with the same title, can provoke such contrasting points of view.

Much depends, of course, on the context in which a perception or opinion is expressed. An individual's response to a telephone survey is likely to be more measured than a comment on an internet blogging or social networking site. Moreover, such perceptions are just that, an individual's more or less well informed point of view. Perceptions or opinions become 'public' when they are expressed in a forum other individuals have reasonably untrammelled access to and so become available in the public domain. 'Public opinion' is the collective view that is expressed when many individuals' views are taken together.

It is possible that public opinion may be divided over whether public perceptions of physical education are important and whether physical educators should pay them any heed. According to Williams (1985), these perceptions *are* crucially important. Writing in the 1980s, she argued that there were at least three public categories that gave legitimacy to physical education's place in the school curriculum at that time, 'sport', 'health' and 'recreation'. The 'legitimating publics' that clustered around these categories effectively were sources of advocacy for school physical education, arguing the case for or against the subject's inclusion in the curriculum. More than this, the categories themselves were means by which to think about physical education, its nature and purposes, aspirations and benefits.

Given the apparent range of opinion about physical education and the importance of legitimating publics for the nature and existence of the subject in schools, perhaps some consideration of public perceptions of physical education is appropriate. But how do we get to grips with such an ambiguous notion? We will propose here that there are at least two major sources of the perceptions that eventually come to form public opinion. The first is an individual's own direct experience of physical education in one or more roles, as a pupil certainly, and possibly as a parent. The second is representations of physical education in various media, including televisual media such as movies, video clips on YouTube and textual representations in, for example, social networking and blogging sites.

We think both sources of individuals' perceptions are powerful, and we focus on each in this chapter. As we do so, we will compare and contrast the views of physical education each source produces with what we know from the published research on perceptions, particularly the perceptions of young people, but also the perceptions or 'philosophies' of teachers. We think policy at various national, district and local levels is a response to, but also a means of shaping, the individual views that become public perceptions. We consider public perceptions in action, in relation to the so-called obesity crisis, before concluding with a brief discussion of how physical educators might respond to public perceptions of their subject.

Personal experience and public perceptions

Most children in the UK now experience some form of physical education at school. A majority of adults will also most likely have experienced physical education in their school days. This means that a large proportion of the population have some direct experience of school physical education on which to base their perceptions. Despite the ubiquity of experience, and apart from the occasional survey, opportunities to express an opinion about physical education in a public forum would for most people be rare. Indeed, it is only relatively recently that researchers have begun to pay attention to pupils' perspectives on physical education (MacPhail *et al.*, 2003; Dyson, 2006; O'Sullivan and MacPhail, 2010). So it takes an exceptional event of some kind to elicit people's opinions on the nature and purposes of physical education based on their personal experiences.

Just such a happening occurred in October 2010. The event was the UK Conservative-led government's proposed cuts to funding School Sport Partnerships (SSPs) following the expenditure of over £2 billion over the previous decade by the former (Labour) government. Pages sprung on up Facebook and Twitter. On them people voiced their opinions about the cuts and in so doing provided us with some insights into their perceptions. As we noted with the comment quoted in the introduction to this chapter, internet media such as blogging and networking sites facilitate a particular style of communication that might be less considered than other forms such as surveys. And most of the contributors who posted comments were in 'protest mode', since they were reacting either for or against a proposal to cut funding. Nevertheless the postings on two sites we examined, a Facebook page titled 'Save School Sport'[2] and the *Guardian* newspaper blog site, revealed considered and nuanced perceptions of physical education alongside more stereotypical opinions.

For example, someone claiming to be a GCSE pupil wrote that participation in extra-curricular activities was important for her CV. She also commented that the SSPs provided young people with valuable leadership experiences and role models: 'I feel strongly that you CANNOT cut school sport partnerships as from a young age, leaders from other schools were who I aspired to be' ('Student', Facebook page 'Save School Sport', 28 November 2010). A parent, commenting on the *Guardian* site, mentioned the benefits to her/his daughter of opportunities sport provided for volunteering ('Rarebite', *Guardian* site, 28 November 2010). One contributor claiming to be a student mentioned that her/his sport of cheerleading had provided opportunities to make friends. Another contributor writing as a parent also mentioned leadership alongside 'hard work, physical and psychological well-being, taking responsibility' as benefits of physical education. Reflecting on her/his own experience of non-competitive activity, this parent claimed:

> Adventure activities in the mountains are not usually competitive but they give young people a great deal. I know, because when I was 15 I was taken down a cave and at 43 I can look back over 28 years of active cave exploration. It's kept me fit, at times kept me sane and enriched my life in so many ways. That one trip had a more positive impact on my life than just about anything else I experienced in the education system.
>
> ('Parent', Facebook page 'Save School Sport', 7 November 2010)

These notions centred on leadership, friendship and volunteering provide an additional category to the three Williams (1985) wrote about, which we might describe as 'public service' or 'citizenship'. At the same time, a majority of the contributors to these two debates reflected a view of physical education that was strongly centred on the category of sport. The caving enthusiast we have just quoted is clearly speaking about this activity as a form of active leisure, and he also mentions keeping fit. Another parent contributing to the Facebook page wrote 'this government thinks children's health and well-being is expendable', an issue we come to shortly. The prominence of sport is perhaps unsurprising when we consider the context of the debates, which was the School Sport Partnerships programme. Nevertheless, many contributors were referring to physical education, and so we might assume with some confidence that 'sport' remains an important category among the public for the legitimation of physical education's place in the school curriculum.

Some of the contributors to the *Guardian* site clearly had a particular view of physical education-as-sport in mind. For instance, one commentator suggested the government should ask the pupils what they want in terms of 'Do you want to go out in the freezing cold and play netball?' ('Emma21', *Guardian* site, 28 November 2010). Another contributor who claimed to be a teacher was rather less temperate:

> I am a teacher and sport in schools just gives scum-children who cannot or will not behave and achieve in other lessons an outlet to 'achieve' and win praise for their amateur sporting prowess when in fact they should be locked up and told in no uncertain terms what they are, until they hang their heads in shame and start learning something useful.
>
> (realgonekid, *Guardian* site, 28 November 2010)

This perception clearly builds on a stereotypical notion that, as the Munn Report (Scottish Education Department Consultative Committee on the Curriculum, 1977) notoriously put it, physical education is a 'non-cognitive' activity. As such, it is assumed, there is little value in 'achieving' in physical education in comparison to other school subjects including, no doubt, this 'teacher's' own. So in order to excel in physical education a pupil needs to have little or no ability in these subjects and may well be prone to misbehaviour as well.

And yet some contributors were prepared to challenge such perceptions. In response to the comment quoted in the introduction, that 'school physical education is nothing but licensed bullying', one blogger wrote:

> As probably the only person young enough on this wall to have actually been at school in the last decade and benefited from the scheme [SSPs], I feel entitled to put forward my view … I would stress that I am no 'sporting hearty', instead a fairly shy young woman, and the idea of PE as being shouted at while running around on a freezing, muddy pitch perhaps only goes to show your age. Things have changed a bit since them days.
>
> ('elfyelf', *Guardian* site, 28 November 2010)

Things may indeed have changed in physical education over the course of time, though it may be these contrasting views simply show that different individuals have had different experiences of physical education regardless of the era in which they attended school. Nevertheless, and despite the positive benefits of physical education listed by some individuals in these debates, the idea that physical education is closely associated with sport and moreover that the experience of it is unpleasant, even for those prepared to take a broad view of the issue, stands out as a recurring aspect of public opinion, as we see in this comment:

> I hated sports as a child, and can't say I've been able to muster up any enthusiasm since. School sports seems rather too much like an exercise in sadism; I'm not a 'team member' so I got nothing from it apart from bruises and humiliation. But, and this is the crucial bit, I don't want to see sports axed from schools due to funding worries. Because a lot of children like sports and get something from playing them, I think it's right and proper that they should still have the same opportunities shown to me.
>
> (annonick, *Guardian* site, 28 November 2010)

For the most part, the contributors to this debate reflect a recurring theme in the research literature on pupils' perceptions of physical education, that it is loved by some and hated by others (Tinning, 2010). Indeed, Flintoff and Scraton (2001) reported that the young women they interviewed enjoyed physical activity outside school despite rather than because of their experiences of school physical education. The contributions to these debates over the SSPs, like the research literature, arguably seem to confirm that opinion is indeed divided about the value of physical education. Another recurring theme of the research literature which is not so evident in these contributions, though it may be echoed in the comment by 'realgonekid', is that, according to Smith and Parr (2007), physical education for many young people is often viewed as a welcome break from the rigours of 'serious' academic subjects, and is certainly not viewed as a 'serious' subject in itself.

Q1

One group of citizens who do not necessarily need a specific set of circumstances such as a financial crisis to air their views on school physical education is politicians, including cabinet ministers. It is a commonplace fact that public opinion can sometimes influence government policy, whether this is on the building of new airport runways or the location of new prisons. At the same time, it is, in principle at least, more common to find that government policy is based on research-based evidence and expert opinion. This approach to policy does not seem to apply in the case of physical education, where even the research commissioned by government itself is rarely used to inform policy (Jung *et al.*, 2011). Instead, it would appear that it is politicians' personal experiences that inform their views on the nature and purpose of physical education, just like ordinary members of the public.

For instance, when ministers give speeches addressing physical education audiences they often appear to feel the need to recount their own physical education and sporting achievements, or lack thereof. In October 2011, in an address to the newly appointed School Games Organisers at the Youth Sport Trust Conference, Secretary of State Jeremy Hunt opened his speech with a story about his school years, saying

> I was always one of the most unsporty children at school ... 'the academic swot', my brother the 'sporty' one.... I can never claim any talent at sport but I've always been totally passionate about the impact sport can have on young people.

Moreover, it is in the House of Commons in Britain where we regularly learn about politicians' perceptions of physical education. As a case in point, in November 2010 an exchange took place between between Labour MP Andy Burnham and the Conservative Secretary of State for Education Michael Gove as they debated Mr Gove's decision to reduce funding to School Sport Partnerships. Recollecting his own school physical education experiences, Burnham called into question Mr Gove's qualifications to make decisions about policy in this field.

> I had the great misfortune to be in a Merseyside comprehensive under Maggie (former Prime Minister Thatcher), and I remember after-school competitive sport vanishing with the teachers' dispute in the 1980s. Ever since, I have worked in politics to put school sport back on its feet. It is the right of every child to have good sport while at school, and it cannot be left to random chance and the occasional good will of teachers.... I also want to know what sport means to the right hon. Gentleman. Last week, he goaded me about my drama career at school. I have looked up his school sports career. It did not take long. One article on him mentions it: 'In 1979, he won a scholarship to Robert Gordon's school in Aberdeen, where he spent the next seven years excelling in every subject, except sport.' There was also a lovely quote from Mrs Gove, his mum: 'When he had finished all his school work, he would more or less revert to reading his encyclopaedia.' (...) It is a lovely image, but it worried me. Did he ever use the encyclopaedia as a goalpost, or anything like that? Stumps? Anyway, that worried me a little. It also made me wonder – so inexplicable is his decision on this matter – whether this whole thing might be Gove's revenge. I get the distinct impression that he harbours some unpleasant memories of his own sporting experiences at school, and that he is lashing out at the school sport system, now that he has the chance to do so.
>
> (Hansard, 2010: 694–9)

These exchanges and recollections of school days by members of Parliament and the government are clearly shaped by their experience, opinions and perceptions of physical education. Indeed, it would appear that Mr Burnham believes positive experiences ought properly to be the basis of policy-making in physical education and sport more broadly and that anyone who has shown a lack of interest in or talent for sport should be immediately suspect as a policy-maker.

Q2

Perceptions of physical education in televisual media

Physical education has occasionally featured in films and on television and these appearances in televisual media are both a source and a reflection of public opinion. Given the massive reach of film and TV as forms of popular culture, these portrayals have the potential to be a powerful influence on public perceptions of the nature and purposes of physical education and related activities such as school sport and coaching. McCullick *et al.* (2003: 8) have examined how physical education and in particular its teachers have been portrayed in movies. On the basis of their analysis they proposed that there are at least four issues concerning the ways in which physical education teachers and, through them, physical education-as-sport is portrayed.

The first issue they identified is that, particularly in the USA, physical education teachers and coaches are viewed as more or less synonymous. If anything, the school sports coach would appear to be a more recognisable character for American viewers than the physical education teacher, even though what he is doing with his players is *teach*. This point is well illustrated in the movie *Coach Carter* (2005), based on a true story, which could not have had the same emotive power if Carter had been portrayed as a teacher. Carter becomes the school basketball coach who decides that his players have to be good students and good people as well as good players. His teaching soon produces results both on and off the court. However, before long, the players' commitment to their academic work wanes. When Carter receives the low grade reports for the players he benches the team, cancels practice and locks up the gym. In an emotional climax to the movie, a debate follows in which the school board and the parents fight back against Carter's actions. Carter remains committed to his methods, and resigns his job. But on returning to pack up his possessions he finds the players sitting at their school desks in the gym, with their teachers tutoring them. Carter stays and the team improve their grades but lose the state championship by two points. Over the closing credits information is provided on the future of the players with six of the team of ten going on to college from a high school from which an average of only 50 per cent of students graduated and a meagre 6 per cent then went onto college. The movie portrays sport as a vehicle for the realisation of other social goods beyond winning championships and Coach Carter as at root a teacher.

In contrast to *Coach Carter*, McCullick *et al.*'s (2003) second issue in their study is that physical education teachers do not 'teach' since, echoing 'real-gonekid' in the previous section, there is little to learn in physical education.

The British film *Kes* (1969) offers Mr Sugden as a 'non-teaching' physical educator. Mr Sugden's 'lessons' merely provide him with an opportunity to play out his own sporting fantasies. In an iconic scene from the movie, he appears on the football pitch dressed in a Manchester United strip. He imagines he is Bobby Charlton and we are provided with the commentary that is running through his head. Helped by compliant pupils and the fact that Mr Sugden is not only the centre-forward but also the referee, he is also able to award free kicks and penalties in order to play out his success. Despite the comedic effect of the scene, a serious point is being made about physical education. The 'teacher' is first and foremost a sportsman, and he is the centre-point of the lesson. By merely 'rolling out the ball' and playing a game, no teaching is taking place.

Mr Sugden is also a bully and a fine example of McCullick *et al.*'s (2003) third issue. Another example is to be found in the BBC TV series *Grange Hill*, a school-based series made for young people that began in 1978. Grange Hill was a fictional co-educational comprehensive school based in the fictional London Borough of Northam. At the beginning of the series, Mr 'Bullet' Baxter is a physical education teacher who is feared, whose lessons include harsh discipline, and competition and success are demanded. When he learns Grange Hill pupils were involved in a fight in a shopping mall with pupils from another school his response to the news is 'Did we win?', epitomising his approach to physical education. In the 1980s a new teacher, Mr Robson, replaces Mr Baxter. Mr Robson, in contrast to his predecessor, believes physical education and sport are about taking part rather than winning, which brings him directly into conflict with the boys' football captain. Later in the series Mr Robson is replaced by Mr Dai 'Hard' Jones, who is ex-military and whose approach to physical education and sport signals a return to the hyper-competitive bullying ethos of 'Bullet' Baxter.

While the physical educator-as-bully is in these cases associated with sport, the movie *Kindergarten Kop* (1990), featuring Arnold Schwarzenegger, draws on military associations. During its pre-sport era, prior to the 1950s in Britain, physical education took the form of drilling and exercising with teachers using 'words of command' from military training books. In *Kindergarten Kop*, undercover policeman Schwarzenegger attempts to tame an unruly class of five-year-olds by use of exercises, marching and strict discipline. While he is a surprising though temporary success, behind the comedic effect of this very large muscular man (a former Mr Universe body builder) and these small children, was the more serious implication that physical activity is a useful and appropriate means of controlling children's behaviour and the physical education teacher is a near neighbour of the army drill sergeant-major.

McCullick *et al.*'s (2003) fourth issue is that female physical education teachers are invariably portrayed differently from male teachers. For example, in the American television series *Glee* we are introduced to Sue Sylvester, the cheerleading coach and a strong female character. While Sylvester is tough and straight-talking, she is demanding of her cheerleaders to be the best they can be, and she is compassionate. She may hang out in a tracksuit most of the time, but we never doubt that she is a very intelligent woman. But as with the portrayal of sport in schools, competitive success is proof that Sylvester is good at what she does, with her cheerleading team, the Cheerios, winning six consecutive national championships. While female physical educators can be attractive, even sexy, they also have to be winners.

Part of the success of a movie at the box office or a TV series in terms of ratings is that the stories they tell capture something of the mood of the times. It is interesting, for example, that Mr Sugden of *Kes* represents a teacher of an era in which few physical educators had degree-level qualifications and their training was college- rather than university-based. Schwarzenegger's *Kindergarten Kop* appeared at a time when Americans were warming to the idea that the problems of unruly youth could be solved through boot-camp discipline. The temporary change of types of teacher in *Grange Hill* also captures a brief moment in which physical educators allegedly eschewed competition for participation, a topic studied in some detail by Evans (1990) and Kirk (1992). The use of sport as a powerful medium for expressing a range of social values, such as those exemplified by the movie *Coach Carter* and the TV series *Glee*, offers continuity to how physical education and related activities are represented by televisual media. The collective effect of these images is to portray a complex, diverse and at times contradictory practice which, arguably, may account for the range of public opinion we discovered in the previous section.

Q3

Public perception in action: the case of physical education and the war on obesity

> The skills taught through PE are not just about creating athletes, they underpin everything we do in life.... Many children will continue to struggle with obesity, children from poorer families will be denied access to organised sport and competition and the quality of life for all children will be affected because healthy, active children achieve more, learn more, enjoy more and cope better.
>
> ('Primary School Teacher', Facebook 'Save School Sport' page, November 2010)

Despite the strong association of physical education with sport demonstrated in the previous two sections, when it comes to the 'war on obesity' it would appear there is a perception among the public and professionals alike that physical education has a key role to play. In part, this perception has been reinforced by what Thorpe (2003) describes as a 'crisis discourse', whereas Gard and Wright (2005) have argued, the impression is created that 'everyone everywhere' is at risk of becoming obese. Of course, a health agenda is not new within physical education and physical educators have argued for the health benefits of their subject since at least the late 1800s (Kirk, 1992). However, pupils' weight and fitness are now, according to Azzarito (2007), 'under siege' and 'schools are becoming accountable for obesity in children'.

In creating the fear of an obesity crisis, the interlinking of key ideas have been crucially important in shaping public opinion. Kirk and Colquhoun (1989) argued that the 'exercise = slenderness = health' trio plays a key role. The assumptions that create the linkages between these key ideas are that exercise is crucial to the maintenance of a slender body and that slenderness is proof of health. These relationships are often represented by sectional interests who benefit from a crisis discourse around obesity as necessary and causal when in fact they are merely contingent and co-relational. That is to say, while exercise may indeed contribute to the maintenance of a slender body, it does not guarantee this outcome. Nor is it possible to vouchsafe that slenderness is proof of health when clearly victims of anorexia experience life-threatening health problems.

There would appear then to be widespread public support for the idea that physical education should be in the vanguard of the fight against obesity, and the range of policy developments in physical education and related activities illustrates a trend in this direction. For example, in England the National Curriculum includes lessons on personal, social, health and economic (PSHE) education. Schools look to achieve the 'Healthy Schools' standard by providing PSHE and opportunities for healthy eating and physical activity and fostering emotional health. Alongside this provision there are also 'active travel plans' to increase the number of children walking or cycling to school, the physical education and sport strategies (PESSCL/PESSYP) for achieving two hours or more of physical education per week and the numerous interventions aimed at increasing participation in lunch, and after-school clubs, many now sponsored by the Department for Health through the Change 4 Life programme. In primary schools the National Child Measurement Programme (NCMP) requires teachers to weigh and measure pupils in Reception year and year 6, with parents being sent letters confirming their child's body mass index (BMI).

While these school-based interventions seem to be focused on increasing the amount of physical activity children do, they all fall short of the Chief Medical Officer's recommendation that 'children and young people should achieve a total of at least 60 minutes of at least moderate intensity physical activity each day' (DoH, 2004: 3). In Britain in 2009, 55 per cent of school pupils were reported to be accessing three hours of physical education and school sport a week (DfE, 2009). In the USA, the Harvard Forums on Health in 2003 examined the opinions of 1,002 Americans aged 18 plus. When they were questioned about children's obesity 76 per cent identified the need for more physical education in schools. Whilst the Center for Disease Control and Prevention (CDC) guidelines promote daily physical education for all pupils 'only 5.8 percent of senior high schools require daily PE or its equivalent for the entire school year for students in all grades in the school' (Burgeson et al., 2001). In 2009, however, less than 10 percent of the public schools in the USA offered physical education classes and the numbers of physical education teachers in schools are becoming fewer and fewer (Ygoy, 2009).

The perception that physical education and related activities play an important role in combating obesity seems to be robust and resistant to counter-claims (e.g. Gard and Wright, 2005; Kirk, 2006). In 2006, research undertaken by Reilly *et al.* in Glasgow assessed whether a physical activity intervention reduced the BMI in young children. Following a clustered randomised controlled trial the research concluded that 'whilst physical activity can significantly improve motor skills it did not reduce body mass index in young children' (Reilly *et al.*, 2006: 1041). In 2009, the UK media published a variety of headline articles discussing the research findings of Plymouth University. A headline in the *Daily Mail* newspaper (7 May 2009) provides a concise summary of the results: 'Child obesity will not be solved by physical education classes in schools.' Alissa Fremeaux, a biostatistician at the Pennisula Medical School, explained:

> we discovered that the children who got a lot of physical education time at school were compensating by doing less at home. While those who got very little physical education time compensated by cranking up their activity at home, so that over the week they all accumulated the same amount.
>
> (Thornhill, 2009)

On the same topic Alleyne wrote in the *Daily Telegraph* that 'the findings throw into doubt drives to increase physical education at schools and suggest that efforts should be targeted at diet to control Britain's spiralling levels of child-hood obesity' (Alleyne, 2009).

Kirk (2006) has argued that physical educators have often been ambivalent about their contribution to the health agenda, in part due to the power of the sport discourse. Nevertheless, as the discourse around obesity has intensified in the first decade of the twenty-first century and the legitimating public clustered around the category of health has appeared to grow, some physical educators and their supporters have seen an opportunity to shore up the subject's place in the school curriculum. The manufacturing of propaganda materials through policy and press outlets as well as paraphernalia by the fitness industry to sustain the illusion of a crisis has supported a consensus in opinion by the public at large that physical education is a necessary part of the school curriculum (Gard and Wright, 2005). Physical education has protected itself from 'loss of support from interested publics' that 'can lead to alienation and ultimately to failure' (Williams, 1985: 408).

Physical education's response to public perceptions

As we noted earlier in this chapter, Williams (1985) argued that the legitimating publics for physical education are important, clustered around the categories of 'sport', 'health' and 'recreation' or 'active leisure' and, as we suggested, an additional category of 'citizenship'. This is because they not only provide arguments for physical education's place in the curriculum or, indeed, against it, they also provide a means of thinking about physical education, its nature and purposes, what it can and cannot be. Yet despite these important points, we know very little about physical educators' views about public perceptions of their subject, far less their responses to these perceptions.

There is some indirect evidence, however, for example in Green's (2000a) study of physical education teachers' 'philosophies'. This study provides us with some insights into how teachers think about their subject. Green himself places 'philosophies' in quotes and suggests that the phenomenon he studied was more like 'beliefs' than 'philosophies'. Given the range of public opinion about physical education we should not be surprised to learn that physical education practitioners similarly, according to Green, have a range of beliefs about their subject that are at times contradictory and superficial, even incoherent. Many of the teachers he interviewed stated that pupils' 'enjoyment' of physical activity was of crucial importance in physical education, with Green noting that this aspiration would not be typical in other subject areas. At the same time, if we think of enjoyment as another way of saying 'motivation', then perhaps the teachers in his study were right to make this claim, since we know that motivation is crucial to sustainable participation in physical activities (e.g. Lirgg, 2006).

Furthermore, Green's teachers (2000a) often used the term 'sport' synonymously with 'physical education', believed in the importance of 'sport for all', and considered physical education's main mission is to inspire young people to be lifelong participants in physical activity, another aspiration, like 'enjoyment', that is ubiquitous to school physical education programmes around the world. The teachers also believed that they had a role to play in the maintenance of pupils' health, though Green notes that their commitment to health was based most often on personal intuition or what was in the news, than academic study of physical education's contribution to healthy lifestyles.

In other words, Green discovered among this group of physical education teachers very many of the same or similar perceptions of physical education that we have discovered in public opinion more generally, with the caveat that physical education teachers, as we would expect, are more or less wholly supportive of their subject. There was, at the same time, a range of views among teachers about where the emphasis should be placed, on one or more of the major categories identified above, for example health. If we are correct in this claim, it might be argued that the apparent congruence between physical education practitioners' perceptions and public perceptions is a good thing. We are all, in this sense, 'singing from the same hymn sheet'. But then we might ask what influence four years of professional education has had on these teachers if their beliefs about their subject are, in Green's unflattering terms, at times incoherent and contradictory. It might be argued that physical educators' role, as the experts in their field, should be to *lead* public opinion about their subject rather than follow it.

Q4

Conclusion

Public perceptions of physical education are informed, rightly or wrongly, primarily by individual experiences gained throughout their school life. This is the foundation on which future opinions are based. Some may change but ultimately every individual will recall their physical education lessons and their teachers. These opinions are magnified or reinforced by portrayals of bullying physical education teachers and appalling lessons. The subject is open to influence and subject content is easily changed to suit the agenda of the day, particularly when it is a politician who is expressing an opinion on physical education. Clearly, as we have shown, there are conflicting and contradictory views of the nature and purposes of physical education within public opinion. The question that physical education practitioners need to answer, perhaps, is how to minimise fluctuating opinions, and to develop instead a coherent message about the nature and purposes of physical education.

In England, with over a decade of investment in physical education and school sport, we wait to see if there has been a change in public perceptions and whether a younger generation will express different views from their parents and grandparents. Perhaps there is also a part to be played by teacher education? After all, if physical education has, as Kirk (2010) claims, remained unchanged in the UK for over 60 years then perhaps new views of the nature and purposes of the field need to be established during teacher education. Perhaps teachers need to address the washout effect on new younger teachers entering the profession who remain silent about what needs to be done in order to be accepted into physical education departments. A change in public perception could start within the physical education profession, through a commitment to becoming reflective practitioners in order to bring about change (see Chapter 9).

Questions for consideration

Q1 To what extent do you think your perceptions of physical education are based in your own experiences of the subject, as a pupil, student, teacher or parent?

Q2 Should public opinion be taken into account by policy-makers? Relatedly, should policy in physical education be made on the basis of research and expert opinion, or based on the past personal experiences of politicians?

Q3 How much impact on public perceptions of physical education do you think the mass media has?

Q4 Should teachers follow or lead public opinion on physical education? If they should, how might they do this?

Notes

1 www.guardian.co.uk/education/2010/nov/28/school-sport-partnerships-abolition-gove (accessed 8 December 2011).
2 www.facebook.com/pages/Save-School-Sport-Partnerships/159893774044860.

Further reading

Dyson, B. (2006) Students' perspectives of physical education, in D. Kirk, D. Macdonald and M. O'Sullivan (eds), *The Handbook of Physical Education*. London: Sage, pp. 326–46.
This chapter provides a comprehensive overview of research on pupil perspectives on physical education, including the main research methods employed.
Evans, J. (1990) Defining a subject? The rise and rise of the new PE. *British Journal of Sociology of Education* 11(2): 155–69.
Evans analyses the impact of a television documentary and a public debate about the nature and purposes of physical education in the run up to the 1987 general election in which Margaret Thatcher secured a third term in office.
Green, K. (2000) Exploring the everyday 'philosophies' of physical education teachers from a sociological perspective. *Sport, Education and Society* 5(2): 109–29.
This study was based on interviews with a number of physical education teachers and explored their beliefs about their subject.
Kirk, D. (2006) The 'obesity crisis' and school physical education. *Sport, Education and Society* 11(2): 121–33.
This paper argues that, despite the noisy public debate around childhood obesity and sedentary behaviour, physical educators remain ambivalent about the place of exercise for health in physical education.

The following physical education journals should support further reading. There are also many education journals which contain articles related to relevant topics across education more generally, which are useful to extend debate further. They may also contain physical education specific articles.

- *European Physical Education Review*
- *Journal of Teaching in Physical Education*
- *Quest*
- *Physical Education Matters*
- *Physical Education and Sport Pedagogy*
- *Sport, Education and Society.*

Part V

Looking ahead

Introduction to Part V

Part V comprises two chapters – 'Conceptualising teaching as learning: the challenge for teacher education' and 'What is the future for physical education in the twenty-first century?' Each in their different way challenges you to reflect seriously on the state of the profession and the future development of the subject area. Chapter 13 argues for the need for teachers to be learners to keep abreast of the rapidly changing world in which we work and Chapter 14 warns the profession that without a serious re-evaluation of our practices our long-term future is far from assured.

Chapter 13, 'Conceptualising teaching as learning: the challenge for teacher education' opens by posing a question: what would be the outcome if teachers were conceptualised not as teachers, but rather as learners? This chapter presents an argument for conceptualising physical education teachers as learners. The arguments are organised around five interlinked assumptions the authors have made about teaching, learning, and teaching as learning: teaching is a profession; teacher education is a career-long process; teachers have a right (and a responsibility) to engage in effective forms of career-long professional development; mentoring is a core professional development activity for all members of the teaching profession; professional development activities for teachers should be based on consistent theories of learning. In relation to each of these assumptions, the chapter presents a rationale underpinning their validity, illustrating the ways in which, taken together, they make a strong case for conceptualising teachers first and foremost as learners rather than as teachers. You are asked to debate this conceptualisation of teaching as learning and to consider the implications for your professional development.

Chapter 14, 'What is the future for physical education in the twenty-first century?' is a most challenging and somewhat disturbing piece of writing that aims to set out, in very clear terms, the uncertain future for physical education in schools. Of all the chapters this asks most of you, as readers. You are strongly advised to relook at your aims and practices, to stand back from your day-to-day involvement in physical education and re-evaluate realistically how far you are making an impact on long-term attitudes to involvement in physical activity in respect of the public at large. It is proposed that the profession is trapped in the present and to some extent in the past, has made very little change in its practices, and questions if our work is fit for the twenty-first century. It is argued that in order to secure a middle to longer-term future for some form of physical education in schools, a radical reform is needed. A models-based approach to physical education is proposed that is learner-centred, inclusive and motivating. You are urged to take the points raised very seriously and face up to the difficult decisions you may have to make. This may well involve risking hard-won recognition of, and achievements in, physical education and a commitment to effecting radical reform. The chapter warns that it is a real possibility that resistance to change will lead to the demise of the subject in the longer term.

Chapter 13

Conceptualising teaching as learning

The challenge for teacher education

Kathleen Armour, Fiona Chambers and Kyriaki Makopoulou

Introduction

What would happen if teachers were to be conceptualised not as *teachers*, but rather as *learners*? At first glance, this might appear to be something of a riddle. Yet we will argue in this chapter that it is a serious question, with answers that could have profound implications for the ways in which teachers are supported in their professional learning from initial teacher education (ITE) through career-long, in-service development. The issues discussed are of particular relevance to those just entering the teaching profession, given that many can expect to be in it for over 30 years. The arguments presented are organised around five interlinked assumptions that the authors have made about teaching, learning and teaching as learning:

> **Assumption 1:** Teaching is a profession, therefore teachers have a *professional responsibility* to their 'clients' (children and young people).
> **Assumption 2:** Teacher education is a *career-long* process, so the different stages in the process need to be understood as a continuum.
> **Assumption 3:** Teachers have a right (and a responsibility) to engage in *effective* forms of career-long professional development.
> **Assumption 4:** *Mentoring* is a core professional development activity for all members of the teaching profession.
> **Assumption 5:** Professional development activities for teachers should be based on *consistent* theories of learning.

In the following sections, we will present the rationale underpinning each of these five assumptions, illustrating the ways in which, taken together, they make a strong case for conceptualising teachers first and foremost as learners rather than as teachers. We will conclude by posing questions about the profound implications of our argument; in other words, we will be making the case that the 'riddle' is a serious business in practice.

'Teaching' and 'learning'

It is useful to begin a complex discussion with some fundamentals, so our starting point for this chapter is the outcome of a dictionary and thesaurus search using the terms 'teaching' and 'learning'. These generic searches for definitions are helpful because they tend to illustrate popular understandings of the terms as they are currently used. Definitions below are taken from the *Encarta Online Dictionary* (English) and the synonyms from the online thesaurus.

Teaching

- The profession or practice of being a teacher.
- Education, lessons, instruction, coaching, training, schooling

Learning

- The acquisition of knowledge or skill (gained through education).
- Knowledge, education, erudition, scholarship, culture, wisdom.

Teacher

- Somebody who teaches especially as a profession.
- Educator, tutor, instructor, coach, trainer, lecturer, professor, governess, educationalist, schoolteacher.

Learner

- Somebody who studies or learns to do something.
- Beginner, apprentice, student, pupil, novice.

This simple exercise throws up a number of issues that recur throughout this chapter. For example, the definitions of teaching and learning have some degree of overlap, but it is in the term *learning* that we find notions of wisdom and erudition. On the other hand, whereas (as might be expected) a teacher is defined in terms of a professional educator or instructor, and the term 'learner' is aligned with terms such as beginner and novice, it is interesting to note that the antonym of learner is identified as 'expert'. Yet, it is argued in this chapter that although successful engagement in ITE leads to certification to become a teacher, it is only by *learning* over a career that a teacher can ever hope to become an expert. So, we might argue that the definition of a teacher should include 'career-long professional learner' – or even 'lead learner'. This leads us into the five assumptions around which this chapter is structured.

Q1

Five assumptions about teachers as learners

Assumption 1: Teaching is a profession and teachers have a professional responsibility to their 'clients' (children and young people)

Teaching is a profession although, over the years, there have been questions raised about the status of teaching in comparison to other professions (Shulman, 2000; Hargreaves *et al.*, 2007). A dictionary definition of a profession is 'an occupation that requires extensive education or specialised training' and those who practise a profession are understood as professionals who conform to clear standards. Based on these definitions, it is clear that teaching qualifies as a profession and, in many countries, the existence of a set of professional standards for teachers at different stages of their career seems to confirm it. This suggests that questions around the designation of teaching are less about the technical definitions of a profession and more about understandings of the standing of different professions in society. New entrants to the teaching profession may – or may not – be aware of these issues.

Etzioni (1969) is often cited on questions about teaching as a profession because he described teaching as a 'semi-profession' on the grounds that it lacks the levels of professional autonomy and respect that are defining characteristics of established professions (such as medicine and law). Perhaps the more interesting point to be made, however, is that teaching could be regarded as a *curious* profession because its primary clients are children and young people. So, whereas most other recognised professions have branches or specialities within a wider professional body to serve this young client group, teaching is focused exclusively on it. Parents are clearly important, but it is children and young people who are the direct recipients of the professional services of teachers. This unusual focus might provide one explanation for some of the questions that have been raised about teaching as a fully fledged profession.

There have been numerous attempts to identify exactly what it is that sets professions apart from other occupational groups. Day (1999: 5) identified four distinguishing features that all professions share:

1   a specialised knowledge base – technical culture;
2   a commitment to meeting client needs – service ethic;
3   a strong collective identity – professional commitment;
4   collegial as against bureaucratic control over practice and professional standards – professional autonomy.

It might be argued that teaching meets some – although perhaps not all – of these criteria. Certainly in some countries, and the UK is a good example, there is evidence of an increase in bureaucratic control over teaching in the last 30 years, the implication being that teachers as professionals are, in some way, unable to monitor the quality of their own practice.

Another key distinguishing feature of professions is that they are assumed to 'serve' their client groups and, in so doing, are required to uphold high ethical and moral standards in the best interests of their clients. For example, the Australian Council of Professions defines a profession as follows:

A disciplined group of individuals who adhere to high ethical standards and uphold themselves to, and are accepted by, the public as possessing special knowledge and skills in a widely recognised, organised body of learning derived from education and training at a high level, and who are prepared to exercise this knowledge and these skills in the interest of others.
(www.accc.gov.au/content/index.phtml/itemId/277772 accessed 26 June 2011)

Central to this definition is the notion that professions have a specialised body of knowledge that results from high levels of education and training and which can be deployed to serve their clients. In other words, if the knowledge base is inadequate, out of date or inappropriate, then a profession cannot fulfil its primary function. From this standpoint, it would be argued that members of a profession cannot choose whether or not to learn continuously throughout their careers because it is a mandatory part of being a professional. Indeed, Brunetti (1998: 62) argued that 'a well developed, readily available continuing education program is the hallmark of a true profession'. This leads to important questions about teachers as learners and about continuing professional development (CPD) within the teaching profession.

It has long been argued by teachers and researchers across curriculum areas and around the world, that existing systems of professional development are inadequate (Borko, 2004; Wayne et al., 2008). Darling-Hammond (2006: 19) argued forcibly that governments need to address this issue by creating 'an infrastructure for ongoing intensive professional development' in order to 'ensure that all teachers can get access to high quality training'. This is, however, only part of the picture. Falk (2001: 137) claimed that 'professional learning is *the* job of teaching' and James et al. (2007: 217) argued that teachers need to 'move away from "performing teaching" to "supporting learning"'.

What these comments seem to suggest is that if teachers are to learn effectively across their careers, it is important both that professional development structures are in place to support them, *and* that they have the disposition to learn from their daily practice. In other words, new entrants to the profession need both the personal drive and the structural opportunity to engage in professional learning. Moreover, in order to discharge their professional responsibility to their young clients, teachers must be continuous learners who learn in and through practice; hence the suggestion that the process of teaching can usefully be regarded as a process of learning. This simple switch of words, from teacher to learner, means that teaching can never be regarded as mere 'delivery' of curriculum material to children and young people because this approach would be unlikely to meet their diverse needs. In turn, teachers would be failing in their professional duty to their clients.

Q2

Assumption 2: Teacher education is a career-long process, so the different stages in the process need to be understood as a continuum

Day (2002: 431) argued that schools and teachers are 'the single most important asset in the achievement of the vision of a learning society'. From this standpoint, teachers are at the heart of visions for a learning society which, for new entrants to the profession, may be a daunting prospect. It should certainly be obvious that teachers need to engage in CPD, and that this should take the form of a series of professional learning engagements that, over time, build on each other incrementally to create a rich, career-long learning experience. This expectation is, however, a little too optimistic. There is a plethora of research evidence in physical education and beyond which shows that CPD fails to support teachers to learn progressively over their careers (Garet et al., 2001; Armour and Yelling, 2004b, 2007). Indeed, it is interesting to consider how far teachers could progress if they were offered the ideal of continuous, rich and meaningful learning experiences.

In the UK, CPD for the teaching profession is defined as 'all formal and informal learning that enables individuals to improve their practice' (Department of Education and Skills, 2010: 2). The Teaching Council of Ireland, however, uses the notion of a *continuum of professional learning*, and this seems to better capture the notion of both accumulating and developing higher levels of knowledge over time:

> The continuum of teacher education describes those formal and informal educational and developmental activities in which teachers engage, as lifelong learners, during their teaching career. It encompasses initial teacher education, induction, early and continuing professional development and, indeed, late career support, with each stage merging seamlessly into the next and interconnecting in a dynamic way with each of the others.
>
> (Teaching Council of Ireland, 2011: 5)

Coolahan (2007) has broken down this continuum into three distinct yet connected stages defined as the '3 Is': Initial teacher education (ITE), Induction and In-service teacher education. Thus, it is recognised that the process of becoming a teacher starts at the beginning of the formal period of ITE

(Cochran-Smith, 2001) and continues throughout a teacher's career; in other words, a teacher is always in the process of learning.

This notion of a continuum can be traced back to the work of John Dewey (1958) who argued that each learning encounter must be designed to build capacity for the next: 'Every experience both takes up something from those which have gone before and modifies in some way the quality of those which come after' (p. 27). From this viewpoint, it can be argued that each stage and element of teacher education – or learning – should be designed to *build future learning capacity*. More recently, Hodkinson *et al.* (2008) and Hager and Hodkinson (2009) defined learning as a holistic process of 'becoming' within a transitional process of boundary crossing, arguing that learning is both social and embodied:

> thus when a learner constructs or reconstructs knowledge or skills, they are also reconstructing themselves. ... That is, people become through learning and learn through becoming whether they wish to do so or not, and whether they are aware of the process or not.
>
> (Hager and Hodkinson, 2009: 633)

These theorists remind us that learners do not 'become' to a fixed endpoint, and 'learning is more fruitfully viewed as an ongoing process rather than a series of acquisition events' (Hager and Hodkinson, 2009: 620). From this point of view, teacher education must, indeed, be viewed as a continuum.

There is no question that experiences in ITE and early career development provide an enduring foundation (positive or negative) for later learning. The Organisation for Economic Cooperation and Development (OECD, 2005b) posited that professional experiences in the early years of teaching are a vital influence on teachers' professional learning and the formation of later career intentions. As Anderson (1987: 63) explains:

> The challenge for [initial] teacher education is to foster commitment to school teaching and to prepare trainees for the reality of classroom practice, but at the same time to provide them with a broad general education, including the capacity to be critical and self-critical, and a familiarity with diverse viewpoints and experiences.

Moreover, it is in ITE that prospective teachers learn across contexts in order to begin to develop 'conceptual unity' (Smagorinsky, 2008). As teachers then progress into and through their careers as continuous learners, Lieberman (1995) suggested that professional learning and development should 'become as varied and engaging for teachers as they are supposed to be for students' and that helping to produce new knowledge must become 'as compelling as consuming already existing knowledge; in fact, one feeds the other' (p. 71). Lieberman argued that this could lead to 'an expanded conception of teacher development' (p. 75). In many ways, Lieberman is stating the blindingly obvious, so the fact that the point needs to be made at all is a concern. It would not be unreasonable, for example, to expect that of all professions, teaching as an *education* profession would have the best and most effective forms of professional development available. You may be surprised to learn, however, that there is little evidence to suggest this is the case.

In physical education there is a wealth of research illustrating the ways in which CPD provision (PE-CPD) falls far short of the ideal of a rich, continuous career-long learning experience. Studies have found, consistently, that structured PE-CPD provision tends to be brief, unsystematic, haphazard, 'transmission-oriented', irrelevant to individual teachers' needs and lacking in challenge (Ko *et al.*, 2006; O'Sullivan and Deglau, 2006; Armour and Yelling, 2007; Armour *et al.*, 2008). There is, however, a growing body of research that has identified more effective forms of CPD that can support teachers – as members of a profession – to learn in ways that will enable them to meet their clients' diverse needs.

Q3

Assumption 3: Teachers have a right (and a responsibility) to engage in effective forms of career-long professional development

There is a large body of research evidence to suggest that improving the quality of teachers, through on-going, systematic CPD opportunities is fundamental to raising standards in schools (WestEd, 2000; Meiers and Ingvarson, 2005). CPD has, therefore, been of growing interest to the education community in the quest to find effective structures and processes (Borko, 2004; Bechtel and O'Sullivan, 2006; Desimone, 2009). Relying principally on teacher–school case studies or teacher self-report surveys (Gersten *et al.*, 2010), CPD researchers have attempted to articulate the features of effective and ineffective CPD. For example, WestEd (2000), Sparks (2002), Guskey (2003) and Bolam and Weindling (2006) identified a range of effective CPD practices including:

1   involving teachers as active and collaborative learners with opportunities to inquire and problem-solve;
2   focusing on subject knowledge but also crucially on pupils and their learning;
3   embedding professional development activities in the school day; and
4   ensuring that engagement in CPD is coherent, progressive, challenging and sustained.

It is also recognised that effective professional learning is often collaborative, and there is a growing consensus that teachers should be able to interact with one another and develop their capacity for 'critical colleagueship' (Lord, 1994, cited in Nicholls, 1997) both within their schools and with colleagues in other settings (EPPI, 2004). Examples include working on a one-to-one basis as mentors/coaches with an explicit focus on teaching and learning, or participating in professional networks, study groups, or professional learning communities (PLCs) (Wenger, 1998). It is possible that you may have experienced some of these collaborative learning approaches.

In physical education, as was noted earlier, research findings tend to mirror those of the wider research. There is also research that points to some successful PE-CPD initiatives, although in each case barriers to professional learning were also identified (e.g. Deglau and O'Sullivan, 2006; O'Sullivan, 2007; Armour and Makopoulou, 2008; Patton and Griffin, 2008). Keay (2006) encountered numerous challenges in trying to establish and sustain effective professional learning communities within physical education settings. Furthermore, in physical education, as elsewhere, there is an enduring concern about the quality of the evidence available on establishing links between teachers' professional learning and pupils' learning outcomes (Armour, 2006).

It is clear from CPD research that there can be no 'one size fits all' approach to effective teacher professional development (Guskey, 2003) but rather CPD effectiveness rests on developing an 'optimal mix' of professional development processes and strategies that will work best in a specific context at a particular point in time (Guskey, 1995). It is widely recognised, for example, that what works in one setting is unlikely to work in quite the same way in another (Meiers and Ingvarson, 2005). On the other hand, there is some agreement that collective participation by teachers on the school site is a key element of an effective CPD strategy (Bredeson, 2003). Moreover, Garet et al.'s (2001) seminal work highlights the importance of a focus on subject-matter content as a significant factor in effectiveness, suggesting that the *form* of professional development may be less important than the substance or content of the experience. This is, perhaps, unsurprising given the earlier points made about the centrality of specialist knowledge for professions to enable them to serve their clients.

As was noted earlier, teaching is a profession so teachers have a responsibility to engage in professional development. Teachers also, however, have a right to be supported to learn in ways that are most likely to be effective; in other words this is both an individual and a structural issue. 'Transforming' schools into learning organisations is acknowledged as a key factor in facilitating ongoing teacher learning. Little (2002: 936) argued that 'strong professional development communities are important contributors to instructional improvement and school reform'. Moreover, in exploring the factors that enabled eight case study schools to 'turn students' performance around', WestEd (2000) identified the establishment of a school-wide professional culture of learning (for both teachers and pupils) as the key to success. WestEd defined the following six elements as central to such a culture:

- Ensure that student-centred goals underpin all professional development.
- Accept an expanded definition of professional development, embracing a wide range of formal and informal learning experiences.
- Recognise, value and make space for 'ongoing, job-embedded informal learning' (p. 22).
- Structure a collaborative learning environment.
- Ensure there is time for professional learning and collaboration.
- Check (constantly) whether professional development is having an impact on pupils' learning.

Yet, although there is a level of conceptual understanding about what is most likely to make CPD and PE-CPD 'effective', there remain significant barriers to developing such systems in practice. There is little doubt that there is a need to develop ongoing, inquiry-oriented, active and collaborative professional learning opportunities which can encourage a conceptual shift from a focus on the performance dimension of teaching to the support of meaningful pupil learning (Armour, 2008). As Elmore (2002: 23) argued, 'investing in more professional development in low-capacity, incoherent systems is simply to put more money into an infrastructure that is not prepared to use it effectively'. In this regard, the contents, structures and processes of CPD need careful examination if they are to support teachers to be learners in the interests of their clients.

Q4

Assumption 4: Mentoring is a core professional development activity for all members of the teaching profession

It has been argued to this point that teachers have a professional responsibility to their young clients which, in turn, means that teachers must be career-long learners. In other words, engagement in (effective forms of) continuous, career-long professional learning is an essential part of teaching. It has also been noted that traditional forms of CPD are not always effective and that forms of school-based and job-embedded learning are often perceived to be effective by teachers. One mechanism through which such embedded learning can occur is mentoring. Although the process of mentoring is fraught with challenges, it could be argued that taking responsibility for the development of newer entrants is a key feature of a profession and, moreover, that mentoring offers potentially rich learning opportunities for teachers at all stages in their careers. In some countries, notably England, mentoring in teacher education has been developed extensively in recent years.

Forging strong, school–university partnerships is widely advocated in research literature as the bedrock of successful mentoring programmes: 'Internationally, the development of mentoring in schools in conjunction with university–school partnerships has become a key feature of re-designed teacher education over the last decade' (Conway *et al.*, 2009: 118). Zeichner (2010) supports this argument, advocating the creation of 'hybrid spaces to more closely connect campus courses and field experiences in university-based pre-service teacher education' (p. 89). This view is in stark contrast to the traditional (and, in the UK, largely historical) structure of school–university partnerships where the university has maintained hegemony over mentoring and school-based experience programme design. Certainly the nature and structure of school–university partnerships vary considerably around the world from formal partnerships to voluntary arrangements based on goodwill.

A system of formal partnerships between schools and university in ITE, including clearly defined mentor roles and training, has become firmly established in the UK over the last ten years. In this example, schools have taken an increasingly leading role in ITE and there are signs that the Coalition government (elected in 2010) wants to shift the balance in the partnerships even further towards schools. In Ireland, which until recently has operated a very traditional university-led model of ITE, there have been calls for closer school–university partnerships in order to ensure that teachers are supported through training and into their professional lives (Drudy, 2009: 196). As Coolahan (2007: 11–12) reports, a key feature of current government thinking is encouragement to forge closer partnerships and to make 'more use of mentors on teaching practice'. Cochran-Smith and Zeichner (2005: 131) argue that increasing the effectiveness of school–university partnerships can 'decrease the discrepancies between advocated practice and situated practice'.

It is of course pertinent to note that in both of these examples, there is an implicit assumption that mentoring is understood, primarily, as being of benefit to the novice (mentee) through an encounter with an experienced teacher (mentor). Although mentors often recognise that they, too, can learn from their mentees, the formal structures around the process appear to place most emphasis on a traditional mentoring model. Yet if, as was argued earlier, teachers are career-long learners and school-based, job-embedded professional learning is effective, then multi-directional mentoring seems to be the ideal learning process in which teachers can engage.

A recent study by Chambers *et al.* (2011) investigated current mentoring practices in three physical education initial teacher education (PE ITE) programmes in Ireland, Northern Ireland and England. The research led to a position statement on mentoring in PE ITE programmes and a number of recommendations for effective mentoring, one of which was that the core purpose of the mentor–mentee relationship is the engagement in professional *sharing* which should continue beyond the school-based experience. This is an interesting point. What seems to be missing in many mentoring structures is an understanding of mentoring as a learning activity in which all teachers are encouraged to engage as a matter of professional responsibility. Indeed, it could even be argued that the introduction of formal structures supporting ITE could militate against an understanding of mentoring as a wider profession-building activity. As Zachary (2000: 167) points out: 'Mentoring programs enjoy sustainability over time when mentoring is embedded in an organisational culture that values continuous learning.' Indeed, Veenman (1984) argued that, in their research, mentor training led to successful mentors who developed fertile and complex pedagogical content knowledge. The mentors also had strong listening and communication skills with which to motivate and provide emotional support for the mentee. Thus, the claim made by Chambers *et al.* (2011), as a result of their research, is that mentor pedagogies need to align with the notion of teachers as career-long learners. As one of the mentors in their research commented:

> It's absolutely essential that those relationships between the university and colleagues that are out in schools [are] fostered, maintained and valued. The best practice demands this. Student teachers thrive in situations where we have a good professional relationship with placement colleagues and the university.
>
> (Chambers *et al.*, 2011: 73)

Another mentor commented on the purpose of mentoring:

> Develop trainee teachers into critical practitioners, into reflective practitioners and empower them to actually develop into those. So develop into people who are reflective of their own practice and into people who are also prepared to take new things on board as they're finding their feet.
>
> (Chambers *et al.*, 2011: 80)

What this and the earlier arguments suggest is that mentoring is a core professional activity supporting the learning of student and early career teachers and that ideally, in practice, the process is multi-directional. In addition to the need to build strong university–school partnerships, however, there is the need to consider the coherence and the consistency of learning theories underpinning mentoring and wider professional learning structures and process.

Q5

Assumption 5: Professional development activities for teachers should be based on consistent theories of learning

> Theories of learning provide a starting point for principles of teaching. Any curriculum or training course has views of learning built into it and any teaching plan is based upon a view of how people learn.
>
> (Tusting and Barton, 2003: 5)

It would seem obvious to state that CPD policies and practices for teachers should be grounded in a sound understanding of learning theory (Borko, 2004; Armour, 2006; Darling-Hammond, 2006). The question is: which learning theory? Learning is conceptualised differently from different theoretical orientations, so understanding which theories are being used both to inform the design of formal CPD, and to conceptualise teachers as learners, is important.

Sfard (1998) argued that there are two basic metaphors underpinning current conceptualisations of learning; namely, 'learning as acquisition' and 'learning as participation'. Hager (2005) added a third metaphor: 'learning as construction' and, Hager and Hodkinson (2009) developed this further with their notion of learning as 'becoming'. It has been argued that the distinction between these metaphors is at the level of ontology, that is, in relation to where knowledge, learning and cognition are located (Vosniadou, 2007). The acquisition metaphor, described as the 'standard paradigm of learning' (Lee et al., 2004), locates knowledge in the minds of individuals and assumes that it can be acquired, developed and changed. This outside-in view of learning has influenced the design and structure of teachers' CPD, leading to individualistic and deductive CPD pedagogies that position the CPD provider as the transmitter of knowledge and the teachers as receivers. The key message conveyed by this 'training model' (Little, 1993) is that professional knowledge is a static, given commodity or product that can be picked up and internalised by teachers. It also assumes that professional practice can change automatically as a result of CPD participation (Stein et al., 1999; Bredeson, 2002).

The metaphor of learning as construction recognises the importance of learners' engagement in the learning process. From a constructivist perspective, and in line with the literature on effective CPD, this kind of learning is viewed as essentially active. In other words, the learner must engage actively in the learning process for learning to be effective. Constructivist learning theories emphasise the importance of 'authentic' experiences over decontextualised 'delivery' of concepts or skills. Thus, in the context of CPD, it becomes clear that in order to be effective, training events should be designed in ways that enable teachers to bring aspects of their professional lives into the CPD context, thereby engaging in construction or reconstruction of meanings and practices (Loughran and Gunstone, 1997). Another point emerging from constructivism, and clearly linked with teacher learning and development, is the notion of teacher reflection (Schon, 1983) where teachers are encouraged to generate and/or construct theories based on their practice (Attard and Armour, 2006) and engage in 'transformative' learning (Mezirow, 1997).

Lave and Wenger (1991) introduced a theory of learning as social practice, where the focus is placed on the person 'as a person in the world' (p. 52). This participation metaphor locates knowledge and learning in the social context, thereby drawing attention to the location and context where learning takes place and focusing on complex social, interactive systems (Greeno et al., 1998), social entities (Salomon and Perkins, 1998) or communities of practice (Wenger, 1998). From a situated learning perspective, learning is not an isolated event that occurs in specific places and at specific times, and it cannot be captured and explored by unravelling the processes of mind (Lave and Wenger, 1991). Instead, learning is part of all human activities through the process whereby interactions with others occur and participation in a range of 'social practices' is enabled (Wenger, 1998). From a situated perspective, crucially, the context within which these 'social practices' and specific activities take place, the patterns of participation encouraged, and the individuals involved determine, to a great extent, what is learnt and how learning takes place (Greeno *et al.*, 1998). The adoption of a situated view of learning calls into question yet again, therefore, the value and effectiveness of traditional one-day, off-site, one-shot CPD activities.

As Tusting and Barton (2003) noted, all learning activities are underpinned by learning theories. Sometimes, however, these theories are implicit, unrecognised or contradictory. What this means is that teachers can be engaged in CPD activities that have little conceptual consistency. One example might be attempting to set up professional learning communities in an out-of-school CPD event in order to develop new knowledge, but then sending teachers back to their schools to develop that knowledge in isolation in their practice. An analysis at the level of underpinning learning theory can help to explain why teachers find CPD activities to be ineffective in meeting their specific learning needs. Such analysis might prove helpful to you as you embark upon CPD activities.

Q6

Summary

Conceptualising teaching as learning: the challenge for teacher education

The five assumptions around which this chapter is built are both interlinked and overlapping. They have been presented in a linear manner for textual clarity, but in reality the picture is much more complex. It has been argued that teaching is a profession therefore, by definition, physical education teachers must be active career-long learners in order to discharge their professional responsibility to their clients: children and young people. For this to happen, the different phases of teacher education should be viewed as a continuum, thus recognising that learning is an ongoing and embodied social process. It has also been argued that CPD should be based on what is known to be effective for teachers and pupils (which should be uncontroversial) and that mentoring, if structured appropriately, has the potential to become the cornerstone of continuous, collaborative and situated professional development. Underpinning all these aspirations is an urgent requirement to reflect critically on the learning theories – both implicit and explicit – that underpin the design and conduct of existing professional development structures and processes.

We have made the claim that one of the key factors restricting the capacity, scope and reach of professional development in teaching is the belief that teachers are just that – 'teachers' – and that viewing them (primarily) as learners leads to a deep conceptual shift in the ways in which professional training and development are understood. Indeed, it might be useful to conceptualise teachers as 'leading learners' and to reflect on the impact of this for CPD. In short, we have claimed that a key challenge for teacher education is to conceptualise teachers as learners – and teaching as learning – and to consider the implications for the design and conduct of teachers' career-long professional education.

Questions for reflection

Q1 What are your initial reactions to the suggestion that teachers should be conceptualised, *primarily*, as learners?

Q2 Consider what the notion of a 'profession' means to you and analyse why you hold these views.

Q3 From your experience to date, do you recognise the conceptualisation of teacher professional learning as a continuum?

Q4 Analyse the professional learning environment of a school with which you are familiar and map its key features against WestEd's (2000) six features of a professional learning culture.

Q5 What are the barriers to continuous, multi-directional professional peer mentoring in education generally and physical education specifically?

Q6 How would an understanding of learning as a process of 'becoming' alter the ways in which career-long teacher education should be structured?

Further reading

Armour, K.M. and Yelling, M.R. (2007) Effective professional development for physical education teachers: the role of informal, collaborative learning. *Journal of Teaching in Physical Education* 26(2): 177–200.

This paper reports data from the third phase of a two-year investigation into continuing professional development (CPD) for physical education teachers in England. It argues that the traditional relationship between teachers and CPD provision needs to be altered so that teachers become 'lead learners' from their professional learning communities or networks. (This paper was awarded the Metzler Freedman Exemplary Research Paper Award, AERA, New York, March, 2008.)

WestEd (2000) *Teachers Who Learn, Kids Who Achieve. A Look at Schools with Model Professional Development.* San Francisco: WestEd.

This reports findings from an unusual approach taken in the USA where case study schools were tasked with 'turning around' an aspect of their provision by improving teacher professional development. The findings are remarkable and the case reports are both interesting and accessible.

The following physical education journals should support further reading. There are also many Education journals which contain articles related to relevant topics across education more generally, which are useful to extend debate further. They may also contain physical education specific articles.

- *European Physical Education Review*
- *Journal of Teaching in Physical Education*
- *Quest*
- *Physical Education Matters*
- *Physical Education and Sport Pedagogy*
- *Sport, Education and Society.*

Chapter 14

What is the future for physical education in the twenty-first century?

David Kirk

Introduction

Futures studies have become a serious business in a range of fields but have occupied the thinking of only a few researchers in physical education (e.g. Massengale, 1987; Penney and Chandler, 2000; Laker, 2003). This relative lack of interest is somewhat paradoxical given, on the one hand, the colourful and dramatic history of the field in schools and colleges (Fletcher, 1984; Kirk, 1992) and, on the other, rapid development in physical culture, including the commercialisation, commodification and technologisation of sport, exercise and active leisure (Kirk, 1999). This lack of curiosity about the future has not been helped by developments in the academic field of sport-related studies (in which physical education is located) where the study of history, where it exists at all at undergraduate level, is dominated by sport rather than physical education. Arguably, physical educators lack a perspective on their field; they are, effectively, trapped in the present tense.

One of the symptoms of being trapped in the present tense is the tendency to be astonished by what appear to be unprecedented developments. Who could have predicted that the rapid academicisation of physical education teacher education would result in a loss of physical activity subject matter knowledge? Or that, in England, the government would spend in just over a decade around £2 billion on physical education and school sport? Or that obesity levels among children and young people would allegedly rise even though we now have degree-qualified physical education teachers in schools more or less worldwide? Or that the development of community-based sport for children under 12, supported by poorly trained volunteer coaches, would undermine the role of physical education teachers in secondary schools? Or that by 2014 four-year physical education initial teacher education (PE ITE) programmes in the UK would have been replaced completely by one-year postgraduate certificates?

Q1

As one small contribution to counteracting this tendency towards being trapped in the present tense, this chapter considers whether and to what extent physical education might be considered fit for purpose in the twenty-first century. I begin by asking whether physical education has a future in the twenty-first century and attempt to define what we might mean by 'the future'. I then consider the relevance of today's physical education for the twenty-first century, and in particular focus on the physical cultural legitimacy of the currently dominant form of physical education. Building on a critique of this dominant version of physical education, I propose a possible middle- to longer-term future that is based on pedagogical models. This futuristic models-based proposal is supplemented by a brief discussion of the need for pupil-centred physical education that facilitates the development of young people's perceived physical competence and their motivation for engagement in physical activities. The chapter ends with a comment on the extent to which physical education teachers might be able and willing to participate in the radical reform of the subject in order to ensure medium- to longer-term futures, and some of the challenges that must also be met for the renovation of physical education to proceed.

Physical education futures: some scenarios

Does physical education have a future? Before we can begin to form a response to this question, we need to decide the period of time we will count as 'the future'. On the one hand, such has been the rate at which 'innovations' have come and gone in physical education during the last decade of Physical Education, School Sport and Club Links (PESSCL) and then Physical Education, School Sport and Young People (PESSYP) in England, for example, it is tempting to frame the future in terms of months rather than years. This timeframe is somewhat limiting, however if we wish to gain some perspective on and analytical distance from the present. On the other hand, if we frame the future as much longer then 20 years, the speed of technological innovation and the effects of forces as varied as climate change, the economy, the greying population, technology, bioscience and the so-called obesity crisis, to name just a few, we risk attempting to talk about a world that could be quite different from the present day.

With these considerations in mind, it might be more acceptable to think in terms of short-, middle- and longer-term futures, with the short term over the next three to five years, the longer term around 20 years, and the middle term somewhere in between. Working with these timeframes, we can perhaps provide some reasonably well-grounded responses to the question 'Does physical education have a future?'

If the form of physical education that currently dominates practice (to be discussed next) in many countries around the world remains as it is, my response is that physical education most certainly does have a future in the short term. With recognition of the importance of physical education to a wide-ranging agenda of social 'goods' such as citizenship, health enhancement and obesity reduction, and growing the pool of talented sports people, there should be little to no possibility of physical education's place in the school curriculum being at risk.

In the middle term, however, as increasing scrutiny of and accountability for the use of scarce public resources begin to provide genuine evidence of physical education's current deficiencies, the possibility of a radically different but (for physical educators) unacceptable future may become more likely. Hoffman's (1987) brilliant satire of a commercialised and commodified future for physical education, in which only those who can afford to pay-to-play receive physical education and the rest are merely supervised in unstructured activity time, may be the most likely middle-term scenario. While Hoffman's 'impossible dream' was not realised within his own timeframe, Tinning's (1992; 2001) successive follow-ups showed that we could well be on our way to this kind of middle-term future.

If this middle-term future is a strong possibility, then the longer-term future indeed looks bleak, at least for the survival of physical education as it is currently understood. But then, when we begin to explore the form of physical education that dominates school practice today and its relevance to the twenty-first century, we might agree that this longer-term future, in which physical education as we know it no longer exists, may be no bad thing.

The relevance of today's physical education to the twenty-first century

We could respond to this issue with the remark that, far from being relevant to the twenty-first century, today's physical education has been scarcely relevant for at least the last 30 years of the twentieth century. Between the 1920s and the 1950s there was a seismic shift in physical education as it was transformed from a gymnastics-based field of practice to a sports-based field. Due to a complex interplay of forces, ranging from the school timetable and the subject-centred academic curriculum to the sheer number and diversity of physical activities that make up contemporary physical education programmes, a sports-based, multi-activity form of the field emerged.

In terms of the day-to-day practice of this form of physical education, we might more accurately speak about physical education-as-sport-techniques. This is because the mainstay of the standard length lesson and short units of work is the teaching and learning of the techniques of a wide range of sports. The term 'technique', rather than 'skill', is appropriate to describe this form of physical education since it is the decontextualised movements of, for example, passing, dribbling and shooting, rather than their appropriate, thoughtful application in games and sports, that form the basic stuff of lessons. And since teachers typically work with relatively large groups of 20 or more pupils, within relatively short lessons, and since they are rightly ever-mindful of safety, a directive, command style of teaching predominates. Within this context, all of the research evidence shows that learning progression seldom occurs (e.g. Lounsbery and Coker, 2008), and so introductory units of work tend to be taught over and over again (Siedentop, 2002a).

This is the dominant form of physical education in schools currently and has been more or less since the 1960s in the UK, and is widespread in many other countries around the world (Puhse and Gerber, 2005). Despite the serious limitations of the subject suggested in the preceding paragraphs, physical educators have consistently argued that physical education can provide children and young people with a range of physical, cognitive, affective, social and health benefits (Bailey *et al.*, 2009). Moreover, preparation for lifelong physical activity is viewed as the subject's *raison d'être*. Indeed, physical educators have continued to state this aspiration despite evidence to the contrary, from over 50 years of surveys of the physical activity habits of the adult population, that only a small number are physically active and a much smaller minority continue to play the games and sports that they experienced at school (Kirk, 2002a).

This sport-technique-based form of physical education has been spectacularly resistant to change. For instance, the notion of 'teaching games for understanding' (TGfU), first developed in the 1980s by Bunker and Thorpe (1982), is still regarded in many school physical education programmes as an innovative idea, some 30 years later. Indeed, this resistance to change is not due to a shortage of good ideas such as TGfU (Oslin and Mitchell, 2006). There has in fact been a proliferation of genuinely innovative forms of practice, including sport education (Siedentop, 1994; Hastie, 2011), play practice (Launder, 2001), physical literacy (Whitehead, 2010a), personal and social responsibility (Hellison and Martinek, 2006), and health-based physical education (Haerens *et al.*, 2011). In the UK, the expenditure of over £2 billion of public money on the PESSCL and PESSYP programmes has arguably done little to impact this dominant form of physical education. In the UK and elsewhere, there has been serious and sustained criticism of physical education-as-sport techniques with arguably little result in terms of radical change (e.g. Hoffman, 1987; Locke, 1992; O'Sullivan *et al.*, 1994; Almond, 1997; Penney and Chandler, 2000; Lawson, 2009).

Physical culture and cultural legitimacy

One way to think about the relevance of the form of school physical education for the twenty-first century is to consider some of the changes that have occurred within the broader physical culture of society since the 1950s which legitimate (Williams, 1985) physical education's place in the curriculum. The field of sport, for example, has become increasingly professionalised, commercialised and commodified. In the 1950s, there were few professional sports, and amateurism retained a stranglehold on sport from beginner to elite levels. Sports that were professional, such as football (soccer), rugby league and boxing, were the reserve mainly of men of the working classes who were not generously remunerated. Nowadays, in contrast, sport is a big money business, generating billions of pounds of profits for owners, investors and some sportsmen and women. Some sports have changed their rules and formats to suit the televisual media, including cricket, rugby union and field hockey. Billions of pounds more are generated from sports merchandise, including replica sportswear and other paraphernalia.

Despite these radical and far-reaching changes to sport and other forms of physical culture such as exercise and active leisure, school physical education is practised in much the same way as it was in the 1950s. So while the physical cultural forms that provide physical education with much of its public legitimacy have altered in tandem with technological advances such as television, the internet, and digitisation, the dominant practice in schools is the teaching and learning of introductory-level sports techniques. In this respect we might argue that this form of physical education is now and has been for some time culturally obsolete. The forms of physical culture that gave physical education-as-sport techniques its cultural legitimacy in the 1950s and 1960s, such as amateurism, have now disappeared.

On the basis of this argument we might reasonably ask what might be done to address this problem. Such a question becomes even more pressing when we acknowledge that public expectations for physical education have actually increased, rather than decreased. Advocates for physical education have been successful in persuading a once sceptical public, including governments, that physical education can make a meaningful contribution to a range of urgent social issues such as health, citizenship and elite sport. Could any of the good ideas mentioned earlier provide a means of responding to this conundrum of cultural obsolescence and raised expectations to achieve a range of important outcomes?

The role of pedagogical models in the future of physical education

The notion of pedagogical models builds on the ground-breaking work of Jewett *et al.* (1995) on curriculum models and Metzler (2005) on instructional models. Both authors argue for an approach to physical education that is 'models-based' (Lund and Tannehill, 2005), in which the curriculum or subject matter (physical activity experiences) and teaching strategies are brought into alignment with distinctive learning outcomes to create a design specification for the creation of school- and district-level programmes.

The term pedagogical model is preferred to 'curriculum' or 'instructional' model since these latter two use only one of the three aspects of pedagogy to describe the entire model. The term 'pedagogical', however, includes all three aspects of learning, curriculum (subject matter) and instruction (teaching strategies). Other pedagogical models include some of the 'good ideas' listed earlier

such as teaching games for understanding, play practice and health-based physical education (HBPE). In each case, a set of unique learning outcomes is identified and aligned with appropriate subject matter and teaching strategies to
form the basis of programmes at local levels. This is the basic idea behind the
notion of pedagogical models.

A good example of a pedagogical model is sport education, developed by
Daryl Siedentop (1994) and his colleagues during the 1980s and early 1990s.
The learning outcomes for sport education are the development of competent,
literate and enthusiastic sportspersons. In order to achieve these learning outcomes, Siedentop argued that the subject matter of sport education is sport,
which includes the key features of seasons, record-keeping, festivity, a culmi-
nating event, persisting groups, and roles in addition to player such as captain,
umpire, scorekeeper, equipment officer and so on. Teacher strategies included
directive teaching when appropriate, but also more pupil-centred strategies
such peer and reciprocal teaching and problem-solving. Metzler (2005)
developed a series of teacher and pupil benchmarks which can be used to
ensure programmes designed for specific locales such as individual schools or
community sports clubs remain consistent with the key features of the sport
education model.

A problem with the multi-activity, sport-technique-based ('one size fits all')
approach to physical education is that a wide range of cognitive, affective,
health, social and motor skill learning outcomes are pursued using the same
programmes, typically involving short units of work focused on techniques and
utilising predominantly a directive teaching strategy. Since the 1950s, we have
traditionally sought to achieve a range of arguably incompatible learning outcomes all through this same approach (Siedentop, 2002b).

In contrast, a models-based approach seeks to retain this range of legitimate learning outcomes for physical education but to align relevant subject
matter and teaching strategies with each set of learning outcomes to create a
package or a model for programme design. So instead of attempting to achieve
health-related learning outcomes through a multi-activity, sport-technique-
based form of physical education, we would bring together the subject matter
and teaching strategies best suited to facilitate the achievement of these outcomes. Rather than leave health outcomes as a hoped-for by-product of a
sport-based programme, we would seek to align subject matter and teaching
strategies that aim specifically and explicitly to achieve health-related learning
outcomes.

A models-based form of physical education might feature a school term of
physical literacy, for example, followed by a term of play practice, then a term of
sport education followed by a term of HBPE or personal and social responsibility. Each model provides a design specification for local versions of physical
education programmes that can cater for the specific needs, interests and circumstances of pupils and teachers, schools and communities. So long as the
local versions of physical education are consistent with the teacher and pupil

benchmarks for each model, we can be sure that pupils are being given opportunities to achieve worthwhile learning outcomes.

A models-based approach could offer middle- to long-term futures for physical education. There are two main reasons why. First, a models-based approach provides a means for physical education to pursue the wide range of legitimate physical, cognitive and social goals that its proponents have claimed for it for many years (Bailey *et al.*, 2009). Second, by aligning learning outcomes with relevant subject matter and teaching strategies, there is a strong chance that these learning outcomes might be achieved by a majority, if not all, pupils. In this respect, a critical mass of research on pedagogical models such as sport education (Hastie, 2011) and TGfU (Harvey *et al.*, 2010) has already produced promising results.

Q2

While pedagogical models that align learning outcomes, subject matter and teaching strategies might provide the possibility of middle- to long-term futures for physical education, this renovation in itself may not be enough to ensure a future for the field.

A focus for change: engaging pupils in physical education

Some physical educators have in the past attempted to establish pupil-centred forms of physical education, but without any profound or lasting success. Their relative failure is an indication of the power of the teacher-centred multi-activity, sport-technique-based form of physical education to resist change. But there can be no doubt, as we understand more and more about the social psychology of learning, that the ways in which we seek to engage pupils in physical education are at least as important as, and some would argue more important than, the design of pedagogical models.

There are two key concepts that must guide any efforts to change physical education to meet the challenges of the early to mid-twenty-first century: perceived competence and motivation. The phenomena they name are closely linked. Goudas and Biddle (1994) found that perceived competence explained over 60 per cent of variance in internal motivation. While actual competence forms the basis for young people's perceptions from age nine onwards (Nichols, 1989), based both on past experience and others' judgements, young people's perceptions of what they can and cannot do play a critical mediating role in both the level and the quality of their engagement in physical activity.

Motivation is probably the most studied psychological concept in the physical education literature (Lirgg, 2006). There are a range of 'mini-theories' of motivation, each stressing slightly different aspects, the emphasis often formed by the tools psychologists use to measure motivation. Irrespective of the theories we might consult, in summary terms a shared conclusion of research is that pupils are more likely to persist in learning when their motivation to do so derives from an internal rather than an external source. In other words, if the source of motivation to learn is either anticipation of reward or fear of punishment, learning is less likely to be sustained and so is less likely to be effective. In contrast, if the source of motivation is internal, particularly if it involves participation in physical activities for their own sake or, as one philosopher expresses it, for the 'goods' internal to the activity itself (MacIntyre, 1985), learning is likely to be sustained.

If the psychologists are correct, and it would seem there is growing evidence that they are, then we must consider the pedagogical implications for physical education. It would seem that the traditional approach has not been entirely successful in facilitating internal motivation among generations of pupils of physical education and, indeed, may have had the opposite effect (Tinning, 2010). One theory suggests that in order to promote internal motivation, young people must be able to fulfil their need for autonomy. In other words, they must feel that they have a genuine say in the form of physical education they experience, that they have real choices that reflect their individual preferences (Shen *et al.*, 2007).

Sport education provides a good example of the kinds of practices that might fulfil this need (Pearlman and Goc Karp, 2010). By providing pupils with opportunities to take on roles in addition to player, sport education engages them in practising skills such as teamwork, conflict resolution and negotiation. Some practices, such as the formation of a student sports council for the sport education season, engage pupils in authentic decision-making on behalf of their team and their competition, with appropriate levels of responsibility and accountability facilitating the development of active citizenship (O'Donovan *et al.*, 2010).

Just how these two concepts of perceived competence and motivation might be applied will depend to a large extent on the form physical education might take. Clearly, on the basis of the discussion so far in this chapter, it might be argued that the teacher-centred, multi-activity, sport-technique-based form of physical education cannot easily facilitate the development of these key psychological characteristics in young people. Some pedagogical models, such as sport education for example, which are explicitly designed for inclusiveness, to reward particular kinds of behaviour, and to offer opportunities for choice and responsibility, might prove more likely to foster perceived competence and motivation. An already substantial and still growing literature suggests that genuinely pupil-centred approaches promoting perceived competence and motivation are vital to the future prosperity of physical education.

Q3

The role of physical education teachers in the radical renovation of physical education

Physical education teachers in post at the end of the first decade of the twenty-first century are heir to a struggle for recognition and status by their predecessors throughout most of the previous century (Kirk, 1992). Recognition of the subject as a core curriculum topic in schools and a very popular examination-based subject in senior secondary schools where this option is available, a profession of degree-qualified teachers, opportunities to undertake postgraduate studies, parity of remuneration with teachers of other school subjects, and a thriving research field in the university sector all represent major achievements of physical educators over this period. In this context, of apparent success, why would physical education teachers as a professional group choose to radically reform their subject? Indeed, the fact that it is widely understood that there is little agreement about the nature and purposes of physical education (Green, 2008), even though there has been genuine progress, might suggest it would be risky to do anything more than defend the status quo.

Even though physical education teachers clearly understand that motivation and perceived competence (or in their terms 'enjoyment' and 'self-confidence', Green, 2000a) are of central importance to physical education, and even though they might recognise that the currently dominant form of the field does not deliver the benefits it aspires to, there may nevertheless be little taste for radical reform. When we appreciate just *how* radical reform would have to be to bring about genuine change for the future survival of physical education, we can begin to better understand teachers' reluctance to jeopardise their achievements to date.

Reform is not simply a matter of teachers agreeing to take a models-based approach to physical education. We would also require reform of what Lawson (2009) has described as the 'Industrial-Age school', with its attendant lack of organic connection with many young people's everyday lives. At secondary school level, where most specialist physical education teachers practise, physical education is shoehorned into a timetable 'just like any other subject', even when this arrangement clearly does not suit the requirements of many of the physical activities that constitute programmes. We would also require the reform of PE ITE. It is clear that we have achieved universal degree-level qualifications to teach physical education at the expense of our knowledge of the core subject matter of our field, which is physical activity, or as Siedentop (2002a) puts it rather more precisely, sport. The challenge here would be to develop what Shulman (1987) describes as teachers' content knowledge alongside their pedagogical content knowledge and still maintain 'degree-worthiness' of PE ITE programmes.

As if reform of the Industrial Age school and PE ITE programmes were not enough, the radical reform of physical education would also need to account for a range of other challenging developments. For example, in the past 20 to 30 years it has become commonplace for children in many economically advanced countries to have their first experiences of sport in a community rather than a school context. Children as young as five or six can be found playing a range of sports in community clubs, often taught by volunteer coaches who have little or no professional education as sports teachers or coaches. Meanwhile, the majority of specialist teachers of physical education do not meet these children until they enter secondary schools around ages 11 or 12. As I have argued elsewhere (Kirk, 2005), while this arrangement might have made some sense prior to the 1980s when opportunities to play sport in the community were rare for the majority of children, it now represents an untenable misdirection of valuable resource. There is strong evidence from a variety of sources to suggest that physical education specialists need to be working in both primary schools and secondary schools. If, however, there is resource available for teachers to work in only one of these sites, then I would strongly vote in favour of the primary school option. This is because by the time most children reach secondary schools their perceived competence and motivation, and hence their likely engagement in physical activity, have already been formed and there is little that physical educators can do to change these dispositions.

Q4

Teachers have some very difficult decisions to make about physical education's future. On the one hand, in order to support radical reform of their subject, they could put at risk the substantial achievements of the past 50 to 100 years. On the other hand, if they do not support radical reform, the middle- to longer-term future of the field looks bleak, at least in relation to many of the achievements listed earlier. To make matters even more difficult, the short-term future looks very favourable, as physical education enjoys the confidence of politicians and policy-makers, if not the public at large (see Chapter 6). It would be entirely reasonable for physical education teachers to ask complacently, 'Crisis? What crisis?'

Informed opinion within the research community, however, is that the current dominant form of the subject makes more enemies than friends of children, does not progress their learning and thus fails to develop their perceived competence and motivation for physical activity, and ultimately fails to achieve the ubiquitous aspiration, common to programmes around the world, of a long-term active lifestyle. How long can this state of affairs continue before this truth about physical education in its current form, that it is in Locke's (1992) colourful prose a 'programmatic lemon', is finally out?

Q5

Summary

Chapter 14 offers a possible antidote to being trapped in the present tense and draws on an analysis of the present and the past in order to consider the extent to which physical education in its current form may be fit for the twenty-first century. The author argues that in order to secure middle- to longer-term futures for some form of physical education in schools, a radical reform is needed. A models-based approach to physical education that is pupil-centred, inclusive and motivating is proposed as key to securing a future for the subject. It is concluded that teachers have some difficult decisions to make in terms of risking hard-won achievements for their subject by engaging in radical reform, while failure to reform may lead to demise in the longer term.

Questions for consideration

Q1 What does it mean to say that physical educators are trapped in the present tense?

Q2 What forms of physical education might more accurately reflect and be legitimised by developments in the wider physical culture of society?

Q3 How can physical education best facilitate the development of physical competence, perceived competence and motivation?

Q4 What are the arguments for and against specialist physical education teachers in the primary school?

Q5 What should teachers' role be in the radical reform of their subject?

Further reading

Bailey, R., Armour, K., Kirk, D., Jess, M., Pickup, I. and Sandford, R. (2009) The educational benefits claimed for physical education and school sport: an academic review. *Research Papers in Education* 24(1): 1–27.

This review critically examines the theoretical and empirical bases of claims made for the educational benefits of physical education and school sport (PESS). It concludes that many of the educational benefits claimed for PESS are highly dependent on contextual and pedagogic variables, which leads the authors to question any simple equations of participation and beneficial outcomes for young people.

Fernandez-Balboa, J.-M. (2003) Physical education in the digital (postmodern) era, in A. Laker (ed.), *The Future of Physical Education: Building a New Pedagogy*. London: Routledge, pp. 137–52.

Fernandez-Balboa frames physical education's future within Toffler's three waves of civilisation. He predicts physical education will be delivered remotely in a digital age, university study of sport will be undertaken from the comfort of the student's living-room with an increasing privatisation of educational programmes in which the profit motive dominates.

Hoffman, S.J. (1987) Dreaming the impossible dream: the decline and fall of physical education, in J.A. Massengale (ed.), *Trends Toward the Future in Physical Education*, Champaign, IL: Human Kinetics, pp. 121–35.

Hoffman's future involves the commercialisation of provision in which parents who could afford to pay for their children's participation, while others who couldn't went without. Only a few of the physical education teachers made redundant were re-employed since pupils chose their teacher, and teachers were paid only if they were in demand. He tells a satirical tale of grim decline and fall.

Kirk, D. (2010) *Physical Education Futures*. London: Routledge.

Kirk draws on extensive historical analysis to consider three future scenarios for physical education, 'more of the same', 'radical reform' and 'extinction'. He argues that the future survival of physical education depends on the field's alignment with four relational issues of physical culture, transfer of learning, excellence and ability, and cultural reproduction and renewal.

Penney, D. and Chandler, T. (2000) Physical education: what future(s)? *Sport, Education and Society* 5: 71–87.

The authors' concern is to connect with and impact on social issues by considering future physical education as a 'connective specialism'. Their vision is shaped by questions about the type of citizen physical education can nurture, and how the subject can become more connected across its own subject matter, across the school curriculum, and to society beyond the school.

The following physical education journals should support further reading. There are also many education journals which contain articles related to relevant topics across education more generally, which are useful to extend debate further. They may also contain physical education specific articles.

- *European Physical Education Review*
- *Journal of Teaching in Physical Education*
- *Quest*
- *Physical Education Matters*
- *Physical Education and Sport Pedagogy*
- *Sport, Education and Society.*

Conclusion

Chapter 15

Conclusions

Drawing the threads together

Margaret Whitehead and Susan Capel

Throughout the book you have been challenged to consider a range of issues relating to physical education. The questions at the end of each chapter have been designed to facilitate debate on the issues highlighted in that particular chapter. There have, however, been a number of recurring themes throughout the book and it is useful to conclude with the identification of some key areas of debate that warrant serious consideration. We **highlight** these below and post more questions designed to support you in considering the need to address issues together rather than in isolation in order to support your development and enhance pupils' learning in physical education. These questions should be considered alongside those in the individual chapters.

For us, it is important that you are clear about what you are trying to achieve as we believe this should inform all decisions in relation to teaching and learning. Discussion and proposals concerning **the aims of physical education** and therefore what should be learnt in physical education were addressed in a variety of ways in Part I 'The nature of physical education' and Part II 'Learning in physical education'.

A key issue to consider here is what your views are concerning the aims, objectives and intended learning outcomes of physical education in schools in the twenty-first century.

For example how important is a focus on developing lifelong commitment to participation in physical activity? To what degree should the subject be designed to promote health-related fitness? Is it the responsibility of the profession to develop world-class athletes? This leads to consideration of how these views manifest themselves in teachers' thinking about, and practice of, physical education. It is useful to consider, too, how you have come to hold these views and how far your own experiences and the views of significant others, for example, parents, teachers and peers, have influenced your thinking.

These deliberations relate closely to identifying what physical education is for you, in other words articulating your own values, beliefs, attitudes and philosophies concerning physical education. Significant here is how far you feel you can justify physical education as an end in itself rather than a means to other ends. Do you support the notion of nurturing physical literacy as the prime goal for the subject? How do you interpret the 'education' in physical education and what approach would you take to argue for the place of physical education in the curriculum?

In a good many chapters you have been challenged to reflect on the **strengths and weaknesses of current practice of physical education** in school and the ways in which perceived weaknesses might be remedied (see, for example, Chapters 3, 4, 6, 7, 8, 11, 14).

In respect of this area you have been asked to consider issues concerned with what, how and who, in relation to learning and teaching in physical education. Where do you stand in relation to the content covered in curriculum time? What are your views on the number of activities taught, and whether they are taught for too short a time for learners to make real progress? Do you agree that it is not in the interests of many learners to spend a high proportion of the time playing competitive team games? What are your views on the best ways to use extra-curricular time?

In relation to your views on the overall aims of the subject and on what should be taught, there is the issue of how success is measured and, hence, how the issue of assessment is to be resolved. How far do you feel that norm-referenced assessment is appropriate and how far would you support much more ipsative assessment with individual profiles to chart the progress of each learner?

With reference to how the subject is taught, you might consider whether the prevailing pedagogy of the subject is appropriate to learners in the twenty-first century? Is the subject delivered in an overly didactic way? Should there be a difference in how the teaching is conducted in curriculum time and extra-curricular time? Should learners be given far more responsibility for their own learning, thus developing independence? How far does your philosophy of physical education match the teaching approaches you employ?

Significant in these deliberations is who should teach physical education in the curriculum and in extra-curricular time. Who is best placed to initiate learners into a lifelong commitment to participation in physical activity? Is there a place for coaches to make a contribution? If coaches are involved in what ways can you ensure that their expertise is used appropriately and to best advantage?

Throughout the book there has been a recurring theme relating to the way that **our history stalks the subject** – not necessarily to our advantage (see, for example, Chapters 1, 7, 12, 14). This view is seen alongside the apparent problem of resistance to change exhibited throughout the profession (see, for example, Chapters 6, 7, 10, 11).

It is valuable to consider if you agree that the subject, in respect of both content and method, has changed very little over the last 30 years, despite the advent in England of the National Curriculum for Physical Education (NCPE) and the rapidly changing culture in this country. Do you agree that the physical education curriculum could be described as sports-technique focused, with competitive team games having the lion's share of curricular and extra-curricular time? Would it be true to say that we are more concerned with the most able learners? Are either of these situations in the *long-term* interests of the subject as taught in schools?

You might think carefully about why change has been so difficult to effect; whether physical education teachers are resistant to change, and if so why might this be. Are there peculiar and particular barriers to change encountered by the profession? Has our history so firmly embedded expectations of the subject in education and beyond that we feel change will not be accepted? Have we missed significant opportunities to remodel our work, in relation perhaps to the unique contribution of our subject to the holistic education of pupils and the use of ICT, new physical activities or new learner interests?

You might consider if change is, in fact, in our hands and whether others are, in part, responsible for our inertia. Who are the key stakeholders who we need to work with to make change more readily achievable and/or to make radical changes in our practices? Have the media and public opinion generally been influential in our inability to change? Does the profession need to 'educate' the public and change their perceptions of and attitudes towards the subject? If so, how might we go about doing that?

It would be salutary to consider if you have, yourself, been involved in and/ or party to significant changes in physical education as a school learner, a student teacher or a teacher. Have you, personally, realigned your philosophy of physical education and modified your practices in line with these new perspectives?

In many of the chapters, and particularly in Part V, you have been confronted with challenges about how the profession and the subject might develop to ensure **the long-term high status and effectiveness of physical education** (see Chapters 7, 8, 9, 10, 11, 13, 14). In other words you have been confronted with questions about ways to effect change. What knowledge do physical education teachers need to teach physical education in the twenty-first century? Significant here is to create a profession of reflective, learning physical education teachers to take the subject forward into the next 20 years and beyond. It is suggested that physical education teachers must be reflective practitioners, readily reassessing their views and practice, and willing to make changes in all aspects of their work. Is this type of open-minded and flexible attitude essential for the continued acceptability of the subject?

While there is agreement that we need to look hard at ourselves in the interests of the long-term future of the subject, you might consider what knowledge and understanding both physical education initial teacher education (PE ITE) and continuing professional development (CPD) currently cover, and how content, design and delivery could be modified to support physical education for the twenty-first-century context and other long-term outcomes.

In addition, what are your views on ways that PE ITE and CPD can assist teachers in becoming reflective practitioners? Do the particular philosophies and characteristics with which student teachers enter PE ITE significantly affect the process of becoming reflective practitioners?

You also need to consider what physical education professionals need to do, both individually and collectively, to achieve change. How can PE ITE and CPD help teachers to be more alert and responsive to changes in respect of both learners' needs and cultural attitudes? What should be the aims, objectives and intended learning outcomes of physical education in schools to ensure the subject thrives in the future? How can teachers be empowered with the confidence and commitment to effect radical change in respect of aims, content, curricular organisation and teaching method?

You are challenged to consider if physical education has a future – in its current form or in a new configuration. You are also encouraged to clarify what that future might be and what you need to do to enhance the learning of your pupils in physical education in the twenty-first century.

The authors wish you fulfilment, satisfaction and success in your physical education teaching careers. The future of the profession is in your hands.

References

Abraham, A. and Collins, D. (1998) Examining and extending research in coach development. *Quest* 50: 59–79.

ACSM (American College of Sports Medicine) (2000) Exercise testing and prescription for children, the elderly and pregnant women, in *ACSM's Guidelines for Exercise Testing and Prescription*, 6th edn. New York: Lippincott Williams and Wilkins, pp. 217–34.

afPE (Association for Physical Education) (2008) Health position paper, www.afpe.org.uk/public/downloads/Health_Paper Sept08.pdf

afPE (Association for Physical Education) (2009) www.afpe.org.uk/advocacy-a-leadership (accessed 21 January 2012).

AGQTP (Australian Government Quality Teacher Programme) (2008) *Innovative and Effective Professional Learning*, Canberra: Department of Education, Employment and Workplace Relations.

Alfrey, L., Cale, L. and Webb, L.A. (2012) Physical education teachers' continuing professional development in health-related exercise. *Physical Education and Sport Pedagogy*, DOI: 10 1080/17408989.2011.594429.

Alleyne, R. (2009) Diet, not exercise, is best way to tackle childhood obesity, *Daily Telegraph*, 7 May.

Almond, L. (ed.) (1997) *Physical Education in Schools*, 2nd edn. London: Kogan Page.

Almond, L. and Harris, J. (1997) Does health related exercise deserve a hammering or help? *British Journal of Physical Education* 28(2): 25–7.

Anderson, D.S. (1987) The professional socialisation of school teachers, in P. Hughes (ed.), *Better Teachers for Better Schools*. Carlton, Victoria: Australian College of Education, pp. 45–65.

Andrews, J.G. (1970/71) The curricular aims of physical education, in *ATCDE, Conference Reports on the Philosophy of Physical Education 1970 and 1971*, London: ATCDE, pp. 17–31.

Argyris, C. and Schon, D. (1974) *Theory into Practice: Increasing Professional Effectiveness*. San Francisco: Jossey Bass.

Armour, K.M. (2006) Physical education teachers as career-long learners: a compelling agenda. *Physical Education and Sport Pedagogy* 11(3): 203–7.

Armour, K.M. (2008) The physical education profession and its professional responsibility (or … why '12 weeks paid holiday' will never be enough). Scholar Lecture at the SIG meeting in the British Educational Research Association Annual Conference, September.

Armour, K.M. and Harris, J. (2008) Great expectations … and much ado about nothing?

Physical education and its role in public health in England. Paper presented at the American Educational Research Association (AERA) Annual Conference, New York, March 2009.

Armour, K.M. and Makopoulou, K. (2008) *Independent Evaluation of the National PE-CPD Programme*, Final report. Loughborough, UK: Loughborough University.

Armour, K.M. and Yelling, M. (2004a) Continuing professional development for experienced physical education teachers: towards effective provision. *Sport, Education and Society* 9(1): 95–114.

Armour, K.M. and Yelling, M. (2004b) Professional 'development' and professional 'learning': bridging the gap for experienced physical education teachers, *European Physical Education Review* 10(1): 71–93.

Armour, K.M. and Yelling, M.R. (2007) Effective professional development for physical education teachers: the role of informal, collaborative learning. *Journal of Teaching in Physical Education* 26(2): 177–200.

Armour, K.M., Makopoulou, K. and Chambers, F. (2008) Progression in PE teachers' career-long professional learning: practical and conceptual concerns. Paper presented at the Annual Meeting of the American Educational Research Association, New York, April.

Arnold, P.J. (1979) *Meaning in Movement, Sport and Physical Education*. London: Heinemann.

ASK (Advisory Service Kent) (2007) *Assessing to Learn, Learning to Assess: Removing the Barriers to Achievement in Physical Education*. Maidstone: Kent County Council.

Attard, K. and Armour, K.M. (2006) Reflecting on reflection: a case study of one teacher's early-career professional learning, *Physical Education and Sport Pedagogy* 11(3): 209–30.

Ayers, W. (1993) *To Teach: The Journey of a Teacher*. New York: Teachers College Press.

Azzarito, L. (2007) 'Shape up America!': Understanding fatness as a curriculum project. *Journal of the American Association for the Advancement of Curriculum Studies* 3: 1–25. Available at www2.uwstout.edu/content/jaaacs/vol3/azzarito.htm (accessed 13 March 2011)

Azzarito, L. and Solomon, M.A. (2005) A reconceptualization of physical education: the intersection of gender/race/social class. *Sport, Education and Society* 10(1): 25–47.

Baalpe (British Association of Advisers and Lecturers in Physical Education) (2005) *Workforce Reform: Essential Safe Practice in Physical Education and School Sport*. Leeds: Coachwise Business Solutions.

Bailey, R., Armour, K., Kirk, D., Jess, M., Pickup, I. and Sandford, R. (2009) The educational benefits claimed for physical education and school sport: an academic review. *Research Papers in Education* 24(1): 1–27.

Bailey, S. and Vamplew, W. (1999) *100 Years of Physical Education 1899–1999*. London: Physical Education Association of the United Kingdom.

Ball, S.J. (1990) *Politics and Policy Making in Education: Explorations in Policy Sociology*. London: Routledge.

Barber, M. and Mourshed, M. (2007) *How the World's Best-performing School Systems Come Out on Top*. London: McKinsey and Company.

Barlow, S.E. and the Expert Committee (2007) Expert Committee recommendations regarding the prevention, assessment and treatment of child and adolescent overweight and obesity: summary report. *Pediatrics* 120: S164–S192.

Barnett, R. (1997) *Higher Education: A Critical Business*. Buckingham: Open University Press.

Barton, L. (1993) Disability, empowerment and physical education, in J. Evans (ed.), *Equality, Education and Physical Education*. London: The Falmer Press, pp. 43–54.

Barton, L. (2009) Disability, physical education and sport: some critical observations and questions, in H. Fitzgerald (ed.), *Disability and Youth Sport*. London: Routledge, pp. 39–50

Battle, E.K. and Brownell, K.D. (1996) Confronting a rising tide of eating disorders and obesity: treatment vs. prevention and policy, *Addictive Behaviours* 21: 755–65.

Baxter Magolda, M. (1999) *Creating Contexts for Learning and Self Authorship*, San Francisco: Jossey Bass.

Beattie, M. (2000) Narratives of professional learning: becoming a teacher and learning to teach. *Journal of Educational Enquiry* 1(2): 1–22.

Bechtel, P.A. and O'Sullivan, M. (2006) Chapter 2: Effective professional development – what we now know. *Journal of Teaching in Physical Education* 25: 363–78.

Behets, D. (1996) Comparison of visual information processing between preservice students and experienced physical education teachers. *Journal of Teaching in Physical Education* 16(1): 79–87.

Behets, D. and Vergauwen, L. (2006) Learning to teaching in the field, in D. Kirk, D. Macdonald and M. O'Sullivan (eds), *Handbook of Physical Education*. London: Sage, pp. 407–24.

Benn, T., Dagkas, S. and Jawad, H. (2011) Embodied faith: Islam, religious freedom and educational practices in physical education. *Sport, Education and Society* 16(1): 17–34.

Bennett, N. (1976) *Teaching Styles and Pupil Progress*. London: Open Books.

BERA (British Educational Research Association) (2011) *Revised Ethical Guidelines for Ethical Research*. Southwell: BERA.

Beveridge, S.K. and Gangstead, S.K. (1988) Teaching experience and training in the sports skill analysis process. *Journal of Teaching in Physical Education* 7(2): 103–14.

Black, P. and Wiliam, D. (1998) *Assessment and Classroom Learning: Assessment in Education*. London: King's College School of Education.

Black, P., Harrison, C., Lee, C. and Marshall, B. (2003) *Assessment for Learning: Putting it into Practice*. Maidenhead: Open University Press.

Blair, R. and Capel, S. (2008) Intended or unintended? Issues arising from the implementation of the UK government 2003 Schools Workforce Remodelling Act, *Perspectives in Education* 26(2): 105–25.

Blair, R. and Capel, S. (2009) Coaching in schools. Unpublished report to the Football League Trust.

Blair, R. and Capel, S. (2011) Primary physical education, coaches and continuing professional development. *Sport, Education and Society* 16(4): 485–506.

Bolam, R. and Weindling, D. (2006) *Synthesis of Research and Evaluation Projects Concerned with Capacity-Building Through Teachers' Professional Development*. London: General Teaching Council for England.

Bolton, G. (2010) *Reflective Practice, Writing and Professional Development*, 3rd edn. Thousand Oaks, CA: Sage Publications.

Booth, M. (1993) The effectiveness and role of the mentor in school: the students' view, *Cambridge Journal of Education* 23(2): 185–97.

Borko, H. (2004) Professional development and teacher learning: mapping the terrain. *Educational Researcher* 33(8): 3–15.

Boud, D. and Miller, N. (1996) *Working with Experience: Animating Learning*. London: Routledge.

Boud, D., Keogh, R. and Walker, D. (eds) (1985) *Reflection: Turning Experience into Learning.* London: Kogan Page.

Bredeson, P.V. (2002) *Designs for Learning: A New Architecture for Professional Development in Schools.* Thousand Oaks, CA: Sage Publications.

Brookfield, S. (1995) *Developing Critical Thinkers: Challenging Adults to Explore Alternative Ways of Thinking and Acting.* San Francisco: Jossey Bass.

Brophy, J. (1979) Teacher behaviour and its effects. *Journal of Educational Psychology* 71: 733–50.

Brown, D. and Rich, E. (2002) Gender positioning as pedagogic practice in teaching physical education, in D. Penney (ed.), *Gender and Physical Education: Contemporary Issues and Future Directions.* London: Routledge, pp. 80–100.

Brown, J. (2011) An investigation into the impact of a sport intervention in three London secondary schools. Unpublished PhD thesis, Brunel University.

Bruner, J. (1966) *Towards a Theory of Instruction.* Cambridge, MA: Harvard University Press.

Bruner, J. (1996) *The Culture of Education.* Cambridge, MA: Harvard University Press.

Brunetti, G.J. (1998) Teacher education: a look at its future. *Teacher Education Quarterly* (Fall): 59–64.

Bucher, C.A. (1983) *Foundations of Physical Education and Sport,* 9th edn. St Louis, MO: C.V. Mosby Company.

Bunker, D. and Thorpe, R. (1982) A model for the teaching of games in the secondary school. *Bulletin of Physical Education* 10: 9–16.

Burgeson, C.R., Wechsler, H., Brener, N.D., Young, J.C. and Spain, C.G. (2001) Physical education and activity: results from the School Health Policies and Programs Study 2000. *Journal of School Health* 71: 279–93.

Burkitt, I. (1999) *Bodies of Thought: Embodiment, Identity and Modernity.* London: Sage.

Cale, L. (2000) Physical activity promotion in schools – PE teachers' views. *European Journal of Physical Education* 5: 158–68.

Cale, L. (2011) The promotion of healthy, active lifestyles through physical education: challenges and opportunities. Proceedings of the AIESEP Conference, La Coruña, Spain, October, 2010.

Cale, L. and Harris, J. (2005) (eds) *Exercise and Young People: Issues, Implications and Initiatives.* Basingstoke: Palgrave Macmillan.

Cale, L. and Harris, J. (2006) School based physical activity interventions: effectiveness, trends, issues, implications and recommendations for practice. *Sport, Education and Society* 11(4): 401–20.

Cale, L. and Harris, J. (2009a) *Getting the Buggers Fit: The Complete Guide to Physical Education.* London: Continuum.

Cale, L. and Harris, J. (2009b) Fitness testing in physical education: a misdirected effort in promoting healthy lifestyles and physical activity? *Physical Education and Sport Pedagogy* 14(1): 89–108.

Cale, L. and Harris, J. (2011a) Learning about health through physical education and youth sport, in K. Armour (ed.), *Sport Pedagogy: An Introduction for Teaching and Coaching,* Harlow: Prentice Hall, pp. 53–64.

Cale, L. and Harris, J. (2011b) Every child (of every size) matters in physical education! Physical education's role in childhood obesity, *Sport, Education and Society,* DOI: 10.1080/13573322.2011.601734.

Cale, L., Harris, J. and Chen, M.H. (2007) More than 10 years after 'the horse is dead…': surely it must be time to 'dismount'?! *Pediatric Exercise Science* 19(2): 115–31.

Capel, S. (2005) Teachers, teaching and pedagogy in physical education, in K. Green and K. Hardman (eds), *Physical Education Essential Issues*. London: Sage, pp. 111–27.

Capel, S. (2007) Moving beyond physical education subject knowledge to develop knowledgeable teachers of the subject. *Curriculum Journal* 18(4): 493–507.

Capel, S. (2010) Starting out as a PE teacher, in S. Capel and M. Whitehead (eds), *Learning to Teach Physical Education in the Secondary School: A Companion to School Experience*, 3rd edn. London: Routledge, pp. 1–12.

Capel, S. and Blair, R. (2007) Making physical education relevant: increasing the impact of initial teacher training. *London Review of Education* 51(1): 15–34.

Capel, S. and Whitehead, M. (eds) (2010) *Learning to Teach Physical Education in the Secondary School: A Companion to School Experience*, 3rd edn. London: Routledge.

Capel, S., Breckon, P. and O'Neill, J. (2006) *A Practical Guide to Teaching Physical Education in the Secondary School*. London: Routledge.

Cardon, G. and De Bourdeaudhuij, I. (2002) Physical education and physical activity in elementary schools in Flanders. *European Journal of Physical Education* 7(1): 5–18.

Carr, W. and Kemmis, S. (1986) *Becoming Critical: Education, Knowledge and Action Research*, Lewes: Falmer Press.

Carroll, B. and Loumidis, J. (2001) Children's perceived competence and enjoyment in physical education and physical activity outside of school. *European Physical Education Review* 7(1): 24–43.

Cassidy, T., Jones, R.L. and Potrac, P. (2009) *Understanding Sports Coaching: The Social, Cultural and Pedagogical Foundations of Coaching Practice*. London: Routledge.

Castelli, D. and Williams, L. (2007) Health-related fitness and physical education teachers' content knowledge. *Journal of Teaching in Physical Education* 26(1): 3–19.

Chambers, F.C., Armour, K., Bleakley, E.W., Brennan, D.A., Herold, F.A. and Luttrell, S. (2011) *Effective Mentoring in Physical Education Teacher Education*. Armagh: Standing Conference on Teacher Education North and South.

Chedzoy, S. (2000) Students' perceived confidence to teach physical education to children aged 7–11 years in England. *European Journal of Physical Education*, 5: 104–27.

Chen, A. and Rovegno, I. (2000) Examination of expert and novice teachers' constructivist-orientated teaching practices using a movement approach to elementary physical education. *Research Quarterly for Exercise and Sport* 71: 357–72.

Chen, M.H. (2010) Health, physical activity and fitness monitoring within the secondary physical education curriculum in England. Unpublished doctoral thesis, Loughborough University.

Clarke, G. (2002) Difference matters: sexuality and physical education, in D. Penney (ed.), *Gender and Physical Education: Contemporary Issues and Future Directions*. London: Routledge, pp. 41–56.

Clarke, S. (2005) *Formative Assessment in the Secondary Classroom*. London: Hodder Murray.

Claxton, G. (1984) *Live and Learn*. London: Harper and Row.

Cochran-Smith, M. (2001) Learning to teach against the (new) grain. *Journal of Teacher Education* 52(1): 3–4.

Cochran-Smith, M., and Lytle, S. (1999) The teacher research movement: a decade later. *Educational Researcher* 28(7): 15–25.

Cochran-Smith, M. and Zeichner, K.M. (eds) (2005) *Studying Teacher Education: The Report of the Panel on Research and Teacher Education*, Washington, DC: American Educational Research Association.

Cohen, L., Manion, L. and Morrison, K. (2007) *Research Methods in Education*, 6th edn. London: RoutledgeFalmer.

Conway, P.F., Murphy, R., Rath, A. and Hall, K. (2009) *Learning to Teach and Its Implications for the Continuum of Teacher Education: A Nine-Country Cross-National Study.* Maynooth: Teaching Council of Ireland.

Coolahan, J. (2007) *A Review Paper on Thinking and Policies Relating to Teacher Education in Ireland.* Maynooth: Teaching Council of Ireland.

Corbin, C. (2007) Commentary on over ten years on from 'The horse is dead…': surely it must be time to 'dismount'?! *Pediatric Exercise Science* 19(2): 123–5.

Cox, C.B. and Dyson, R.E. (eds) (1975) *Black Paper 1975: The Fight for Education.* London: Dent.

Craig, R. and Shelton, N. (eds) (2008) *Health Survey for England 2007:* Volume 1, *Healthy Lifestyles: Knowledge, Attitudes and Behaviour,* Leeds: NHS Information Centre for Health and Social Care.

Curtner-Smith, M.D. (1999) The more things change the more they stay the same: factors influencing teachers' interpretations and delivery of national curriculum physical education. *Sport, Education and Society* 4(1): 75–97.

Curtner-Smith, M.D. (2001) The occupational socialization of a first-year physical education teacher with a teaching orientation. *Sport, Education and Society* 6(1): 81–105.

Dagkas, S. and Benn, T. (2006) Young Muslim women's experiences of Islam and physical education in Greece and Britain: a comparative study. *Sport, Education and Society* 11(1): 21–38.

Daley, A. (2002) Extra-curricular physical activities and physical self-perceptions in British 14–15 year old male and female adolescents. *European Physical Education Review* 8(1): 37–49.

Darling-Hammond, L. (2006) Securing the right to learn: policy and practice for powerful teaching and learning. *Educational Researcher* 35(7): 13–24.

Darling-Hammond, L. and Bransford, J. (eds) (2005) *Preparing Teachers for a Changing World: What Teachers Should Learn and Be Able to Do.* London: Jossey Bass.

Davidson, F. (2007) Childhood obesity prevention and physical activity in schools. *Health Education,* 107(4): 377–95.

Day, C. (1999) *Developing Teachers: The Challenges of Lifelong Learning.* London: Falmer Press.

Day, C. (2002) The challenge to be the best: reckless curiosity and mischievous motivation. *Teachers and Teaching: Theory and Practice* 8(3/4): 421–34.

Day, C., Stobart, G., Sammons, P., Kington, A., Gu, Q., Smees, R. and Mujtaba, T. (2006) *Variations in Teachers' Work, Lives and Effectiveness (VITAE).* Research Report RR743: Department for Education and Skills.

DCMS (Department for Culture, Media and Sport) (2002) *Game Plan: A Strategy for Delivering Government's Sport and Physical Activity Objectives.* London: DCMS Strategy Unit.

DCMS/DfES (Department for Culture, Media and Sport and Department for Education and Skills) (2006) *School Sport Survey 2005–2006.* London: HMSO.

DCSF (Department for Children, Schools and Families) (2008) *Personalised Learning – A Practical Guide,* Nottingham: DCSF.

Deglau, D. and O'Sullivan, M. (2006) The effects of a long-term professional development programme on the beliefs and practices of experienced teachers. *Journal of Teaching in Physical Education* 25: 379–96.

Dening, G. (1993) *Mr Bligh's Bad Language: Passion, Power and Theatre on the Bounty.* Cambridge: Cambridge University Press.

Denzin, N. (1984) *On Understanding Emotion.* San Francisco: Jossey Bass.

Department of Education and Skills (2010) *Continuing Personal and Professional Development Needs of Teachers in Ireland.* Dublin: The Stationery Office.

Department of Education, Tasmania (2008) *The Tasmanian Curriculum. Health and Wellbeing. K–10 Syllabus and Support Materials.* www.education.tas.gov.au/curriculum/standards/health (accessed 22 November 2010).

DES (Department of Education and Science) (1991) *Physical Education for Ages 5 to 16.* London: DES.

DES/WO (Department of Education and Science and the Welsh Office) (1992) *Physical Education in the National Curriculum.* London: HMSO.

Desimone, L.M. (2009) Improving impact studies of teachers' professional development: toward better conceptualisations and measures. *Educational Researcher* 38(3): 181–99.

Dewar, A. (1989) Recruitment in physical education teaching: Toward a critical approach, in T. Templin and P. Schempp (eds), *Socialization into Physical Education: Learning to Teach.* Indianapolis, IN: Benchmark Press, pp. 39–58.

Dewey, J. (1922) *Human Nature and Conduct.* Austin, TX: Holt.

Dewey, J. (1933) *How We Think: A Restatement of the Relation of Reflective Thinking to the Educative Process.* Boston: DC Heath and Company.

Dewey, J. (1958) *Experience and Education.* London and New York: Simon and Schuster.

DfE (Department for Education) (1995) *Physical Education in the National Curriculum.* London: HMSO.

DfE (Department for Education) *Personal Learning and Thinking Skills.*Available at: http://curriculum.qcda.gov.uk/key-stages-3-and-4/skills/perlearning-and-thinking-skills/index.aspx (accessed 20 July 2011).

DfEE/QCA (Department for Education and Employment and Qualifications and Curriculum Authority) (1999) *Physical Education: The National Curriculum for England.* London: HMSO.

DfES (Department for Education and Skills) (2003a) *Every Child Matters.* Green Paper, Cm. 5860. London: The Stationery Office.

DfES (Department for Education and Skills) (2003b) *Time for Standards: Guidance Accompanying the Section 133 Regulations Issued Under the Education Act 2002.* Nottingham: DfES.

DfES (Department for Education and Skills) (2005) *Implementing the Disability Discrimination Act in Schools and Early Years Settings.* Nottingham: DfES.

DfES/DCMS (Department for Education and Skills/Department for Culture, Media and Sport) (2004) *Learning through PE and Sport.* Nottingham: DfES.

DfES/DCMS (Department for Education and Skills/Department for Culture, Media and Sport) (2008) *Learning through PE and Sport,* Nottingham: DfES.

Dinan Thompson, M. (ed.) (2009) *Health and Physical Education: Issues for Curriculum in Australia and New Zealand.* Melbourne, Australia: Oxford University Press.

DoH (Department of Health) (2004) *At Least Five a Week: Evidence on the Impact of Physical Activity and Its Relationship to Health: A Report from the Chief Medical Officer.* London: DoH.

DoH (Department of Health) (2010) *Healthy Lives, Healthy People: Our Strategy for Public Health in England.* London: The Stationery Office.

DoH/DCSF (Department of Health and Department for Children, Schools and Families) (2008) *Healthy Weight, Healthy Lives: A Cross-Government Strategy for England.* London: HMSO.

Doolittle, S.A., Dodds, P. and Placek, J.H. (1993) Persistence of beliefs about teaching during formal training of pre-service teachers. *Journal of Teaching in Physical Education* 12(4): 355–65.

Douge, B. and Hastie, P. (1993) Coach effectiveness. *Sport Science Review* 2(2): 14–29.

Drudy, S. (2009) *Education in Ireland, Challenge and Change.* Dublin: Gill and Macmillan.

Dyson, B. (2006) Students' perspectives of physical education, in D. Kirk, D. Macdonald and M. O'Sullivan (eds), *The Handbook of Physical Education.* London: Sage, pp. 326–46.

Edelman, G.M. (2006) *Second Nature.* New Haven, CT, and London: Yale University Press.

Elmore, F.R. (2002) *Bridging the Gap Between Standards and Achievement: The Imperative for Professional Development in Education.* New York: Albert Shanker Institute.

Ennis, C. (2003) Using curriculum to enhance student learning, in S.J. Silverman and C.D. Ennis (eds), *Student Learning in Physical Education.* Champaign, IL: Human Kinetics, pp. 109–29.

Entwistle, N.J. (1990) *Handbook of Educational Ideas and Practices.* London: Routledge.

Entwistle, N.J. (1993) *Styles of Learning and Teaching,* 3rd edn. London: David Fulton.

EPPI (Evidence for Policy and Practice Information and Co-ordinating Centre) (2004) *The Impact of Collaborative CPD on Classroom Teaching and Learning: What Do Teachers' Impact Data Tell Us about Collaborative CPD?* London: Institute of Education.

ERA (Education Reform Act) (1988) *Education Reform Act, 29 July 1988.* London: HMSO.

ETUCE (European Trade Union Committee for Education) (2008) *Teacher Education in Europe: An ETUCE Policy Paper.* Brussels: ETUCE.

Etzioni, A. (1969) *The Semi-Professions and Their Organization.* New York: Free Press.

Evans, J. (1990) Defining a subject? The rise and rise of the new PE. *British Journal of Sociology of Education* 11(2): 155–69.

Evans, J. (2004) Making a difference? Education and 'ability' in physical education. *European Physical Education Review* 10(1): 95–108.

Evans, J. (2007) Health education or weight management in schools? *Cardiometabolic Risk and Weight Management* 2(2): 12–16.

Evans, J. and Davies, B. (1986) Sociology, schooling and physical education, in J. Evans (ed.), *Physical Education, Sport and Schooling: Studies in the Sociology of Physical Education.* London: Falmer Press, pp. 11–37.

Evans, J. and Davies, B. (2008) The poverty of theory: Class configurations in the discourse of physical education and health (PEH). *Physical Education and Sport Pedagogy* 13(2): 199–213.

Evans, J. and Davies, B. (2010) Family, class and embodiment: why school physical education makes so little difference to post-school participation patterns in physical activity. *International Journal of Qualitative Studies in Education* 23(7): 765–85.

Evans, J., Davies, B. and Penney, D. (1996) Teachers, teaching and the social construction of gender relations. *Sport, Education and Society* 1(2): 165–83.

Evans, J., Rich, E. and Davies, B. (2004) The emperor's new clothes: fat, thin and overweight. The social fabrication of risk and ill health. *Journal of Teaching in Physical Education* 23: 372–91.

Evans, J., Rich, E., Davies, B. and Allwood, R. (2008) *Education, Disordered Eating and Obesity Discourse: Fat Fabrications.* London: Routledge.

Evans, J., Rich, E. and Holroyd, R. (2004) Disordered eating and disordered schooling: what schools do to middle-class girls. *British Journal of Sociology of Education* 25: 123–42.

FA (Football Association) Learning (2008) *The FA Youth Award, Module 1: Developing the Environment*. Leeds: Coachwise.

FA (Football Association) Learning (2009) *The FA Youth Award, Module 2: Developing the Practice*. Leeds: Coachwise.

FA (Football Association) Learning (2010) *The FA Youth Award, Module 3: Developing the Player*. Leeds: Coachwise.

Fairclough, N. (1998) *Discourse and Social Change*. Cambridge: Polity Press.

Fairclough, S. (2003) Physical activity lessons during Key Stage 3 physical education, *British Journal of Teaching Physical Education* 34(1): 40–5.

Fairclough, S. and Stratton, G. (2005) Physical education makes you fit and healthy: physical education's contribution to young people's physical activity levels. *Health Education Research* 20(1): 14–23.

Falk, B. (2001) Professional learning through assessment, in A. Lieberman and L. Miller (eds), *Teachers Caught in the Action: Professional Development that Matters*. New York: Teachers College Press, pp. 118–40.

Faulkner, G., Reeves, C. and Chedzoy, S. (2004) Nonspecialist, preservice primary-school teachers: predicting intentions to teach physical education. *Journal of Teaching in Physical Education* 23: 200–15.

Feiman-Nemser, S. (1990) Teacher preparation: structural and conceptual alternatives, in W.R. Houton, M. Haberman and J. Sikula (eds), *Handbook of Research on Teacher Education*. New York: Macmillan, pp. 212–33.

Fernandez-Balboa, J.-M. (1997) Knowledge base in physical education: a proposal for a new era. *Quest* 49(2): 161–81.

Fernandez-Balboa, J.-M. (2003) Physical education in the digital (postmodern) era, in A. Laker (ed.), *The Future of Physical Education: Building a New Pedagogy*. London: Routledge, pp. 137–52.

Fletcher, S. (1984) *Women First: The Female Tradition in English Physical Education 1880–1980*. London: Athlone.

Flintoff, A. (2008) Targeting Mr Average: participation, gender equity and school sport partnerships. *Sport, Education and Society* 13(4): 393–411.

Flintoff, A. and Scraton, S. (2001) Stepping into active leisure? Young womens' perceptions of active lifestyles and their experiences of school PE. *Sport, Education and Society* 6(1): 5–22.

Flintoff, A. and Scraton, S. (2006) Girls and physical education, in D. Kirk, D. Macdonald and M. O'Sullivan (eds), *The Handbook of Physical Education*. London: Sage, pp. 767–83.

Flintoff, A., Fitzgerald, H. and Scraton, S. (2008) The challenges of intersectionality: researching difference in physical education. *International Studies in Sociology of Education* 18(2): 73–85.

Folsom-Meek, S.L., Nearing, R.J., Groteluschen, W. and Krampf, H. (1999) Effects of academic major, gender and hands-on experience on attitudes of preservice professionals. *Adapted Physical Activity Quarterly* 16(4): 389–402.

Fox, K. (1992) Education for exercise and the national curriculum proposals: a step forwards or backwards? *British Journal of Physical Education* 23(1): 8–11.

Fox, K. and Harris, J. (2003) Promoting physical activity through schools, in J. McKenna and C. Riddoch (eds), *Perspectives on Health and Exercise*. Basingstoke: Palgrave Macmillan, pp. 181–201.

Fox, K., Cooper, A. and McKenna, J. (2004) The school and promotion of children's health-enhancing physical activity: perspectives from the United Kingdom. *Journal of Teaching Physical Education* 23: 338–58.

Freedson, P.S., Cureton, K.J. and Heath, W. (2000) Status of field-based fitness testing in children and youth. *Preventive Medicine* 31: S77–S85.

Freire, P. (1972) *Pedagogy of the Oppressed*. Harmondsworth: Penguin.

French, S.A., Story, M. and Jeffery, R.W. (2001) Environmental influences on eating and physical activity. *Annual Review of Public Health* 22: 309–35.

Gallagher, S. (2005) *How the Body Shapes the Mind*. Oxford: Clarendon Press.

Galton, M. and Croll, P. (1980) *Inside the Primary Classroom*. London: Routledge and Kegan Paul.

Gard, M. (2004a) Desperately seeking certainty: statistics, physical activity and critical enquiry, in J. Wright, D. Macdonald and L. Burrows (eds), *Critical Inquiry and Problem Solving in Physical Education*. London: Routledge, pp. 171–83.

Gard, M. (2004b) An elephant in the room and a bridge too far, or physical education and the 'obesity epidemic', in J. Evans, B. Davies and J. Wright (eds), *Body Knowledge and Control*. London: Routledge, pp. 66–83.

Gard, M. and Wright, J. (2001) Managing uncertainty: obesity discourses and physical education in a risk society. *Studies in Philosophy and Education* 20: 235–49.

Gard, M. and Wright, J. (2005) *The Obesity Epidemic*. London: Routledge.

Garet, M.S., Porter, A.C., Desimone, L., Birman, B.F. and Yoon, K.S. (2001) What makes professional development effective? Results from a national sample of teachers. *American Educational Research Journal* 38(4): 915–45.

Garrett, R. and Wrench, A. (2007) Physical experiences: primary teachers' conceptions of sport and physical education. *Physical Education and Sports Pedagogy* 12(1): 23–42.

Garrett, R. and Wrench, A. (2008) Fitness testing: the pleasure and pain of it. *ACHPER Healthy Lifestyles Journal* 55(4): 17–22.

Gersten, R., Dimino, J., Jayanthi, M., Kim, J.S. and Edwards, L. (2010) Study group: impact of the professional development model on reading instruction and student outcomes in first grade. *American Educational Research Journal* 47(3): 694–739.

Gibbs, W.G. (2006) *Embodiment and Cognitive Science*. Cambridge: Cambridge University Press.

Gilbert, W. and Trudel, P. (1999) An evaluation strategy for coach education programs. *Journal of Sports Behaviour* 22(2): 34–50.

Gill, J.H. (2000) *The Tacit Mode*. Albany: State University of New York Press.

Gore, J. (1993) *The Struggle for Pedagogies*. London: Routledge.

Goudas, M. and Biddle, S. (1994) Perceived motivational climate and intrinsic motivation in school physical education classes. *European Journal of Psychology of Education* 9: 237–47.

Gower, C. and Capel, S. (2004) Newly qualified physical education teachers' experiences of developing subject knowledge prior to, during and after a postgraduate certificate in education course. *Physical Education and Sport Pedagogy* 9(2): 1–19.

Graber, K.C. (1995) The influence of teacher education programs on the beliefs of student teachers general pedagogical knowledge, pedagogical content knowledge and teacher education course work. *Journal of Teaching in Physical Education* 14(2): 157–78.

Graham, G. (1995) Physical education through students' eyes and in students' voices: introduction. *Journal of Teaching in Physical Education* 14(4): 364–71.

Graham, H. (1965) *The Leaflet* 66(2): 15.

Great Britain, Board of Education (1933) *Syllabus of Physical Training for Schools*, 1933. London: HMSO.

Green, K. (2000a) Exploring the everyday 'philosophies' of physical education teachers from a sociological perspective. *Sport, Education and Society* 5(2): 109–29.

Green, K. (2000b) Extra-curricular physical education in England and Wales: a sociological perspective on the sporting bias. *European Journal of Physical Education* 5(2): 178–207.

Green, K. (2002) Physical education, lifelong participation and the work of Ken Roberts. *Sport, Education and Society* 7(2): 167–82.

Green, K. (2003) *Physical Education Teachers on Physical Education: A Sociological Study of Philosophies and Ideologies.* Chester: Chester Academic Press.

Green, K. (2005a) Examinations: a 'new orthodoxy' in physical education, in K. Green and K. Hardman (eds), *Physical Education: Essential Issues.* London: Sage, pp. 143–60.

Green, K. (2005b) Extra-curricular physical education in secondary schools in England and Wales: reflections on the 'state of play', in K. Green and K. Hardman (eds), *Physical Education: Essential Issues.* London: Sage, pp. 98–110.

Green, K. (2008) *Understanding Physical Education.* London: Sage.

Green, K. and Thurston, M. (2002) Physical education and health promotion: a qualitative study of teachers' perceptions, *Health Education*, 102(3): 113–23.

Greeno, J.G. and the Middle School Mathematics Through Applications Project Group (1998) The situativity of knowing, learning and research. *American Psychologist* 53(1): 5–26.

Grehaigne, J.-F., Richard, J.-F. and Griffin, L.L. (2005) *Teaching and Learning Team Sports and Games.* London: RoutledgeFalmer.

Griggs, G. (2008) Outsiders inside: the use of sports coaches in primary schools. *Primary Physical Education Matters* 3(1): 33–7.

Grimmett, P.P. and MacKinnon, A.M. (1992) Craft knowledge and the education of teachers, in G. Grant (ed.), *Review of Research in Education 18*, Washington DC: American Educational Research Association, pp. 385–456.

Grimmett, P.P., Mackinnon, A., Erickson, G. and Riechen, T. (1990) Reflective practice in teacher education, in R. Clift, W. Houston and M. Pugach (eds), *Encouraging Reflective Practice in Education: An Analysis of Issues and Programs.* New York: Teachers College Press.

Guskey, T.R. (1995) Professional development in education: in search of the optimal mix, in T.R. Guskey and M. Huberman (eds), *Professional Development in Education: New Paradigms and Practices.* New York: Teachers College Press, pp. 114–32.

Guskey, T.R. (2003) Analysing lists of the characteristics of effective professional development to promote visionary leadership, *NASSP Bulletin* 87(637): 38–54.

Haerens, L., Kirk, D., Cardon, G. and Bourdeauhuji, I. (2011) The development of a pedagogical model for health-based physical education. *Quest* 63: 321–38.

Hager, P. (2005) Philosophical accounts of learning. *Educational Philosophy and Theory* 37(5): 649–66.

Hager, P. and Hodkinson, P. (2009) Moving beyond the metaphor of transfer of learning. *British Educational Research Journal* 35(4): 619–38.

Hansard (2010) HC Deb 30 November 2010, vol 519, cols 693–737.

Hardin, B. (2005) Physical education teachers' reflections on preparation for inclusion. *Physical Educator* 62(1): 44–56.

Hardman, K. (2011) Physical education, movement and physical literacy in the twenty-first century: pupils' competencies, attitudes and behaviours. Paper presented at the 6th FIEP European Congress, 18–21 June 2011, Poreč, Croatia.

Hardman, K. and Marshall, J. (2005) Physical education in schools in a European context: charter principles, promises and implementation realities, in K. Green and K. Hardman (eds), *Physical Education: Essential Issues*. London: Sage, pp. 39–64.

Hargreaves, D. (2003) *Teaching in the Knowledge Society: Education in the Age of Insecurity*. Maidenhead: Open University Press.

Hargreaves, L., Cunningham, M., Hansen, A., McIntyre, D., Oliver, C. and Pell, T. (2007) *The Status of Teachers and the Teaching Profession in England: Views from Inside and Outside the Profession*, final report of the Teacher Status Project, DfES Research Report RR831A.

Harris, J. (1993) Young people's perceptions of health, fitness and exercise. *British Journal of Physical Education Research Supplement* 13: 2–5.

Harris, J. (1994) Young people's perceptions of health, fitness and exercise: implications for the teaching of health-related exercise, *Physical Education Review* 17(2): 143–51.

Harris, J. (1995) Physical education: a picture of health? *British Journal of Physical Education* 26(4): 25–32.

Harris, J. (1997) Physical education: a picture of health? The implementation of health-related exercise in the national curriculum in secondary schools in England. Unpublished doctoral thesis, Loughborough University.

Harris, J. (2000) *Health-Related Exercise in the National Curriculum. Key Stages 1 to 4.* Leeds: Human Kinetics.

Harris, J. (2010) Health-related physical education, in R. Bailey (ed.), *Physical Education for Learning: A Guide for Secondary Schools*. London: Continuum, pp. 26–36.

Harris, J. and Elbourn, J. (1992) Highlighting health-related exercise within the National Curriculum – Part 1. *British Journal of Physical Education* 23(1): 18–22.

Harvey, S., Cushion, C.J., Wegis, H.M. and Massa-Gonzalez, A.D. (2010) Teaching games for understanding in American high-school soccer: a quantitative data analysis using the game performance assessment instrument. *Physical Education and Sport Pedagogy* 15: 29–54.

Hastie, P. (2011) A review of research on sport education: 2004 to the present. *Physical Education and Sport Pedagogy* 16: 103–32.

Hattie, J. (2009) *Visible Learning: A Synthesis of Over 800 Meta-analyses Relating to Achievement*. London: Routledge.

Hay, P. and Penney, D. (2011) Inclusivity and physical education: moving beyond the rhetoric, in S. Brown (ed.), *Issues and Controversies in Physical Education. Policy, Power and Pedagogy*. Auckland: Pearson, pp. 92–102.

Hay, P.J. and lisahunter (2006) 'Please Mr Hay, what are my poss(abilities)?': legitimation of ability through physical education practices. *Sport, Education and Society* 11(3): 293–310.

Hay, P.J. and Macdonald, D. (2010) The gendering of abilities in senior PE, *Physical Education and Sport Pedagogy* 15(3): 271–85.

Haycock, D. and Smith, A. (2010) Inadequate and inappropriate? The assessment of young disabled pupils and pupils with special educational needs in National Curriculum physical education. *European Physical Education Review* 16(3): 283–300.

Haydn-Davies, D. (2010) Physical literacy and learning and teaching approaches, in

M. Whitehead (ed.), *Physical Literacy: Throughout the Lifecourse*. London: Routledge, pp. 165–74.

Hellison, D. and Martinek, T. (2006) Social and individual responsibility programs, in D. Kirk, D. Macdonald and M. O'Sullivan (eds), *The Handbook of Physical Education*. London: Sage, pp. 610–26.

Hellison, D. and Templin, T. (1991) *A Reflective Approach to Teaching Physical Education*. Champaign, IL: Human Kinetics.

Hirst, P. (1974) *Knowledge and the Curriculum*. London: Routledge and Kegan Paul.

Hodge, S.R. and Jansma, P. (2000) Physical education majors' attitudes toward teaching students with disabilities. *Teacher Education and Special Education* 23(3): 211–24.

Hodkinson, P., Biesta, G. and James, D. (2008) Understanding learning culturally: overcoming the dualism between social and individual views of learning. *Vocations and Learning* 1: 27–47.

Hoffman, S.J. (1987) Dreaming the impossible dream: the decline and fall of physical education, in J.A. Massengale (ed.), *Trends Toward the Future in Physical Education*. Champaign, IL: Human Kinetics, pp. 121–35.

Hopkins, J. (2002) *A Teachers' Guide to Classroom Research*, 3rd edn. Buckingham: Open University Press.

Hoyle, E. (1974) Professionality, professionalism and control in teaching. *London Education Review* 3(2): 13–19.

Hoyle E. and John, P.D. (1995) *Professional Knowledge and Professional Practice*. London: Cassell.

Hutchings, M., Seeds, K., Coleman, N., Harding, C., Mansoray, A., Mayler, U., Minty, S. and Pickering, E. (2009) *Aspects of School Workforce Remodelling Strategies Used and Impact on Workload and Standards*. London: DCSF.

Hutchinson, G.E. (1993) Prospective teachers' perspectives on teaching physical education: An interview study on recruitment phase teacher socialization. *Journal of Teaching in Physical Education* 12(4): 344–54.

Imwold, C.H. and Hoffman, S.J. (1983) Visual recognition of a gymnastics skill by experienced and inexperienced instructors. *Research Quarterly for Exercise and Sport* 54(2): 149–55.

James, M. and Pollard, A. (2006) *Improving Teaching and Learning in Schools: A TLRP Commentary*. London: TLRP.

James, M., McCormick, R., Black, P., Carmichael, P., Drummond, M.-J., Fox, A., Frost, D., MacBeath, J., Marshall, B., Pedder, D., Procter, R., Swaffield, S. and Wiliam, D. (2007) *Improving Learning How to Learn: Classrooms, Schools and Networks*. London: Routledge.

Jewett, A.E., Bain, L.L. and Ennis, C.D. (1995) *The Curriculum Process in Physical Education*, 2nd edn. Madison, WI: Brown.

Jones, R.L. (2006) How can educational concepts inform sports coaching? in R.L. Jones (ed.), *The Sports Coach as Educator: Reconceptualising Sports Coaching*. London: Routledge, pp. 3–13.

Jones, R.L., Armour, K. and Potrac, P. (2004) *Sports Coaching Cultures: From Practice to Theory*. London: Routledge.

Joyce, B., Calhoun, E. and Hopkins, D. (2002) *Models of Learning, Tools for Teaching*, 2nd edn. Buckingham: Open University Press.

Jung, H., Harvey, S. and Kirk, D. (2011) Identifying the physical cultural discourses informing the PESSCL strategy during a decade of change. Paper presented to the Sport Under Pressure Conference, University of Birmingham, March.

Kagan, D. (1992) Professional growth among pre service and beginning teachers. *Review of Educational Research* 62: 129–69.

Kahn, E.B., Ramsey, L.T., Brownson, R.C., Health, G.W., Howze, E.H. and Powell, K.E. (2002) The effectiveness of interventions to increase physical activity. *American Journal of Preventive Medicine* 22: 4S: 73–107.

Keating, X.D. (2003) The current often implemented fitness tests in physical education programs: problems and future directions. *Quest* 55: 141–60.

Keay, J. (2006) Developing the physical education profession: new teachers learning within a subject-based community. *Physical Education and Sport Pedagogy* 10(2): 139–57.

Kelchtermans, G. (2009) Who I am in how I teach is the message: self-understanding, vulnerability and reflection. *Teachers and Teaching: Theory and Practice* 15(2): 257–72.

Kinchin, G. (2010) Models of pedagogy, in R. Bailey (ed.), *Physical Education for Learning: A Guide for Secondary Schools*. London: Continuum, pp. 118–29.

King, P. and Kitchener, K. (1994) *Developing Reflective Judgement*. San Francisco: Jossey Bass.

Kirk, D. (1992) *Defining Physical Education: The Social Construction of a School Subject in Postwar Britain*. London: Falmer Press.

Kirk, D. (1999) Physical culture, physical education and relational analysis. *Sport, Education and Society* 4: 63–73.

Kirk, D. (2002a) Quality physical education through partnerships: a response to Karel J. van Deventer. Paper presented to the 12th Commonwealth International Sport Conference, Manchester, July.

Kirk, D. (2002b) Physical education: a gendered history, in D. Penney (ed.), *Gender and Physical Education. Contemporary issues and future directions*, London: Routledge, pp. 24–38.

Kirk, D. (2005) Physical education, youth sport and lifelong participation: the importance of early learning experiences. *European Physical Education Review* 11: 239–55.

Kirk, D. (2006) The 'obesity crisis' and school physical education. *Sport, Education and Society* 11(2): 121–33.

Kirk, D. (2010) *Physical Education Futures*. London: Routledge.

Kirk, D. (2011) The crisis of content knowledge. *Physical Education Matters* 6(2): 34.

Kirk, D. and Colquhoun, D. (1989) Healthism and physical education. *British Journal of Sociology of Education* 10: 417–34.

Kline N. (1998) *Time to Think: Listening to Ignite the Human Mind*. London: Cassell Octopus.

Knight, P. (2002) A systemic approach to professional development: learning as practice. *Teaching and Teacher Education* 18(3): 229–41.

Knudson, D.V. and Morrison, C.S. (2002) *Qualitative Analysis of Human Movement*. Champaign, IL: Human Kinetics.

Ko, B., Wallhead, T. and Ward, P. (2006) Professional development workshops: what do teachers learn and use? *Journal of Teaching in Physical Education* 25: 367–412.

Kolb, A. and Kolb, D. (2005) Learning styles and learning spaces: enhancing experiential learning in higher education. *Academy of Management Learning and Education* 4(2): 193–212.

Kolb, D. (1984) *Experiential Learning: Experience as the Source of Learning and Development*. Englewood Cliffs, NJ: Prentice Hall.

Kulinna, P.H. and Zhu, W. (2001) Fitness portfolio calibration for first- through sixth-grade children. *Research Quarterly for Exercise and Sport* 72: 324–34.

Kulinna, P.H., McCaughtry, N., Martin, J.J., Cothran, D. and Faust, R. (2008) The influence of professional development on teachers' psychosocial perceptions of teaching a health-related physical education curriculum. *Journal of Teaching in Physical Education* 27: 292–307.

Laker, A. (ed.) (2003) *The Future of Physical Education: Building a New Pedagogy.* London: Routledge.

Lakoff, G. and Johnson, M. (1999) *Philosophy in the Flesh: The Embodied Mind and Its Challenge to Western Thought.* New York: Basic Books.

Latner, J.D. and Stunkard, A.J. (2003) Getting worse: the stigmatisation of obese children. *Obesity Research* 11: 425–56.

Launder, A.G. (2001) *Play Practice: The Games Approach to Teaching and Coaching Sport.* Champaign, IL: Human Kinetics.

Lave, J. and Wenger, E. (1991) *Situated Learning: Legitimate Peripheral Participation.* Cambridge: Cambridge University Press.

Lavin, J., Swindlehurst, G. and Foster, V. (2008) The use of coaches, adults supporting learning and teaching assistants in the teaching of physical education in the primary school. *Primary Physical Education Matters* 3(1): 9–11.

Lawson, H.A. (1983a) Toward a model of teacher socialization in physical education: the subjective warrant, recruitment and teacher education (part 1). *Journal of Teaching in Physical Education* 2(3): 3–16.

Lawson, H.A. (1983b) Toward a model of teacher socialization in physical education: entry into schools, teachers' role orientations and longevity in teaching (part 2). *Journal of Teaching in Physical Education* 3(1): 3–15.

Lawson, H.A. (1986) Occupational socialization and the design of teacher education programs. *Journal of Teaching in Physical Education* 5(1): 107–16.

Lawson, H.A. (2009) Paradigms, exemplars and social change. *Sport, Education and Society* 14: 77–100.

Leach, J. and Moon, B. (1999) *Learners and Pedagogy.* London: Paul Chapman.

Learning and Teaching Scotland (n.d.) *Curriculum for Excellence: Health and Wellbeing Experiences and Outcomes.* www.ltscotland.org.uk/Images/health_wellbeing_experiences_outcomes_tcm4–540031.pdf (accessed 4 June 2011).

Leder, D. (1990) *The Absent Body.* Chicago and London: University of Chicago Press.

Lee, T., Fuller, A., Ashton, D., Butler, P., Felstead, A., Urwin, L. and Walters, S. (2004) *Learning as Work: Teaching and Learning Processes in the Contemporary Work Organisation.* Working Paper 2, Centre for Labour Market Studies, University of Leicester.

Leggett, G. (2008) A changing picture of health: health-related exercise policy and practice in physical education curricula in secondary schools in England and Wales. Unpublished doctoral thesis, Loughborough University.

Leinhardt, G. (1990) Capturing craft knowledge in teaching. *Educational Researcher* 19(2): 18–25.

Lieberman, A. (1995) Practices that support teacher development: transforming conceptions of professional learning. *Phi Delta Kappan* 76: 591–6.

Light, R. (2008) Complex learning theory – its epistemology and its assumptions about learning: implications for physical education. *Journal of Teaching in Physical Education* 27: 22–37.

Lirgg, C. (2006) Social psychology and physical education, in D. Kirk, D. Macdonald and M. O'Sullivan (eds), *The Handbook of Physical Education*. London: Sage, pp. 141–62.

Little, J.W. (1993) The persistence of privacy: autonomy and initiative in teachers' professional relations. *Teachers College Record* 91(3): 509–36.

Little, J.W. (2002) Locating learning in teachers' communities of practice: opening up problems of analysis in records of everyday practice. *Teaching and Teacher Education* 18: 917–46.

Locke, L.F. (1992) Changing secondary school physical education. *Quest* 44: 361–72.

Logsdon, B., Barrett, K., Broer, M., Ammons, M. and Roberton, M. (1977) *Physical Education for Children: A Focus on the Teaching Process*. Philadelphia: Lea and Febiger.

Loughran, J. and Gunstone, R. (1997) Professional development in residence: developing reflection on science teaching and learning. *Journal of Education for Teaching* 23(2): 159–78.

Lounsbery, M. and Coker, C. (2008) Developing skill-analysis competency in physical education teachers. *Quest* 60(2): 255–67.

Lund, J. and Tannehill, D. (2005) *Standards-Based Physical Education Curriculum Development*. Sudbury, MA: Jones and Bartlett Publishers.

Lund, J.L., Metzler, M.W. and Gurvitch, R. (2008) Pedagogical content knowing for model-based instruction in physical education and future directions for research. *Journal of Teaching in Physical Education* 27(4): 580–9.

MacIntyre, A. (1985) *After Virtue: A Study in Moral Theory*, 2nd edn. London: Duckworth.

MacPhail, A., Kirk, D. and Eley, D. (2003) Listening to young people's voices: youth sports leaders' advice on facilitating participation in sport. *European Physical Education Review* 9(1): 57–73.

Mangan, J.A. (1981) Grammar schools and the games ethic in Victorian and Edwardian eras, *Albion* 15(4): 313–35.

Martino, W., Kehler, M. and Weaver-Hightower, M. (eds) (2009) *The Problem with Boys' Education: Beyond the Backlash*. Abingdon: Routledge.

Martino, W., Mills, M. and Lingard, B. (2005) Interrogating single-sex classes as a strategy for addressing boys' educational and social needs. *Oxford Review of Education* 31(2): 237–54.

Massengale, J.A. (ed.) (1987) *Trends Toward the Future in Physical Education*. Champaign, IL: Human Kinetics.

Matanin, M. and Collier, C. (2003) Longitudinal analysis of preservice teachers' beliefs about teaching physical education. *Journal of Teaching in Physical Education* 22(2): 153–68.

Maude, P.M. (2003) *Observing Children Moving* (CD). Worcester: afPE.

Maude, P.M. and Whitehead, M.E. (2006) *Observing and Analysing Learners' Movement* (CD). Worcester: afPE.

Mazur, J. (1990) *Learning and Behaviour*, 2nd edn. Englewood Cliffs, NJ: Prentice Hall.

McCullick, B.A., Belcher, D., Hardin, B. and Hardin, D. (2003) Butches, bullies and buffoons: images of physical education teachers in the movies. *Sport, Education and Society*, 8: 3–16.

McDiarmid, G.W. and Clevenger-Bright, M. (2008) Rethinking teacher capacity, in M. Cochran-Smith, S. Feiman-Nemser and D.J. McIntyre (eds), *Handbook of Research on Teacher Education: Enduring Questions in Changing Contexts*, 3rd edn. New York: Routledge, pp. 134–56.

McElroy, M. (2008) A socio-historical analysis of US youth physical activity and sedentary behaviour, in A.L. Smith and S.J.H. Biddle (eds), *Youth Physical Activity and Sedentary Behaviour. Challenges and Solutions.* Leeds: Human Kinetics, pp. 59–78.

McInerney, D. and McInerney, V. (2002) *Educational Psychology: Constructing Learning.* Sydney: Pearson.

McIntosh, P.C. (1968) *Physical Education in England since 1800.* London: Bell & Hyman Ltd.

Meegan, S. and MacPhail, A. (2006) Irish physical educators' attitude toward teaching students with special educational needs. *European Physical Education Review* 12(1): 75–97.

Meiers, M. and Ingvarson, L. (2005) *Investigating the Links Between Teacher Professional Development and Student Learning Outcomes.* Australian Government Quality Teacher Programme, Australian Council for Educational Research.

Merleau-Ponty, M. (1962) *Phenomenology of Perception.* London. Routledge & Kegan Paul.

Metzler, M. (2005) *Instructional Models for Physical Education,* 2nd edn. Scottsdale, AZ: Holcomb Hathaway.

Mezirow, J. (1990) *Fostering Critical Reflection in Adulthood: A Guide to Transformative and Emancipatory Learning.* San Francisco: Jossey Bass.

Mezirow, J. (1997) Transformative learning: theory to practice. *New Directions For Adult and Continuing Education* 74: 5–12.

Miles, M.B. and Huberman, M.A. (1994) *Qualitative Data Analysis,* 2nd edn. London: Sage.

Moon, J. (1999) *Reflection in Learning and Professional Development.* London: Kogan Page.

Moon, J. (2005) *We Seek it Here: A New Perspective on the Elusive Activity of Critical Thinking: A Theoretical and Practical Approach.* York: Higher Education Academy, University of Bristol.

Morley, D., Bailey, R., Tan, J. and Cooke, B. (2005) Inclusive physical education: teachers' views of including pupils with special educational needs and/or disabilities in physical education. *European Physical Education Review* 11(1): 84–107.

Morrison, C.S. (2004) Refinement of terminology in qualitative analysis of human movement. *Perceptual and Motor Skills* 99(1): 105–6.

Morrison, C.S. and Reeve, E.J. (1988) Effect of instruction and undergraduate major on qualitative skill analysis. *Journal of Human Movement Studies* 15(6): 291–7.

Mosston, M. and Ashworth, S. (2002) *Teaching Physical Education,* 5th edn. San Francisco: Benjamin Cummings.

Murdoch, E. (1987) *The Desk Study: Sport in Schools.* London: Sports Council.

Murdoch, E. (1993) Education, sport and leisure: collapsing boundaries? in G. McFee and A. Tomlinson (eds), *Education, Sport and Leisure: Connections and Controversies.* Eastbourne: Chelsea School Research Centre, University of Brighton, pp. 65–72.

Murdoch, E. (2004) NCPE 2000 – where are we so far? in S. Capel (ed.), *Learning to Teach Physical Education in the Secondary School: a Companion to School Experience,* 2nd edn. London: Routledge, pp. 280–300.

Nelson, L.J. and Cushion, C.J. (2006) Reflection in coach education: the case of the national governing body coaching certificate. *Sport Psychologist,* 20: 174–83.

NICE (National Institute for Health and Clinical Excellence) (2007a) *Physical Activity and Children. Review 1: Descriptive Epidemiology.* NICE Public Health Collaborating Centre: www.nice.org.uk.

NICE (National Institute for Health and Clinical Excellence) (2007b) *Physical Activity and Children. Review 3: The Views of Children on the Barriers and Facilitators to Participation in Physical Activity: A Review of Qualitative Studies,* NICE Public Health Collaborating Centre: www.nice.org.uk.

Nicholls, G. (1997) *Collaborative Change in Education.* London: Kogan Page.

Nichols, J.G. (1989) *The Competitive Ethos and Democratic Education.* Cambridge, MA: Harvard University Press.

North, J. (2009) *The Coaching Workforce 2009–2016.* Leeds: Sports Coach UK.

Nussbaum, M.C. (2000) *Women and Human Development. The Capabilities Approach.* Cambridge: Cambridge University Press.

O'Bryant, C., O'Sullivan, M. and Raudetsky, J. (2000) Socialization of prospective physical education teachers: the story of new blood. *Sport, Education and Society* 5(2): 177–93.

O'Connor, A. and MacDonald, D. (2002) Up close and personal on physical education teachers' identity: is conflict an issue? *Sport, Education and Society* 7(1): 37–54.

O'Dea, J.A. (2005) Prevention of child obesity: 'first, do no harm'. *Health Education Research Theory and Practice* 20(2): 259–65.

O'Donovan, T., MacPhail, A. and Kirk, D. (2010) Active citizenship through Sport Education, *Education 3–13* 38(2): 203–15.

OECD (Organisation for Economic Cooperation and Development) (2005a) *Teachers Matter: Attracting, Developing and Retaining Effective Teachers: An Overview.* Paris: OECD.

OECD (Organisation for Economic Cooperation and Development) (2005b) *Attracting, Developing and Retaining Effective Teachers – Final Report: Teachers Matter,* Paris: OECD.

Ofsted (Office for Standards in Education) (2004) *The School Sport Partnerships Programme: Evaluation of Phases 3 and 4 2003/04.* London: Ofsted.

Ofsted (Office for Standards in Education) (2005) *Physical Education in Secondary Schools.* London: Ofsted.

Ofsted (Office for Standards in Education) (2009) *Physical Education in Schools 2005–2008.* www.ofsted.gov.uk/resources/physical-education-schools-200508-working-towards-2012-and-beyond (accessed 4 December 2011).

Oliver, K. and Oesterreich, H. (2011) Student-centered inquiry as curriculum in teacher education. Paper presented at the Association for Teacher Education, Orlando, FL.

Opinion Research Corporation (2000) *Public Attitudes Towards Physical Education: Are Schools Providing What the Public Wants?* Princeton: Opinion Research Corporation.

Oslin, J. and Mitchell, S. (2006) Game-centred approaches to teaching physical education, in D. Kirk, D. Macdonald and M. O'Sullivan (eds), *The Handbook of Physical Education.* London: Sage, pp. 627–51.

O'Sullivan, M. (1996) What do we need to know about the professional preparation of teachers? In S.J. Silverman & C.D. Ennis (eds), *Student Learning in Physical Education: Applying Research to Enhance Instruction.* Champaign, IL: Human Kinetics, pp. 315–37.

O'Sullivan, M. (2003) Learning to teach physical education, in S. Silverman and C. Ennis (eds), *Student Learning in Physical Education: Applying Research to Enhance Instruction,* 2nd edn. Champaign, IL: Human Kinetics, pp. 275–94.

O'Sullivan, M. (2005) Beliefs of teachers and teacher candidates: implications for teacher education, in F. Carreiro da Costa, M. Cloes and M. Gonzalez (eds), *The Art and Science of Teaching Physical Education and Sport*. Lisbon: Universidade De Tecnica.

O'Sullivan, M. (2007) Creating and sustaining communities of practice among physical education professionals. Paper presented at the AIESEP-Lboro Specialist Seminar on PE-CPD, Loughborough, 1–3 September.

O'Sullivan, M. and Deglau, D.A. (2006) Principles of professional development. *Journal of Teaching in Physical Education* 25(4): 441–9.

O'Sullivan, M. and MacPhail, A. (2010) *Young Peoples' Voices in Physical Education and Youth Sport*. Abingdon: Routledge.

O'Sullivan, M., MacPhail, A. and Tannehill, D. (2009) A career in teaching: decisions of the heart rather than the head. *Irish Educational Studies* 28(2): 177–91.

O'Sullivan, M., Siedentop, D. and Tannehill, D. (1994) Breaking out: codependency of high school physical education. *Journal of Teaching in Physical Education* 13: 421–8.

Ovens, A. and Tinning, R. (2009) Reflection as situated practice: a memory-work study of lived experience in teacher education. *Teaching and Teacher Education* 25(8): 1125–31.

Pajares, M. (1992) Teachers' beliefs and educational research: cleaning up a messy construct. *Review of Educational Research* 62(3): 307–32.

Parker, J. (1995) Secondary teachers' views of effective teaching in physical education. *Journal of Teaching in Physical Education* 14: 127–39.

Pate, R.R. (1994) Fitness testing: current approaches and purposes in physical education, in R.R. Pate and R.C. Hohn (eds), *Health and Fitness through Physical Education*, Champaign, IL: Human Kinetics, pp. 119–27.

Patton, K. and Griffin, L.L. (2008) Experiences and patterns of change in a physical education teacher development project. *Journal of Teaching in Physical Education* 27: 272–91.

Pearlman, D. and Goc Karp, G. (2010) A self-determined perspective of the sport education model. *Physical Education and Sport Pedagogy* 15: 401–18.

Pendlebury, S. (1995) Reason and story in wise practice, in H. McEwan and K. Egan (eds), *Narrative in Teaching, Learning and Research*. New York: Teachers College Press, pp. 50–65.

Penney, D. (ed.) (2002) *Gender and Physical Education: Contemporary Issues and Future Directions*. London: Routledge.

Penney, D. (2006) Curriculum construction and change, in D. Kirk, D. Macdonald and M. O'Sullivan (eds), *The Handbook of Physical Education*. London: Sage, pp. 565–79.

Penney, D. and Chandler, T. (2000) Physical education: what future(s)? *Sport, Education and Society* 5: 71–87.

Penney, D. and Evans, J. (1995) Changing structures; changing rules: the development of the internal market. *Social Organisation* 15: 13–21.

Penney, D. and Evans, J. (1999) *Politics, Policy and Practice in Physical Education*. London: E. and F.N. Spon.

Penney, D. and Evans, J. (2002) Talking gender. in D. Penney (ed.), *Gender and Physical Education: Contemporary Issues and Future Directions*. London: Routledge, pp. 13–23.

Penney, D. and Evans, J. (2005) Policy, power and politics in physical education, in K. Green and K. Hardman (eds), *Physical Education Essential Issues*. London: Sage.

Penney, D. and Harris, J. (1997) Extra-curricular physical education: more of the same for the more able? *Sport, Education and Society* 2(1): 41–54.

Penney, D. and lisahunter (2006) Guest editorial overview: (dis)abling the (health and) physical in education: ability, curriculum and pedagogy. *Sport, Education and Society* 11(3): 205–9.

Phillpots, L. (2010) Working with partners, in R. Bailey (ed.), *Physical Education for Learning: A Guide for Secondary Schools.* London: Continuum, pp. 158–78.

Piaget, J. (1973) *The Child and Reality*, trans. A. Rosin. New York: Grossman.

Piaget, J. and Inhelder, B. (1969) *The Psychology of the Child*, trans. H. Weaver. New York: Basic Books.

Pinheiro, V.E.D. (2000) Qualitative analysis for the elementary grades. *Journal of Physical Education, Recreation and Dance* 71(1): 18–21.

Pinheiro, V.E.D. and Simon, H.A. (1992) An operational model of motor skill diagnosis. *Journal of Teaching in Physical Education* 11(3): 288–302.

Placek, J.H., Dodds, P., Doolittle, S.A., Portman, P.A., Ratliffe, T.A. and Pinkham, K.M. (1995) Teaching recruits' physical education backgrounds and beliefs about purposes for their subject matter. *Journal of Teaching in Physical Education* 14: 246–61.

Placek, J.H., Griffin, L.L., Dodds, P., Raymond, C., Tremino, F. and James, A. (2001) Middle school students' conceptions of fitness: the long road to a healthy lifestyle. *Journal of Teaching in Physical Education* 20: 314–23.

Polanyi, M. (1966) *The Tacit Dimension.* Garden City, NY: Doubleday.

Pollard, A. (ed.) (2010) *Professionalism and Pedagogy: A Contemporary Opportunity.* London: GTCE/TLRP.

Puhse, E. and Gerber, M. (eds) (2005) *International Comparison of Physical Education: Concepts, Problems, Prospects.* Oxford: Meyer.

QCA (Qualifications and Curriculum Authority) (2003) *The Key Stage 3 National Strategy: Key Messages Pedagogy and Practice.* London: QCA.

QCA (Qualifications and Curriculum Authority) (2007a) *National Curriculum for Physical Education.*

QCA (Qualifications and Curriculum Authority) (2007b) *Physical Education Programmes of Study. Key Stage 3 and Key Stage 4.* Available at: www.qcda.org.uk/curriculum.

QCA (Qualifications and Curriculum Authority) (2007c) *The New Secondary Curriculum: What Has Changed and Why.* London: QCA.

QCA (Qualifications and Curriculum Authority) (2008) *National Curriculum for England.* London: QCA.

Quick, S., Simon, A. and Thornton, A. (2010) *PE and Sport Survey 2009/10 Research Report*, TNS-BMRB on behalf of Department of Education DFE-RR032. Available at www.education.gov.uk.

Reason, P. and Bradbury, H. (2001) *Handbook of Action Research: Participative Enquiry and Practice.* London: Sage.

Reeve, J. (2000) Qualitative analysis: Putting it all together. *Journal of Physical Education, Recreation and Dance* 71(1): 16–17.

Reilly, J.J., Kelly, L., Montgomery, C., Williamson, A., Fisher, A., McColl, J.H., Lo Conte, R., Paton, J.Y. and Grant, S. (2006) Physical activity to prevent obesity in young children: cluster randomised controlled trial, *British Medical Journal* 333(7577): 1041.

Reynolds, A. (1995) The knowledge base for beginning teachers: education professionals' expectation versus research findings on learning to teach. *Elementary School Journal* 95(3): 199–221.

Rich, E. (2010) Obesity assemblages and surveillance in schools. *International Journal of Qualitative Studies in Education* 23(7): 803–21.

Richardson, V. (1996) The role of attitudes and beliefs in learning to teach, in J. Sikula, T. Buttery and E. Guyton (eds), *Handbook of Research on Teacher Education*, 2nd edn. New York: Macmillan.

Rink, J. (2001) Investigating the assumptions of pedagogy. *Journal of Teaching in Physical Education* 20: 112–28.

Rink, J. (2003) Effective instruction in physical education, in S. Silverman and C. Ennis (eds), *Student Learning in Physical Education*, 2nd edn. Champaign, IL: Human Kinetics.

Roberts, K. (1996) Young people, schools, sport and government policies. *Sport, Education and Society* 1: 47–58.

Rosenholtz, C. (1989) *Teachers' Workplace: The Social Organisation of Schools*. New York: Longman.

Rosenshine, B. (1987) Explicit teaching, in D. Berliner and B. Rosenshine (eds), *Talks to Teachers*. New York: Random House, pp. 75–89.

Rossi, T. and Cassidy, T. (1999) Knowledgeable teachers in physical education: a view of teachers' knowledge. In C.A. Hardy and M. Mawer (eds), *Learning and Teaching in Physical Education*, London: Falmer Press, pp. 188–202.

Rovegno, I. (1992) Learning to reflect on teaching: a case study of one preservice physical education teacher. *Elementary School Journal* 92(4): 491–510.

Rovegno, I. (2003) Teachers' knowledge construction, in S. Silverman and C. Ennis (eds), *Student Learning in Physical Education: Applying Research to Enhance Instruction*, 2nd edn. Champaign, IL: Human Kinetics, pp. 295–310.

Rovegno, I. and Dolly, J.P. (2006) Constructivist perspectives on learning, in D. Kirk, D. Macdonald and M. O'Sullivan (eds), *Handbook of Physical Education*. London, Sage, pp. 242–61.

Rust, R. and Sinelnikov, O. (2010) Practicum in a self-contained environment: pre-service teacher perceptions of teaching students with disabilities. *Physical Educator* 67(1): 33–45.

Salmon, J., Booth, M.L., Phongsavan, P., Murphy, N. and Timperlo, A. (2007) Promoting physical activity participation among children and adolescents. *Epidemiological Reviews* 29: 144–59.

Salomon, G. and Perkins, D.N. (1998) Individual and social aspects of learning. *Review of Research in Education* 23: 1–24.

Schempp, P.G. and Graber, K.C. (1992) Teacher socialization from a dialectical perspective: pretraining through induction. *Journal of Teaching in Physical Education* 11: 329–48.

Schommer, M. (1994) An emerging conceptualization of epistemological beliefs and their role in learning, in R. Garner and P. Alexander (eds), *Beliefs about Text and About Text Instruction*, Hillsdale, NJ: Erlbaum, pp. 25–39.

Schon, D.A. (1983) *The Reflective Practitioner: How Professionals Think in Action*. London: Temple Smith.

Schon, D.A. (1987) *Educating the Reflective Practitioner*. San Francisco: Jossey Bass.

Scottish Education Department Consultative Committee on the Curriculum (1977) *The Structure of the Curriculum in Years 3 and 4 of Scottish Secondary Schools*. Edinburgh: HMSO.

Sfard, A. (1998) On two metaphors for learning and the danger of choosing just one. *Educational Researcher* 27(2): 4–13.

Shen, B., McCaughtry, N. and Martin, J. (2007) The influence of self-determination in physical education on leisure-time physical activity behavior. *Research Quarterly for Exercise and Sport* 78: 328–38.

Shephard, R.J. and Trudeau, F. (2000) The legacy of physical education: influences on adult lifestyle. *Pediatric Exercise Science* 12: 34–50.

Shuell, T. (1986) Cognitive conceptions of learning. *Review of Educational Research* 56: 411–36.

Shulman, L.S. (1986) Those who understand: knowledge growth in teaching. *Educational Researcher* 15(2): 4–21.

Shulman, L.S. (1987) Knowledge and teaching: foundations of the new reform. *Harvard Educational Review* 57: 1–22.

Shulman, L.S. (1999) Knowledge and teaching: foundation of the new reform, in J. Leach and B. Moon (eds), *Learners and Pedagogy*. London: Paul Chapman, pp. 61–77.

Shulman, L.S. (2000) From Minsk to Pinsk: Why a scholarship of teaching and learning? *Journal of Scholarship of Teaching and Learning (JoSoTL)* 1(1): 48–53.

Shulman, L.S. (2007) Practical wisdom in the service of professional practice. *Educational Researcher* 36(9): 560–3.

Siedentop, D. (1994) *Sport Education: Quality PE through Positive Sport Experiences*. Champaign, IL: Human Kinetics.

Siedentop, D. (2002a) Content knowledge for physical education. *Journal of Teaching in Physical Education* 21: 368–77.

Siedentop, D. (2002b) Junior sport and the evolution of sport cultures. *Journal of Teaching in Physical Education* 21: 392–401.

Siedentop, D. and Tannehill, D. (2000) *Developing Teaching Skills in Physical Education*, 4th edn. Mountain View, CA: Mayfield.

Skinner, B.F. (1953) *Science and Human Behavior*. New York: Macmillan.

Sloan, S. (2010) The continuing development of primary sector physical education: working together to raise quality of provision. *European Physical Education Review* 16(3): 267–81.

Smagorinsky, P. (2008) Challenges in teaching, learning and teacher education from a Vygotskian perspective. Paper presented at the Sociocultural Perspectives on Teacher Education and Development: New Directions for Research.

Smith, A. and Parr, M. (2007) Young people's views on the nature and purposes of physical education: a sociological analysis. *Sport, Education and Society* 12: 37–58.

Smith, A.L. and Biddle, S.J.H. (eds) (2008) *Youth Physical Activity and Sedentary Behavior. Challenges and Solutions*. Champaign, IL: Human Kinetics.

Sparkes, A. (1991) *Research in Physical Education and Sport: Exploring Alternative Visions*. London: Falmer Press.

Sparkes, A. (2002) *Telling Tales in Sport and Physical Activity*. Leeds: Human Kinetics.

Sparks, D. (2002) *Designing Powerful Professional Development for Teachers and Principals*. Oxford, OH: National Staff Development Council. Available online at: www.nsdc.org/sparksbook.html.

Sport England (2003a) *Young People and Sport in England: Trends in Participation 1994–2002*. London: Sport England.

Sport England (2003b) *Young People and Sport in England, 2002; A Survey of Young People and PE Teachers*. London: Sport England.

Sport, Education and Society (2006) Issue 3: special issue: 'Ability', curriculum and pedagogy.

Sports Coach UK (2004) *Sport Coaching in the UK: Final Report*. Leeds: Sports Coach UK.

Sports Coach UK (2007a) *Sport Coaching in the UK II: Main Report*. Leeds: Sports Coach UK.

Sports Coach UK (2007b) *The UK Coaching Framework, a 3–7–11 year Action Plan*. Leeds: Sports CoachUK.

Stanley, S. (1969) *Physical Education: A Movement Orientation*. Toronto: McGraw-Hill.

Stein, M.K., Smith, M.S. and Silver, E.A. (1999) The development of professional developers: learning to assist teachers in new settings in new ways. *Harvard Educational Review* 69(3): 237–69.

Stenhouse, L. (1975) *An Introduction to Curriculum Research and Development*. London: Heinemann Educational.

Stenhouse, L. (1983) Curriculum, research and the art of the teacher, in L. Stenhouse (ed.), *Authority, Education and Emancipation: a collection of papers*. London: Heinemann Education, pp. 155–62.

Stensel, D., Gorely, T. and Biddle, S. (2008) Youth health outcomes, in A.L. Smith and S.J.H. Biddle (eds), *Youth Physical Activity and Sedentary Behaviour: Challenges and Solutions*. Leeds: Human Kinetics, pp. 31–57.

Stewart, S. and Mitchell, M. (2003) Instructional variables and student knowledge and conceptions of fitness. *Journal of Teaching in Physical Education* 22: 533–51.

Stewart, W. (2006) Time off for staff is big business. *Times Educational Supplement*, 10 November, p. 26.

Stratton, G. (1998) Repetition in health related exercise and physical education: mindless or mindful activity? *British Journal of Physical Education* 29(4): 35–7.

Stratton, G., Fairclough, S. and Ridgers, N. (2008) Physical activity levels during the school day, in A.L. Smith and S.J.H. Biddle (eds), *Youth Physical Activity and Sedentary Behaviour. Challenges and Solutions*. Leeds: Human Kinetics, pp. 321–50.

Strawson, P.F. (1964) *Individuals*. London. Routledge.

Stroot, S.A. and Ko, B. (2006) Induction of beginning physical educators into the school setting, in D. Kirk, D. Macdonald and M. O'Sullivan (eds), *The Handbook of Physical Education*. London: Sage, pp. 425–48.

Stroot, S.A. and Oslin, J.L. (1993) Use of instructional statements by preservice teachers for overhand throwing performance of children. *Journal of Teaching in Physical Education* 13(1): 24–45.

Stroot, S.A. and Whipple, C. (2003) Organizational socialization: factors impacting beginning teachers, in S. Silverman and C. Ennis (eds), *Student Learning in Physical Education: Applying Research to Enhance Instruction*, 2nd edn. Champaign, IL: Human Kinetics, pp. 311–28.

Swann, J. (1999) Making better plans: problem-based versus objectives-based planning, in J. Swann and J. Pratt (eds), *Improving Education Realist Approaches to Method and Research*. London: Cassell, pp. 53–66.

Talbot, M. (1995) The politics of sport and physical education, in S. Fleming, M. Talbot and A. Tomlinson (eds), *Policy and Politics in Sport, Physical Education and Leisure*. Hove: Leisure Studies Association, pp. 3–26.

Talbot, M. (2007) An independent voice for physical education: a precious asset. *Physical Education Matters* 2(4): 6–8.

Talbot, M. (2008) Valuing physical education: package or pedagogy? *Physical Education Matters* 3(3): 6–8.

Tammelin, T., Nayha, S., Hills, A.P. and Jarvelin, M. (2003) Adolescent participation in sports and adult physical activity. *American Journal of Preventative Medicine* 24(1): 22–8.

Taylor, W.C., Blair, S.N., Cummings, S.S., Wun, C.C. and Malina, R.M. (1999) Childhood and adolescent physical activity patterns and adult physical activity. *Medicine and Science in Sports and Exercise* 31(1): 118–23.

Teaching Council of Ireland (2011) *Draft Policy Paper on the Continuum of Teacher Education*. Maynooth: Teaching Council of Ireland.

Thiessen, D. (2007) Researching student experiences in elementary and secondary school, in D. Thiessen and A. Cook-Sather (eds), *International Handbook of Student Experience in Elementary and Secondary School*. The Netherlands: Springer, pp. 1–70.

Thomson, P. (1999) How doing justice got boxed in: a cautionary curriculum tale for policy analysts, in B. Johnson and A. Reid (eds), *Contesting the Curriculum*, Katoomba, NSW: Social Sciences Press, pp. 24–42.

Thorburn, M. (2007) Achieving conceptual and curriculum coherence in high-stakes school examinations in physical education. *Physical Education and Sport Pedagogy* 12(2): 163–84.

Thornhill, C. (2009) Child obesity will NOT be solved by PE classes in schools, say researchers, *Daily Mail*, 7 May. Available at: www.dailymail.co.uk/health/article-1178232/Child-obesity-NOT-solved-PE-classes-schools-say-researchers.html.

Thorpe, S. (2003) Crisis discourse in physical education and the laugh of Michel Foucault. *Sport, Education and Society* 8(2): 131–51.

Tinning, R. (1992) Not so sweet dreams: physical education in the year 2001. *ACHPER [Australian Council for Health, Physical Education and Recreation] National Journal* 138: 24–6.

Tinning, R. (2001) The 2001 Senate inquiry: a non-preferred scenario for physical education. *ACHPER National Journal*, 48: 14–16.

Tinning, R. (2006) Theoretical orientations in physical education teacher education, in D. Kirk, D. McDonald and M. O'Sullivan (eds), *Handbook of Physical Education*, London: Sage, 369–86.

Tinning, R. (2010) *Pedagogy and Human Movement: Theory, Practice, Research*. London: Routledge.

Tinning, R., Kirk, D. and Evans, J. (1993) *Learning to Teach in Physical Education*. London, Prentice Hall.

Tinning, R., Macdonald, D., Wright, J. and Hickey, C. (2001) *Becoming a Physical Education Teacher: Contemporary and Enduring Issues*. Frenches Forest, Australia: Prentice Hall.

Trudel, P. and Gilbert, W. (2006) Coaching and coach education, in D. Kirk, D. McDonald and M. O'Sullivan (eds), *Handbook of Physical Education*. London: Sage, pp. 516–39.

Trudel, P., Gilbert, W. and Werthner, P. (2010) Coach education effectiveness, in J. Lyle and C. Cushion (eds), *Sport Coaching Professionalisation and Practice*. London: Elsevier, pp. 135–52.

Tsangaridou, N. (2006a) Teachers' beliefs, in D. Kirk, D. Macdonald and M. O'Sullivan (eds), *The Handbook of Physical Education*. London: Sage, pp. 486–501.

Tsangaridou, N. (2006b) Teachers' knowledge, in D. Kirk, D. Macdonald and M. O'Sullivan (eds), *The Handbook of Physical Education*. London: Sage, pp. 502–15.

Tsangaridou, N. and O'Sullivan, M. (1994) Using pedagogical reflective strategies to enhance reflection among preservice physical education teachers. *Journal of Teaching in Physical Education* 14(1): 13–33.

Tsangaridou, N. and O'Sullivan, M. (1997) The role of reflection in shaping physical education teachers' educational values and practices. *Journal of Teaching in Physical Education* 17(1): 2–25.

Tsangaridou, N. and Siedentop, D. (1995) Reflective teaching: a literature review. *Quest* 47(2): 212–37.

Tusting, K. and Barton, D. (2003) *Models of Adult Learning: A Literature Review*, Leicester: NRDC for ALN.

UNESCO (United Nations Educational, Scientific and Cultural Organisation) (1994) *The Salamanca Statement and Framework for Action on Special Educational Needs*. Paris: UNESCO.

USDHHS (United States Department of Health and Human Services) (2008) *Physical Activity Guidelines Advisory Committee Report*, Washington, DC: USDHHS. Available at: www.health.gov/paguidelines.

USDHHS (United States Department of Health and Human Services) (2010) *Healthy People 2010. Understanding and Improving Health*, Washington, DC: USDHHS.

Valli, L. (ed.) (1992) *Reflective Teacher Education: Cases and Critiques*. Albany: State University of New York Press.

van Manen, M. (1977) Linking ways of knowing with ways of being practical. *Curriculum Inquiry* 6(3): 205–28.

Veenman, S. (1984) Perceived problems of beginning teachers. *Review of Educational Research* 54(2): 143–78.

Velija, P., Capel, S., Katene, W. and Hayes, S. (2009) Student teachers in their figurations: an exploration of interdependent relationships on a one-year initial teacher training physical education course. *European Physical Education Review* 14(3): 389–406.

Vosniadou, S. (2007) The cognitive-situative divide and the problem of conceptual change. *Educational Psychologist* 42(1): 55–66.

Vygotsky, L. (1978) *Mind in Society*. Cambridge, MA: Harvard University Press.

Vygotsky, L. (1986) *Thought and Language*, revised and edited by A Kozulin. Cambridge, MA: MIT Press (original work published in 1962).

Ward, L. (2009) Physical education teachers' engagement with 'health-related exercise' and health-related continuing professional development: a healthy profile? Unpublished doctoral thesis, Loughborough University.

Ward, L., Cale, L. and Webb, L. (2008) Physical education teachers' knowledge and continuing professional development in health-related exercise: a healthy profile? Paper presented at the British Educational Research Association Conference, Edinburgh, September.

Wayne, A.J., Yoon, K.S., Zhu, P., Cronen, S. and Garet, M.S. (2008) Experimenting with teacher professional development: motives and methods. *Educational Researcher* 37(8): 469–79.

Webster, C. and Schempp, P. (2008) Self-monitoring: demystifying the wonder of expert teaching. *Journal of Physical Education, Recreation and Dance* 79(1): 23–9.

Weinstein, C. (1990) Prospective elementary teachers' beliefs about teaching: implications for teacher education. *Teaching and Teacher Education* 6(3): 279–90.

Wellard, I. (ed.) (2007) *Rethinking Gender and Youth Sport*. Abingdon: Routledge.

Wendt, J. and Bain, L. (1985) Surviving the transition: concerns of the beginning teacher. *Journal of Physical Education, Recreation and Dance* 56(2): 24–5.

Wenger, E. (1998) *Communities of Practice: Learning, Meaning and Identity*, Cambridge: Cambridge University Press.

WestEd (2000) *Teachers Who Learn, Kids Who Achieve: A Look at Schools with Model Professional Development.* San Francisco: WestEd.

Whitehead, J.R., Pemberton, C.L. and Corbin, C.B. (1990) Perspectives on the physical fitness testing of children: the case for a realistic educational approach. *Pediatric Exercise Science* 2: 111–23.

Whitehead, M.E. (2000) Aims as an issue in physical education, in S. Capel and S. Piotrowski (eds), *Issues in Physical Education.* London: RoutledgeFalmer, pp. 7–21.

Whitehead, M.E (ed.) (2010a) *Physical Literacy: Throughout the Lifecourse.* London: Routledge.

Whitehead, M.E. (2010b) The value of being physically literate. Unpublished paper presented in Gothenberg, 2010. Available at: www.physical-literacy.org.uk.

Whitehead, M.E. (2011) Key features of a curriculum to promote physical literacy. Unpublished paper presented at the International Physical Literacy Conference, University of Bedfordshire, June. Available at: www.physical-literacy.org.uk.

Whitehead, M.E with Blair, R. (2010) Designing teaching approaches to achieve intended learning outcomes, in S. Capel and M. Whitehead (eds), *Learning to Teach Physical Education in the Secondary School: A Companion to School Experience*, 3rd edn. London: Routledge, pp. 154–67.

Whitehead, M.E. with Murdoch, E. (2006) Physical literacy and physical education: conceptual mapping. *Physical Education Matters* 1(1): 6–9.

WHO (World Health Organization) (2011) Childhood overweight and obesity. Available at: www.who.int/dietphysicalactivity/childhood/en/index.html.

Wilkinson, S. (1996) Visual analysis of the overarm throw and related sport skill: training and transfer effects. *Journal of Teaching in Physical Education* 16(1): 66–78.

Williams, E.A. (1985) Understanding constraints on innovation in physical education. *Journal of Curriculum Studies* 17(4): 407–13.

Williams, E.U. and Tannehill, D. (1999) Effects of a multimedia performance principle training program on correct analysis and diagnosis of throw-like movements. *Physical Educator* 56(3): 143–54.

Williams, J.F. (1970) Education through the physical, in H.S. Slusher and A. Lockart (eds), *An Anthropology of Contemporary Readings.* Dubuque, IA: W.C. Brown, p. 3.

Wolfenden Report (1960) *Sport and the Community.* London: Central Council for Physical Recreation.

Wright, J. and Dean, R. (2007) A balancing act: problematising prescriptions about food and weight in school health texts. *Journal of Didactics and Educational Policy* 16(2): 75–94.

Wright, J., Macdonald, D. and Groom, L. (2009) Physical activity and young people beyond participation, in R. Bailey and D. Kirk (eds), *The Routledge Physical Education Reader.* London: Routledge, pp. 103–22.

Wright, L. (2002) Rescuing primary physical education: saving those values that matter most. *British Journal of Teaching Physical Education* 33(1): 37–8.

Wright, L. (2004) Preserving the value of happiness in primary school physical education. *Physical Education and Sport Pedagogy* 9(2): 149–63.

Yeung, J. and Hills, A.P. (2007) Childhood obesity: an introduction, in A.P. Hills, N.A. King and N.M. Byrne (eds), *Children, Obesity and Exercise.* Abingdon: Routledge, pp. 1–10.

Ygoy (2009) Physical education and obesity. Available at: http://obesity.ygoy.com/2009/06/11/physical-education-and-obesity.

You, J. (2011) Portraying physical education-pedagogical content knowledge for the professional learning of physical educators. *Physical Educator* 68(2): 98–113.

Zachary, L.J. (2000) *The Mentor's Guide: Facilitating Effective Learning Relationships.* San Francisco: Jossey Bass.

Zeichner, K. (2010) Rethinking the connections between campus courses and field experiences in college and university-based teacher education. *Journal of Teacher Education* 61(1): 89–99.

Zeichner, K. and Tabachnick, B.R. (1981) Are the effects of university teacher education 'washed out' by school experience? *Journal of Teacher Education* 32(2): 7–11.

Zeichner, K.M. and Tabachnik, B.R. (1983) Teacher perspectives in the face of the institutional press. Paper presented at the annual meeting of the AERA, Montreal, ON, Canada: April.

Zeichner, K. and Tabachnick, B.R. (1991) Reflections on reflective teaching, in B.R. Tabachnick and K. Zeichner (eds), *Issues and Practices in Inquiry-Oriented Teacher Education.* London: Falmer Press, pp. 1–21.

Zieff, S.G. and Veri, M.J. (2009) Obesity, health and physical activity: discourses from the United States. *Quest* 61(2): 154–79.

Zwozdiak-Myers, P. (2012) *The Teacher's Reflective Practice Handbook: Becoming an Extended Professional Through Capturing Evidence Informed Practice.* Abingdon: Routledge.

Index